JEROME KANTER is Director of Planning and Consulting for National Industry Operations at Honeywell Information Systems in Wellesley, Massachusetts. He is the author of numerous journal articles and four previous books in the field of management and computer systems.

Prentice-Hall International, Inc., *London*
Prentice-Hall of Australia Pty. Limited, *Sydney*
Prentice-Hall of Canada, Ltd., *Toronto*
Prentice-Hall of India Private Limited, *New Delhi*
Prentice-Hall of Japan, Inc., *Tokyo*
Prentice-Hall of Southeast Asia Pte. Ltd., *Singapore*
Whitehall Books Limited, *Wellington, New Zealand*

TAMING YOUR COMPUTER

A GUIDE FOR BUSINESS AND PROFESSIONAL PEOPLE

Jerome Kanter

A SPECTRUM BOOK

PRENTICE-HALL, INC.
Englewood Cliffs, New Jersey 07632

Library of Congress Cataloging in Publication Data

KANTER, JEROME.
  Taming your computer.

  (A Spectrum Book)
  Bibliography: p.
  Includes index.
    1. Business—Data processing. 2. Data processing
service centers—United States. 3. Computer service
industry—United States. 4. Computers. I. Title.
HF5548.2.K3243   011.64′024658   81-1451
ISBN 0-13-884403-8   AACR2
ISBN 0-13-884395-3 (pbk.)

© 1981 by Prentice-Hall, Inc., Englewood Cliffs, New Jersey 07632.
This is a revised and updated edition of *A Management Guide to
Computers* by Jerome Kanter, published by Honeywell Information
Systems, Inc. © 1977.

A SPECTRUM BOOK

Editorial/production supervision and interior design by Frank Moorman
Cover design by Ira Shapiro
Manufacturing buyer: Barbara A. Frick

10 9 8 7 6 5 4 3 2 1

This Spectrum Book can be made available to businesses and
organizations at a special discount when ordered in large quantities.
For more information, contact:
  Prentice-Hall, Inc.
  General Book Marketing
  Special Sales Division
  Englewood Cliffs, N.J. 07632

Contents

Preface, vii

1 Introduction to Computers, 1

2 Uses and Applications of
Computer Systems, 22

3 Selecting and Implementing
Computer Applications, 65

4 Mini/Micro Mania, 90

5 Understanding Software and
Programming, 106

6 Computer-aided Decision
Making, 128

7 Management Information
Systems, 149

8 Computer-based Teleprocessing
Systems, 175

9 Future Use and Growth of
Computers, 206

Bibliography, 235

Index, 239

Preface

Taming Your Computer is aimed at the business manager who may use computer output or provide computer input but who is not directly involved with the design or implementation of computer systems. The book discusses the computer and the electronic data-processing industry in terms that are familiar to business people. The computer is viewed from "outside in," the vantage point of a user, rather than from "inside out," the view of a computer professional. The book stresses the techniques that managers should employ to gain maximum benefit from computers. The book emphasizes the straightforward and direct presentation of technical elements. It offers an insight into computer technology, illustrating first the needs that computers can fill and then the manner in which they meet these needs.

Chapter 1 reviews the development evolution of computers and describes in simple terms the basic elements that make up a computer system. Chapter 2 discusses examples of computer applications across a broad industry spectrum—from manufacturing and distribution firms to hospitals and schools. Chapter 3 reviews how basic management principles apply to the selection, design, and implementation of computer applications. Management's role in each phase is emphasized. Chapter 4 looks at the proliferation of mini and micro computers and what this means to the manager. Chapter 5 is the most technical chapter. It gives the manager a peak "under the hood" of computer systems, explaining the basics of computer programming. Chapters 6, 7, and 8 elaborate on three of the fastest-growing application areas: computer-aided decision making; management information systems; and computer-based teleprocessing systems, geographic networks providing computer power to remote points. Chapter 9 concludes with a look at what we can expect of computers in the years ahead.

The objective of the book is to give a greater awareness of computers, to explain the application of computers to a variety of jobs, and to enable the businessperson to utilize the benefits that computers afford.

ACKNOWLEDGMENTS

I gratefully acknowledge the assistance of Ollie Miles and Camela Hansen in reviewing specific sections; Eileen Ward for her excellent library research; Carol Dello Russo for the final compilation; and the skillful typing, editing, and general enthusiasm of Pat Roberts. I also thank Jerry Meyer and the management of my company, Honeywell, for their cooperation on this project.

To Jane

1 Introduction to Computers

Computers are being built that are faster and fiercer but smaller and simpler than their predecessors—and they are proliferating at a rapid rate. The first commercial computer was introduced in 1951. Today, some thirty years later, there are more than 900,000 computers (not counting microcomputers) installed in companies throughout the world, and the statement "We couldn't compete without them" is a slogan that has been heard for over a decade now. So-called mainframes, which filled huge rooms, have been complemented and superceded by minicomputers, which in turn are being complemented and superceded by microcomputers. This evolutionary change (some call it revolutionary) from computers on a floor to computers on a chip is one of the most exciting of this century—some say equal in impact to the invention of the steam engine or the printing press.

The faster and fiercer of the breed can perform arithmetic calculations at the rate of 100 million per second. What does this ability really mean? Assume, for example, that each and every one of the 4.5 billion people on earth had to prepare an income tax return. If each tax return required 100 arithmetic operations (add deductions, subtract from income, multiply by appropriate tax rate, and so on), a modern computer could calculate every tax return on earth in one and one-quarter hours. Considerations of computer systems, however, go beyond raw speed and power.

For one thing, this processing power can be put to use only after the data have been recorded in a format that the machine can read. It also takes skilled systems analysts to develop the total system (of which the computer is only a part) to process and produce the required output.

It is true that the computer offers people a device that can take them where they don't want to go faster than any other device ever conceived. It is also true that we must be on our guard lest we fall into the technological trap that because we have the means to do something, that something is worth doing. In a business sense, "worth" means producing dollar and cents benefits to the company; in a social sense, "worth" means improving the quality of life. Later chapters will delve into how these critical elements harness the computer's raw speed and apply it to the things it does best.

It is a thesis of this book that there are things a human does best, even with the advent of computers. Dr. Lawrence J. Peter and Raymond Hull in their book *The Peter Principle* describe "the most penetrating and psychological discovery of the century"—the principle that "In a hierarchy, every employee tends to rise to his level of incompetence." It seems that the computer is not immune to this law. Applied to computers, the Peter Principle states that as the computer succeeds at routine jobs, there is a strong compulsion to apply it to progressively more responsible tasks, until the computer, too, reaches its level of incompetence. I believe the machine's level of incompetence is determined by the type of organization using the computer, by management attitudes, and by the business and technological perspective of the systems designers. A major goal of a computer user should be to determine his particular company's Peter Principle threshold.

IMPACT OF COMPUTERS

There is little doubt that computers play an ever-increasing role in our lives. A prominent business executive foresees a day when computers will make life easier for everyone. They'll let executives work at home, saving commuting time. As the directing forces of automated factories, computers will help reduce the work week and give everyone more leisure time. Computers will enable you to vote at home, and will do a myriad of other tasks to simplify the routine aspects of life. The thoughtful head of a

British electronics firm feels the computer will bring "the greatest change in the whole history of mankind."

The computer has gone beyond the stage where it can be ignored. To think of a computer as a super adding machine or as just another management tool is dangerous. The computer affects people in a variety of ways. I would be surprised if the reader could not relate to one of the following vignettes.

Sam Curtis is president and chief executive officer of Curtis Manufacturing, a $7-million producer of metal products. Sam has seen the company he founded grow from less than $1 million in sales to the current volume in less than ten years. Profits have not kept pace with sales in the inflationary economy, and paperwork and staff matters are taking an increasing amount of Sam's time. At a recent country club dinner a friend mentioned to Sam that his company had just installed a computer and that they had high prospects for getting better control of operations after it was up and running. Last week Sam had a sales call from a representative of a systems house that claimed they had a packaged computer solution for sales order processing, inventory control, and accounting applications. Sam was aware that a close business colleague was using a computer system acquired by the company controller at a computer retail store. Sam had not paid too much attention to this type of talk in the past, but he had the feeling that the time was right for a computer system for Curtis Manufacturing. He was concerned, however, as to how to go about putting the whole computer issue into a proper business framework in order to begin analyzing his needs and then make the decision as to which of the seemingly hundreds of small business systems would prove the best for Curtis. The variety of vendors from whom to buy also clouded his thinking. As he pondered the matter, he had never felt quite as out of control of a situation as this one. He realized he didn't even know what questions to ask and he hated to think he was at the mercy of the market.

The Prudential Investment Company has had a computer for several years. It uses the computer for customer billing, calculating payments to its investment counselors, and producing a variety of sales reports and analyses. Carole Harrison, thirty-eight, has been the senior investment counselor for Prudential for the past five years and is well thought of in the investment community. She is concerned with a new application in the process of being computerized. While the computer has helped her in routine accounting areas, Carole is dubious about its ability to analyze stocks and to perform portfolio analysis based on a stated investor profile. She has attended several sessions where the systems designers explained the new approach, but she didn't quite comprehend the techniques or the benefits to her. She didn't want to appear defensive and antagonistic to the proposed system, but Carole just didn't feel comfortable with what was going on.

Dr. Lloyd Carson is forty-five years old, a graduate of Tufts Medical School and a staff member of a large, prominent Boston hospital. The hospital introduced a computer system to handle patient records and to provide a more automated method of handling the admission, treatment, and billing of patients. The computer also handles lab and test scheduling and monitors the dispensing of drugs and medicine. Previously Dr. Carson had not thought a great deal about computers—now he is forced to, if only to answer the complaints of his secretary and the nurse who have to select the proper codes from a catalog of various transactions that occur daily. In addition, he has agreed to talk with a systems analyst about a computer system that would assist in the initial screening of patients and diagnosis of symptoms.

Calvin Sharpe is thirty years old, a graduate of Massachusetts Institute of Technology, and has a master's degree in Management Information Systems from the University of Minnesota. He has been the staff assistant to the president of Blocker Electronic Company for the past two years. Before that he spent the previous five years in a series of computer-related jobs. Calvin was hired because the president of Blocker wanted a close staff aide to direct the use of computers to aid the management decision process at the company. The president realized that the companies with advanced computer systems would have a competitive edge in the future, and he wanted Blocker to be in the forefront. Sharpe is working on a computerized simulation model—a paper image of how the company operates. When complete, the model could answer such questions as what would happen if sales of particular lines increased or decreased by a certain percentage, or what would be the effect of consolidating distribution channels or expanding sales coverage. Variables such as order rate, cash flow, production capacity, and plant facilities also can be manipulated.

A graduate of Smith College, Helen Swindell is not currently employed, but she is aware that computers affect her life. Her interest in computers was prompted by the computer course

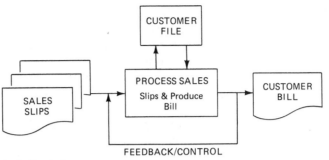

FIGURE 1-2
Credit Application

sales slips are sent to a central administration point (see Figure 1-2). They are the input to the billing system.

The bills are recorded against the customer master file, and this is where we add another element to the information system module—storage. Storage is in electronic form and is a current record of the customer's transaction and balance. The result of the arithmetic and record processing is a customer bill, which is the output of our information system. The feedback is the customer who either accepts the charges and remits payment or who voices a complaint or question via a letter or a telephone call. This, then, is an information system where there is a good deal of human interaction, both on the input and on the output side.

THE COMPUTER AS A SYSTEM

Now that we have the concept of a system in hand, we can view the computer as a system and describe the various elements that comprise it.

The field of computers is called electronic data processing (EDP) and a computer is just that—an electronic data processor. It accepts data (numeric and alphabetic characters) normally via a keyboard but also through optically scanned documents or in some cases by verbal command. The data can be a specific order quantity for a particular product, or they can be the number of hours worked by a particular employee. The computer processes these data; that is, it takes the quantity ordered and multiplies it by the price and weight per unit, or it calculates the wages to be paid to a particular employee. It does all of this electronically. The alphabetic and numerical characters are interpreted from the input media and represented in electronic form within the computer. The subsequent arithmetic or processing operations are accomplished electronically. Thus in its simplest form, the computer can be defined as an electronic data processor. Figure 1-3 depicts the elements comprising a computer system.

The processing part of the computer is the most significant element and is called the central processor. It consists of three basic components, the control section, the arithmetic section, and memory. The control section keeps the system elements (input, processing, storage, and output) in proper working relationship with one another while the arithmetic unit can perform the four mathematical functions as well as compare two quantities to see if one is equal to, greater than, or less than the other. It is interesting and somewhat surprising to realize that these five operations (add, subtract, multiply, divide, and compare) represent the entire processing logic of the computer. You may wonder how a computer can accomplish the variety of exciting things it can with this meager processing logic. However, after you think about it, it becomes clear that this is no mean capability. The majority of decisions made in business and private life involve placing relative weight on diverse factors in order to come to some conclusion. Consider, for example, the decision of whether to take an umbrella to work on a particular morning. This decision is reached after placing relative weight on such factors as (a) the weather report, (b) the percentage of time you plan to spend outside the office, and (c) whether you just had your suit pressed or not. Using the five basic processing

FIGURE 1-3
Computer System Elements

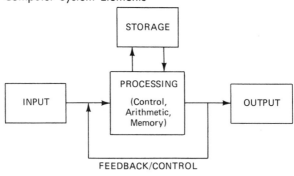

operations, a thought process is developed that gives relative weight to the decision criteria just established. The formula analyzes the input parameters—for example, the percentage of time you actually expect to be out of the office—and on this basis determines whether an umbrella is called for. There are a large number of variables, but this is true whether the electronic computer or the human computer makes the decision.

Memory is the third major element of the central processor and permits the computer to store, in electronic form, data from input devices as well as lengthy series of instructions called programs that tell the machine what to do. It is the memory facility that gives the computer its broad capability and versatility. Internally stored programs enable the computer to execute specified sequences of programmed steps in order to process specific input data and produce specific output data.

Together, high-speed processing and large multifunction programs stored in memory are the elements that make the computer the most advanced information-processing device humans have yet conceived.

Figure 1-4 is a picture of a basic computer system with the systems module elements of input, output, processing, storage, and feedback. The input device in this instance is a video screen terminal with a keyboard. The storage is small diskettes, which look like 45-rpm phonograph records, but each can hold the equivalent of 1 million characters of data (customer files, transactions, and the like). The output device is a printer, which produces the customer bill, inventory status report, or whatever. The processing unit that gives the computer its inherent mathematical and logical power is located in the pedestal under the terminal. The feedback/control element is not visible in the illustration, but is present in the form of internal and external quality checks on the system's operation.

COMMUNICATIONS AND SOFTWARE

There are two additional and important elements of information systems that will be touched on briefly at this point. They will be discussed more completely in later sections. The first element is communications, a vital part of the computer's message delivery system. When we speak of communications, we are talking of the ability to transmit data from a computer or terminal site via telephone lines, microwave, or satellite to another computer

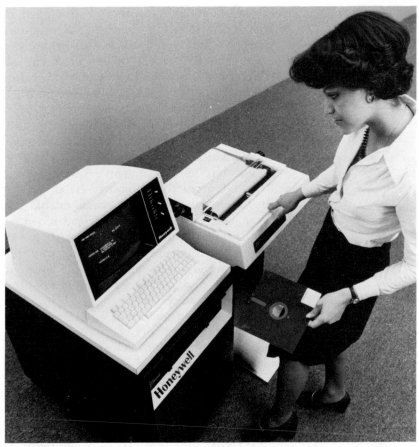

FIGURE 1-4
Basic Computer System (Courtesy of Honeywell Information Systems)

or terminal site. Communications capability is obviously quite crucial for companies with remote locations or the need to gain access to communication networks for a variety of information services. Communication transmission can range from simple data input, such as order entry, to complex file interchange, such as that found in a banking application.

Software is as much an integral part of the information system as the hardware. More and more, the differentiation between information systems comes from the software, the operating and language elements that give the system its inherent capability. Software combines those five rudimentary logic functions referred to earlier into meaningful streams of instructions and application programs. Most systems manufacturers have reached the crossover point where they are expending more than half their research and development funds for software as opposed to hardware. The subject of software will arise frequently as we proceed; the purpose here is to indicate its growing significance to the computer equation.

Now that we know the elements of a system and a computer, we can trace their origins.

HISTORY OF COMPUTERS

In his provocative book *Future Shock*, Alvin Toffler points out that almost as much has happened since we were born as happened before we were born. This barrage of change, scientific acceleration, and technological turnover is causing a psychological shock wave throughout society. Toffler indicates that if the last 50,000 years of human existence were divided into lifetimes of approximately 62 years each, there have been about 800 lifetimes. Of these 800, fully 650 were spent in caves. Only during the last 70 lifetimes has it been possible to communicate effectively from one lifetime to another—as writing made it possible to do. Only during the last 6 lifetimes did masses of people ever see a printed word. Only during the last 4 has it been possible to measure time with any precision. Only in the last 2 has anyone anywhere used an electric motor. And an overwhelming majority of the material goods we use in daily life was developed within the present, the 800th, lifetime. This type of analysis holds for computers and the science of information processing. Certainly computers have been characteristic only of the 800th lifetime—in fact, the last third of the 800th lifetime, if you consider computers on the commercial scene.

You should view the progress of computers with this perspective to avoid reaching the conclusion that computers are overrated and their impact limited. The learning curve has been rapid despite the experience of some, particularly those in the EDP business or those using computers, who have borne the brunt of abortive attempts to reach out too far, too fast. The Toffler "lifetime" concept places the computer in its proper framework in time and projects a sobering view of its potential.

Although the abacus is not a computer, the history of computing really began with this device. The abacus is a manual device combining two fundamental concepts. It uses objects (small beads) to represent numbers, and it uses one object to represent several numbers. On an abacus the number nine is represented by one "five" bead and four "one" beads. In the hands of a skilled user, the abacus makes extremely rapid arithmetic calculations. The abacus is still the most widely used computing device in existence.

The first machine to add numbers mechanically was invented by Blaise Pascal, the French mathematician and philosopher, in 1643. Pascal used geared counter wheels that could be set to any of the positions zero to nine. The geared tooth was used for carrying one to the next position when nine was reached. Following Pascal's lead, G. W. Leibnitz, a German mathematician, invented a machine in 1671 that could control the amount of adding. This was the first multiplying machine. These early machines are the direct ancestors of the electric-powered, but hand-operated adding machines and desk calculating machines that are still very much part of the business scene. These adding machines and calculators accomplish only one operation at a time and are key driven, that is, they are activated by depressing a key.

Charles Babbage, a professor of mathematics at Cambridge University, England, attempted in 1812 to build a difference engine—a machine that could add, subtract, multiply, divide, and perform a sequence of steps automatically. The last function is the forerunner of the stored program. Babbage called his machine a difference engine because he intended to use it to compute mathematical tables by adding differences such as the time between the high and low tides. For example, if the moon rises exactly one hour later each day, and the high and low tides are 6½ hours apart, and if on August 14, high tide is at 12:00 A.M., then low tide will be at 6:30 P.M. On August 15, high tide will be at 1:00 P.M., and low tide at 7:30 P.M., and so on. A table was to be built by adding differences. Babbage failed to get the necessary funds for his machine, and in 1833 the project was dropped. Babbage was also thinking of making an analytical engine with three parts: store (memory), mill (arithmetic), and sequence mechanisms (control). These parts are very similar to the elements of a computer. Babbage didn't have the necessary funds and support for this project either, but his concepts were sound in every respect. It is generally stated that the technology in Babbage's time just didn't permit the development of instruments with the precision required by his analytical engine.

At this state in history we are introduced to one of the few romantic figures in computer history, Ada Lovelace. Ada was the only legitimate daughter of Lord Byron. Unlike ladies of her time and background who occupied themselves with light studies, recreation, and serving tea, Ada took to mathematics and at age fifteen had covered Paisley's geometry alone as a diversion. She became known to Charles Babbage through a translation she did of a French work that helped the development of the difference engine. Ada is described as brilliant, charming, and feminine and became a vital assistant to Babbage. Molly Gleiser, computer historian, writes that at her death at age thirty-six, at her own wish, Ada was buried at the side of Lord George Gordon Byron (also dead at age thirty-six), all passion stilled, passionate and noble daughter of a passionate and noble father. Sometimes an emotion or two crops up even in a book on computers and information systems.

A major development occurred in 1886, when a statistician named Herman Hollerith was working on the 1880 census of the United States. After six years of constant work the census still had not been calculated. Obviously, a new way to handle large amounts of data was needed if this census were to be completed before the next one came around. For eighty years cards with punched holes representing numbers had been used to control the weaving of cloth on Jacquard looms. Hollerith had the idea that these holes could be sensed by a machine that would then sort and manipulate the arithmetic sums represented by the holes. The punched card has withstood the rapid innovations in computer technology for nearly ninety years. Today the Hollerith punched card and punched card number code are still a basic computer input medium.

It was the same Herman Hollerith who became the chief asset of the Tabulating Machine Company (as William Rodgers wrote in his book *Think*, a biography of the Watsons and IBM). Thomas J. Watson left NCR in 1913 and in the following year, through a holding company called the Computer-Tabulating-Recording Company (C-T-R) headed up by a noted American financier, Charles R. Flint, became general manager of one of the component companies, the Tabulating Machine Company. In 1924 C-T-R became known as IBM, with Tom Watson its eventual president. Rodgers points out that Watson never got along with the volatile inventor Hollerith, who was to drive Watson literally out of his senses. Out of his senses or no, Watson parlayed Hollerith's concept of the punched card and the punched card machine into an empire that today employs more than a third of a million people and has sales of over $25 billion per year. Appropriately enough, the formation of C-T-R in 1914 corresponds almost exactly to the beginning of Toffler's 800th life-time.

The first automatic digital computer that worked was constructed at the Bell Telephone Laboratories in New York in 1939 by George Stibitz. Stibitz, an engineer, was faced with the problem of performing arithmetic operations on complex numbers. He decided that ordinary telephone relays could be wired together to do this time-consuming job. Stibitz represented each decimal digit by a code of ones and zeros (the beginning of binary notation) such that four relays arranged in a pattern of being energized or not could represent a number. The machine was completed and successfully demonstrated in 1940. It is interesting to note that mathematicians at Dartmouth College sent problems to the machine via teletype and received answers. This was the beginning of online communications to the computer.

The first general-purpose, automatic digital computer was the Harvard-IBM automatic sequence-controlled calculator called the Mark I. It began operations in 1944, under the pressure of wartime. It was developed by Professor Howard Aiken with the help of engineers from IBM. The Mark I performed about three additions per second and had seventy-two internal storage registers. This is a modest capability compared with the millions of additions per second and the millions of registers of internal storage available in today's computers. The cause of the slow operation was the use of the relay, an electromechanical device, as the major component.

At the same time a group of engineers at the University of Pennsylvania, headed by John W. Mauchly and J. P. Eckert, was working on an automatic electronic digital computer using radio tubes instead of relays. Radio tubes function at higher speed than relays. The ENIAC (Electronic Numerical Integrator and Automatic Calculator) was completed in 1947. It had only twenty storage registers, but it could accomplish 5,000 additions per second, which made it the fastest computer in operation.

At this point it would be inappropriate to proceed without at least the brief mention of three men, who, though not necessarily associated with specific computer hardware development, were instrumental in the introduction of logic and programming elements enabling the computer to execute complex instructions and to control a wide gamut of business and scientific operations. These men are George Boole, Norbert Wiener, and John Von Neumann.

George Boole lived in Babbage's time (early and mid 1800s)

and, though not involved in hardware development, used his genius in mathematics to lay the groundwork for the theory behind computer logic. Modern computers operate with a binary or two-stage operating logic; each instruction or piece of data is converted to this two-stage form before entering the computer and being processed. The data are then converted back to decimal and alpha mode at output time. The binary representation and internal arithmetic manipulation are called Boolean algebra, after George Boole, and this indeed represents a most significant contribution to computer development.

Norbert Wiener, who received a Ph.D. in 1913 at the age of nineteen reincarnated the word *cybernetics* from the Greek *kubernetes*, "steersman," in the 1940s. The science of cybernetics is defined as how automatic machines or computers function including the elements of input, output, processing, communications, and feedback loops. Wiener's work helps us understand the basic concept of a system and indeed underlies the description of the systems module described earlier. Wiener's writings develop an analogy of automatic feedback systems to the human nervous system. Thus intension tremor and parkinsonism are impairments of the normal feedback loops between brain and motor functions. Wiener's work assists us in comprehending the overall science or body of thought in which the computer plays a significant part.

John Von Neumann (1903-1957) is a prominent name to people familiar with the early development of computers in the United States. In a book entitled *The Computer from Pascal to Von Neumann*, Herman Goldstine, who worked with Von Neumann, cannot say enough about the latter's contribution in the computer field. Von Neumann, a brilliant mathematician, had a profound influence on the development of early hardware, but he concentrated on the memory and software side, the latter being an area that to this day has not been fully understood nor properly emphasized. Von Neumann showed earlier hardware developers how to store instructions and what these instructions should do. His initial concept of storage in a mercury delay line is the forerunner of core memory and today's semiconductor memory. Prior to Von Neumann, paper tape was the accepted vehicle for getting instructions to the processor. John Von Neumann's contributions are immense.

From 1946 to 1951 the computer field was dominated by the government, universities, and small companies working with government or university grants. It was five years before the world's first commercial computer was produced by Remington Rand (now the Sperry Corporation). Remington Rand had purchased control of the Eckert-Mauchly Computer Corp., developers of the ENIAC. The first commercial computer, UNIVAC I, was delivered in 1951 to the same U.S. Bureau of the Census that first spurred Dr. Hollerith to use punched cards in calculations. The first nongovernment installation of a UNIVAC I was at General Electric's appliance plant in Louisville, Kentucky, in 1954.

The Commercial Era

The installation of the UNIVAC I's at the Census Department and at General Electric opened up the commercial era of computers, and few could forecast what was to come, in fact several prominent prognosticators of the time proclaimed that no more than one hundred of these machines would be needed to handle the computations for the entire country.

The First Computer Decade

It is difficult to characterize an entire decade with a single development, but Figure 1-5 starts with that premise.

During the 1950s the so-called mainframers—IBM, Sperry, Honeywell, and RCA—predominated. The term *mainframe*, which was not coined until the advent of minicomputers, connoted the large, high-power, high-cost nature of these first computer products.

Remington Rand completely dominated the market during the five-year period between 1951 and 1956. The situation then shifted radically, and by 1957 IBM controlled the computer field, as it had the office machine and punched-card fields. Other companies—Honeywell, General Electric, Control Data, NCR, Burroughs, Digital Equipment Corporation, and RCA—to name some of the larger ones, also began manufacturing computers. General Electric was subsequently bought out by Honeywell in 1970. Sperry Rand purchased the remains of the RCA computer business after RCA left the computer business in 1971. IBM still

FIGURE 1-5.
Computer Decades.

	Mainframes	Minicomputers	Microcomputers
1950s	Coming on		
1960s	Proliferating	Coming on	
1970s	Maturing	Proliferating	Coming on
1980s	Peaking	Maturing	Proliferating

dominates the market, with about 60 percent of all computers installed.

The 1950s can be characterized as the era of the engineer. The demands of engineers, mathematicians, and scientists for raw calculating power created the need for computers. The iterative mathematical process is immense if you want, for example, to solve a complex equation involving hundreds of calculations by assigning values x and y ranging from 1 to 100 in gradations of 0.1. Thus the first computers were big "number crunchers." They also were expensive, and difficult to maintain and use.

Early machines were supported by government and educational funds; cost effectiveness was not the primary focus. This is not all bad in the infancy of a burgeoning new technology, of course, for constraining the scope of research and development too early can hinder progress. Since much of the work given to computers had not been done before, it was hard to determine whether computer benefits offset costs. Cost justification is particularly difficult in experimental R&D.

There were many abortive attempts to build new machines and to improve existing ones. The builders received little help from equipment users. At first there was no great interest in the use of computers for business purposes. Business was not aware of the computer's vast potential in business operations. Also, there were no company planning groups or special-interest organizations to give guidance or direction to computer manufacturers. Frequently a product was developed before its market potential, if any, had been determined. An already-developed product sought a suitable market, instead of being determined by marketplace needs. The 1950s belonged to the mainframes, and there were about 4,000 systems installed by the end of the decade.

The Second Computer Decade

As the first computer decade was the era of the engineer, the second decade was that of the marketeer. Large, well-financed companies, led by IBM, and including Honeywell, Sperry Rand, Burroughs, and NCR, developed powerful marketing and sales forces in this new growth industry. Thousands of sales and systems personnel were sent out to convince the marketplace that the "chicken in every pot" idea applied to computers. These marketeers were young, ambitious, enthusiastic, intelligent, and wrapped up in their new product. Perhaps as a result, they oversold it on a grand scale. The 1960s marked the era of mainframe computer proliferation, with the number of installed computers increasing from 4,000 to over 50,000.

While mainframes were proliferating, the minis were coming on the scene lead by DEC (Digital Equipment Corporation), who had achieved over $100 million sales by the end of the decade. During the 1960s minis hardly made a dent in the installed computer base, but the potential was ominous, to say the least.

What the marketeers failed to understand was the practical company environment in which computers had to operate, and they vastly overestimated their customers' ability to use the equipment. Computer users, however, have to share the rap for this unwise proliferation. Very few users understood the role the computer should play in a company: They didn't select the areas where it should be used; they didn't establish priorities or determine schedules; future systems planning was almost nil. Upper management didn't understand computers and didn't take the time to learn, either because they didn't think they could or because they thought computers were merely another accounting tool that belonged in the controller's shop. So they turned over the computers to the technocrats—systems and programming priesthoods ran the show and managed the new machines.

Buzzwords in the sixties proliferated: on-line, real time, management information systems, central data bases, telecommunications, command and control systems, simulation models. Acronyms flourished: **COBOL, FORTRAN, DOS, ALGOL, I-D-S, RAMP, STET, NEAT, IMS, JOVIAL, RPG, MCP, GCOS, BOMP,** ad infinitum. It was an age of "acronyms anonymous," with the industry running out of clean four-letter words!

The advanced systems or innovative approach was "in." Systems analysts had a tendency to be too cute or too sophisticated. The value of something became a function of its uniqueness or complexity, not its worth to the user: The means justified the ends. Vendors and users alike were subject to a wish-fulfillment syndrome. When a new technique or product on the market bears some relationship (however remote) to a problem, there is a tendency to apply it, regardless of relevance. The computer and the various concepts of management information systems, central data bases, operations research, management science, and the like were facets of this wish-fulfillment syndrome.

This was also the decade of advertising, seminars, general and special-interest groups, trade shows, press conferences and educational institutes. Computers were talked about as never before.

In perspective, however, the 1960s represent the essential phase of growth and expansion of the computer industry. Successful marketing is as important as product development, perhaps even more so. Many experts feel that the demise of GE and RCA in the computer industry resulted principally from their lack of effective marketing organizations.

The Third Computer Decade

The third computer decade began with the business downturn in the early 1970s. At a time when business volume was down, companies found themselves underutilizing their computers, or with excess capacity because of the oversell and overbuy of the late 1960s. For the first time since computers appeared on the commercial scene, EDP managers were forced to cut computer operating budgets. The EDP industry had experienced a kind of chain letter effect: everything growing at an exponential rate. One system this month became two next month, four the next, and eight the following. Similarly, software and services companies proliferated, terminal and peripheral devices multiplied, and the market for trained systems analysts, programmers, and operating personnel expanded. The business recession ended all that. The computer industry was not immune to depressions after all.

This era marked a maturing of the mainframes, with more judicious selection and use on the part of the user community. However, this was the era of minicomputer proliferation, and *extensibility* became a popular buzzword. The less expensive minis led to their use in remote offices and facilities of large companies as well as lowering the entry threshold for small businesses acquiring their first computer. This decade also marked the coming-on phase of the microcomputer. Both the mini and micro explosion will be covered in a later chapter dedicated solely to this most important development.

The third decade of computers belonged to the businessperson and to management, as the first belonged to the engineer and the second to the marketeer. Although the management outlook reveals increasing maturity in a rapidly growing and changing industry, it should not be used to stifle product innovation and expansion. Rather, it should be used to direct the thrust of product development to ensure the greatest return from the development dollar. The user should focus on the applications he foresees for the machine. The computer manufacturer should concentrate on the products required to accomplish these applications most efficiently and economically. When users are overawed by technology, they are, as someone has put it, like the stereo enthusiast who, wild over woofers, intrigued by intermodulation, tantalized by tweeters, and delirious over decibels, hates music.

The Fourth Computer Decade

The last chapter will give a more complete picture of what we can expect in the 1980s. Generally there should be a peaking of the mainframe business. It will grow but much slower than the mini and micro computer areas; in fact, the market will see a blurring of the distinction between mainframes, minis, and micros.

The general-manager framework will carry over to the fourth decade of computer use, causing more emphasis on solid business practice and tighter control over computer and related expenditures. EDP departments are being scrutinized as closely as other operating departments within a company. The computer itself is being treated like other major capital expenditures, coming under stringent analysis regarding return on investment and cash flow.

There is a more formal planning by both the vendor and the customer. A comprehensive, quantitative data base of information about user buying profiles is now available, as is a qualitative data base on application areas, system trends, and future use patterns. The planning cycle now emanates more from user needs and requirements rather than from technology and product considerations. Users dictate the "what" of EDP while vendors supply the "how." This is exactly as it should be. The key justification criteria are becoming ease of use and total user benefit, rather than degree of sophistication. The computer designer works more and more under the constraint of "elegance in simplicity," providing advanced computing equipment and keeping the complexity transparent to the user.

Users no longer want to replace equipment just to have the most modern computer. They want to make sure they can change equipment without losing productivity, without unnecessary cost, and with commensurate benefits.

SUMMARY

Chapter 1 defined electronic data processing and the computer's role in it. After a look at the principal components of a computer system, the chapter reviewed the history of data-processing equipment. Beginning with the abacus, the origin and evolution of computers was traced through Babbage's difference engine, Herman Hollerith's punched cards, IBM, the Mark I at Harvard, and the UNIVAC I at the Department of the Census. Four decades of computer use were described, opening with the 1950s, the era of the engineer and the mainframe, moving to the 1960s, the era of the marketeer, and coming through the 1970s, the era of the businessperson and the mini, when computer systems returned to management.

The fourth decade, with the proliferation of micros, should continue the business perspective established in the 1970s. The brief history of computers has followed the cycle of all high-technology industries: a rapid buildup of the technology, followed by a lag in the ability of users to see the implications of the device or to tap its full potential. This "culture lag," as it has been termed, has certainly been true in the EDP industry.

This background provides the framework for a more comprehensive look at what computers do (Chapter 2) and the why of computerization or cost justification (Chapter 3). The rapid emergence of mini and micro computers (Chapter 4) will be described before discussing how computers accomplish their intended applications (Chapter 5). From there, we will look at several key areas of computer usage: management decision making (Chapter 6), management information systems (Chapter 7), and teleprocessing systems (Chapter 8). A look at the future of computers and computer usage (Chapter 9) concludes the book.

Computers can replace people; relieve people of routine, dull, repetitive jobs; simulate situations; save or lose hundreds of thousands of dollars; power advanced information systems; frustrate a broad spectrum of people; make giant mistakes; improve the accuracy of information; complicate simple procedures; break down repeatedly or run for months without interruption; aid management decision making; make a company competitive; and make some people sorry they ever saw one.

In short, computers can excite and exasperate, challenge and confound, stimulate and stupefy. We are now in the fourth decade of computer use (or misuse, as the case may be). Despite the problems, the learning curve has been rapid, and it is inevitable that computers and information systems will play an increasingly significant role in our lives.

Uses and Applications of Computer Systems

2

This chapter will concentrate on the "what" of computers, exploring the myriad of computer applications throughout industry and government. It is important to focus on the "what" and the "why" (covered in Chapter 3) before delving into the "how" of computers. This chapter first will categorize the general types of computer applications and then will give application profiles in a variety of areas. The applications will range from a simple order-processing program to a complex simulation of submarine warfare. From these examples a manager should be able to discern the wide applicability of computers. When you assess the potential use of computers to improve business operation, always keep in mind that the results of computerization must offer commensurate benefits of savings to the company.

TYPES OF APPLICATIONS

Computer applications can be categorized into three general areas: strategic, operational, and administrative (see Figure 2-1). The strategic area is normally the province of top management assisted by various staff planning groups. Top management determines the short- and long-term objectives of the business; the physical, monetary, and personnel resources to realize these ob-

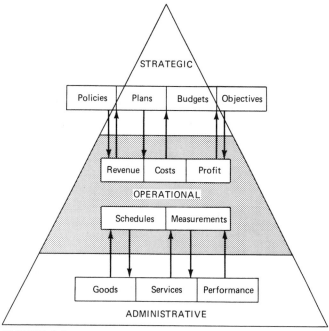

FIGURE 2-1
Application Categories

jectives; and the policies and strategies that best utilize these resources. This activity involves the study of market conditions, the analysis of competition and business opportunities, and the development of alternate product plans and strategies.

The operational area is the province of middle management, translating the strategies of top management into specific schedules, measurements, and implementation plans to achieve the stated business and strategic objectives. While there is an important element of planning in this activity, the emphasis is on management control.

The administrative, or support, area is the actual production of the goods and services and the provision of them to the served marketplace. This is usually performed by lower levels of management supported by production workers and clerical administrative personnel.

Computer application examples in the strategic area are business and financial models that project the results of alternate actions on profitability and other business indicators. Examples of operational applications are production and inventory control systems that schedule and control manufacturing operations. In the administrative area typical applications are order processing, billing, and accounting.

A survey I conducted in 1980 of one hundred company presidents, shows that 88 percent thought the application of computers to administrative applications in their companies has been positive or very positive, while the equivalent statistics for operational applications was 61 percent and for strategic areas was 21 percent.

It is interesting to speculate on the comparatively slow development in strategic and operational applications. A look at the characteristics of basic applications may provide a clue. Basic applications

- Are easy to justify
- Have tangible benefits
- Have been done before
- Represent well-known methodology
- Are in the controller's or accountant's bailiwick
- Involve upper management to a minimal extent
- Are necessary building blocks for advanced applications
- Represent a required learning curve
- Require less-skilled personnel
- Have minimal risk of failure or impact on the organization

While the foregoing list certainly indicates that it is wise to start with the more basic applications, the real payoff of computerization comes when the moneymaking areas of a business are tackled. The basic applications can be building blocks and represent a learning curve if they logically grow into the advanced applications. This happens only if there is proper initial planning. Oftentimes, the advanced applications remain only as potentials because the company faces massive redesign and reimplementation. The importance of systems planning cannot be emphasized too highly. Applications must be designed to allow for later enhancements and to be the springboard into advanced applications.

MODES OF IMPLEMENTATION

Depending upon the nature of the applications and the particular business environment, the systems designer will decide how to get information into and out of the computer. The decision is important because, as in most business decisions, there are trade-offs of cost, complexity, time, capability, need, and benefit to balance in determining which method to use. The basic methods are (1) batch, or sequential, processing; (2) on-line processing; and (3) transaction processing.

Batch, or Sequential, Processing

This type of operation is decreasing but is still the workhorse of today's data processing. Data are collected and saved, then processed in batches at predetermined times. The classic example of batch processing by computer is the oldest application, payroll. Transactions are collected during the week as they occur. At a predefined time, usually the Thursday before Friday payday, the hourly rate, the hours worked, and other data are fed into the computer. The computer prints the paychecks that are distributed to the wage earners. Various payroll reports and registers also can be produced. Batch operation is very efficient in such situations as customer billing and insurance premium collection, where regimentation and orderly process can be achieved. Where the process is less controllable, however, and where time demands are more pressing, another implementation mode may be a wiser choice.

On-Line Processing

On-line processing involves a direct communications link into the central computer system. The link can be local—that is, from within the same locality as the computer—or it can be from a remote location.

A typical on-line operation is the ability to make an inquiry to a central data base in order to ascertain the inventory status of an item being ordered, a credit check on a customer, or a bank balance of a depositor. The distinction between on-line operation and transaction processing described next is that the central file is not altered during the on-line inquiry. Thus, there are two separate subsystems, the inquiry subsystem and the file update subsystem. The file update system can be initiated either by a batch of transactions or periodically as individual transactions occur. On-line operation can be input only, an example of which is sending data to the central computer to be stored for later processing, or it can be what is called real time. Real time operation involves in effect an instantaneous feedback from the central computer to the inquiry point at the remote site.

Transaction Processing

Transaction processing incorporates all of the attributes of on-line processing but in addition updates the central file or data base if an update is called for. For example, if an order is being taken, an inquiry is made as to inventory status and if there is stock on hand, the order is processed, an invoice printed, and the file updated (reduced by the quantity ordered). The next order for the same item will now screen a current balance for availability. When the inventory balance is reduced to a predetermined replenish point, a purchase order or production notice is automatically produced. Transaction processing has obvious advantages over the other application modes described and is the favored approach today. The shift from batch to transaction processing represents a major trend in application development.

INFORMATION CATEGORIES

A basic consideration that runs across the range of application types is the kind of information required for computerization. Information is becoming an increasingly valuable commodity in business. It is considered by many to be as significant a resource as the four M's of men, machines, material, and money. Information has many shapes and forms, but it can be characterized by the matrix shown in Figure 2-2.

Internal information is a by-product of the normal operations of a business. For example, a recording of inventory usage for the past week is typical internal information. Internal information usually is historical, or after-the-fact, data. Category A represents information that is reported but not statistically processed. In the case of inventory usage, if the information is limited to history and no attempt is made to sample statistically or draw correlations from the data, it represents internal reported data. If, however, inventory usage is plotted to project future usage patterns that are used to set optimum inventory levels, it represents an example of Category B, statistically processed internal information.

FIGURE 2-2
Information Matrix

Type of Information	Reported	Processed
Internal	A	B
External	C	D

External information is data whose source is outside the operations of the company. Population growth in the market served by a company or changes in the ethnic makeup of the market are external information. Category C reports such data but makes no attempt to analyze them statistically. In Category D various mathematical techniques have been used to analyze and correlate the data. A sales forecast based on historical sales movement would be Category B information, whereas a sales forecast that also includes external market statistics and trends would be a combination of B and D. The relative use of these various forms of information by a computer system is consistent with the alphabetical sequence. That is, A is found in a computer system more often than B, and so on.

In order for a computer to tackle advanced applications, the applications must be built around processed external information. The difficulty not only in acquiring this information but in developing the decision rules to process it is another reason why the basic applications still predominate.

MANAGEMENT ATTITUDES
AND APPROACH

The International Data Corporation, publisher of the *EDP Report*, studied top management EDP attitudes and expectations several years ago. The sample was drawn from those IDC called the "professional computer user," users who represent the large companies where EDP spending is concentrated. IDC selected its survey sample from less than half the organizations that spend over 95 percent of the total EDP dollars in the country. IDC feels that these are the "pacemaking organizations, where new applications are first implemented and new concepts proved. It is these users who must set the pace if the computer industry is to continue solid growth in the future."

The findings of the study were quite similar to others I have reviewed. They also agreed with my personal observations in discussing EDP with hundreds of users over the past several years. I have summarized the survey results in Figure 2-3.

Management is stating in these surveys that after a decade or so of pioneering, experimenting, and learning, it is time to return to "results orientation." They now are aware of the complexities of advanced systems, as well as the time and cost to implement them. With this realization, management would like

MANAGEMENT ATTITUDE

- Dissatisfied with overall EDP performance
- Implementation of new applications is never on schedule
- Costs are consistently underestimated
- Communication between EDP and the user department is a problem
- Inefficiency often is buried under a cloak of redundancy
- Continue to believe in EDP

MANAGEMENT APPROACH

- Desire realistic new applications
- Recognize need for greater management control of EDP
- Want more emphasis on centralization
- Operate EDP as a cost/profit center
- Need more precise feasibility data
- Need clearer planning procedures
- Develop management steering committees to approve applications

FIGURE 2-3
Management Attitude and Approach to Computer Applications

to see a more practical and pragmatic approach to computer applications. Management must take overall direction of EDP, insisting on stricter feasibility criteria and benefit analyses. They must participate as members of steering committees to select and approve new application development and direction. Most important, management still believes in the value and worth of EDP—despite the rather bleak record in some cases. They feel it is time to regroup and reassess the situation. It is time to re-orient goals and objectives based on a more solid EDP planning process, an enlightened management involvement, and a thorough evaluation of where the computer and advanced EDP approaches can best aid the company.

COMPUTER USE BY INDUSTRY

Figure 2-4 breaks down installed computer value by industry segment. The total of $68 billion of installed value comes from an International Data Corporation 1979 Year End Projection, while the industry split is derived from a study by Quantum

28

Sciences. The figure includes both mainframes and minicomputers.

There are more computers installed in manufacturing companies than in other industries. This holds true for both discrete, or assembly-type, manufacturing (automobiles, electronics) and process manufacturing (food processing, chemicals, or petroleum). Over $20 billion (30 percent of the total) is invested in computers in manufacturing. Banking and Finance is the second-ranking industry, while federal government, insurance and business services (computer service centers, certified public accountants, research firms, lawyers, and personnel services) are next in volume of installed equipment. The federal government, which accounted for as much as 70 percent of the computer value in the early 1960s, now represents only 9 percent. Education and health care are fast-growing segments.

Manufacturing   The basic computer applications are the same in both the discrete type of manufacturing operations and the process type of manufacturing. Accounting, order processing, purchasing, and inventory applications are computerized in most manufacturing companies. Inventory status reports, sales analyses, and cost reports are commonplace documents to the management of manufacturing companies. In more advanced applications, projected sales volume is used as prime input into other subsystems (production scheduling, for example) within the business system. An increasing use is made of numerical control applications where the computer produces a paper tape that is fed into a machine tool controller to control the drilling or milling of a machine part. In design automation an engineer designs a part or product with the aid of a computer that tells how the part will react under stress and other conditions.

In the process, or continuous-flow, type of manufacturing, process control computers are used to control the flow of the product or process automatically. Mix formulation is used to aid petroleum, food processing, or other areas where an optimum blend of raw material is processed to form the finished product while meeting certain cost and other constraints. For example, percentages of different octanes are constraints in petroleum, and nutritional and vitamin content are constraints in food processing. This complex process is materially aided by the computer. Simulation and revenue models are other examples of advanced manufacturing applications.

The following are examples of how two companies in the

FIGURE 2-4

Use of Computers by Industry

Industry Segment	Computer Value (in billions)	Market Share	Basic Applications	Advanced Applications
Discrete manufacturing	$12.9	18.9%	• accounting • order processing • purchasing • inventory control	• forecasting • numerical control • production scheduling • design automation
Process manufacturing	$ 7.7	11.3%	• accounting • order processing • purchasing • inventory control	• mix formulation • process control • simulation • revenue models
Banking and finance	$ 7.1	10.4%	• demand deposit accounting • check processing • proof and transit operations • cost control	• on-line savings • centralized file system • portfolio analysis • cash flow analysis
Federal government	$ 6.3	9.2%	• accounting and administration • tax reporting and auditing • order processing • census analysis	• information retrieval • intelligence • command and control • pollution control
Insurance	$ 5.9	8.7%	• premium accounting • customer billing • external reports • reserve calculation	• actuarial analysis • investment analysis • policy approval • cash flow analysis
Business and personnel service	$ 5.2	7.7%	• service bureau functions • tax preparation • accounting • client records	• econometric models • time sharing • engineering analysis • data base
Education	$ 4.1	6.0%	• attendance accounting • grading and scoring • school administration • alumni records	• student scheduling • computer-aided instructions • library cataloging • student counseling
Utilities	$ 3.9	5.8%	• customer billing • accounting • meter reading • inventory control	• rate analysis • line and generator loading • operational simulation • financial models
State and local government	$ 3.7	5.5%	• utility billing • tax recordkeeping • payroll • school administration	• traffic analysis • budget preparation • police identification • city planning
Retail	$ 2.7	4.0%	• customer billing • sales analysis • accounting • inventory reporting	• point of sale automation • sales forecasting • merchandising • cash flow analysis

FIGURE 2-4 (Continued)

Industry Segment	Computer Value (in billions)	Market Share	Basic Applications	Advanced Applications
Transportation	$ 2.5	3.7%	• rate calculation • vehicle maintenance • cost analysis • accounting	• traffic pattern analysis • automatic rating • tariff analysis • reservation systems
Health care	$ 1.7	2.5%	• patient billing • inventory accounting • health care statistics • patient history	• lab/operation scheduling • nurses' station automation • intensive care • preliminary diagnosis
Distribution	$ 1.6	2.3%	• order processing • inventory control • purchasing • warehouse control	• vehicle scheduling • merchandising • forecasting • store site selection
Printing and publishing	$ 1.0	1.5%	• circulation • classified ads • accounting • payroll	• automatic typesetting • home finder • media analysis • page layout
Other	$ 1.7	2.5%		
TOTAL	$68.0	100.0%		

manufacturing industry are using computers. One shows a small company involved mainly in basic applications; the other shows a large company delving into more advanced computer applications.

USING COMPUTERS TO PRODUCE AND PACKAGE CANDY

Company Background

A Midwest-based candy company is in business to "keep 'em smiling" by selling taste sensations—a line of unusual confections that are completely new additions to the candy industry (as contrasted with redesigned versions of items already available).

To keep this market the company has been a pioneer in product packaging, in machine design, and in new product research that has a twofold objective: to provide ever-increasing consumer enjoyment and ever-increasing profits for dealers and distributors.

**Computer
Applications**

The computerized applications are multilevel, multibased, fixed-variable systems processed for all divisions and subsidiaries. The company developed a financial reporting system that includes accounts payable, standard cost raw material inventory, budget reporting, and job cost reporting.

It also has developed an invoicing application consisting of various subsystems. Accounts receivable generates timely information reports. Sales analysis (detail or combined) shows weekly and monthly territory gross sales, daily gross sales, quarterly customer and bookings reports. The accounting subsystem issues sales commissions and credit memo charges. The finished-goods inventory subsystem maintains daily, weekly, and monthly cumulative inventory and back-order reports and summaries. The invoicing subsystem reports on daily order counts and cancelled and revised orders and prepares a trucking recap. A future-orders report subsystem prepares future orders reports by item, broker, and warehouse.

The accounts payable system has proved a vital asset in the preparation and maintenance of vendor checks, analysis of cash requirements, and handling of bank reconciliations. The system relays all information that has been approved for payment to the stores inventory system, which allows for production adjustments, adjustments to the vendor's invoice, standard loss adjustments, obsolete raw material write-offs, physical end-of-the-month inventories, and so on. A new standard cost system provides the cost of goods for each item by total material, labor, overhead, and standard loss; the cost of goods for each store by product line; and also the cost of goods for each store for each item number.

The accounts payable, stores inventory, and accounting system feed information to the general ledger system, which prepares the necessary financial reports such as the income statement, balance sheet, monthly and YTD general ledger. The general ledger system passes its results to the budget system.

The budget system is a sophisticated application that covers every division. It breaks each division into major areas, such as manufacturing, engineering, marketing, administration, distribution, and other income and expense areas. Within each of these major areas three levels of reporting are provided: a department report, a cost center summary report, and a cost center report.

As has been true with the other phases of business—machine design, packaging, innovative products—so it is with the data-processing operations. The company continues to design and implement effective changes to make outstanding accomplishments in its field, and provide the company with important competitive advantages.

AN INTEGRATED INFORMATION SYSTEM

Company Background

A manufacturing company with 4 plants, 16 assembly departments, about that many fabricating centers, and more than 200 machine centers has installed a pacesetting integrated information system.

The operations are characterized by a nationwide distribution network. The product moves through 38 branch offices and 312 authorized distributors—all of which maintain some inventory. Authorized distributors generate 37 percent of the orders but account for only 24 percent of the sales. Most of the business is done through the branch offices.

The product line is large. Products are classified into 176 family groups, representing 12,000 finished goods (listed in catalog), of which 3,600 are carried in inventory and 8,400 are made to order. Approximately 1,500 new items enter the product line annually, and a similar number are discontinued.

These 12,000 finished goods require 25,000 component parts, of which 6,600 are carried in inventory and 18,400 are made to order.

Computer System Benefits

The integrated system has already paid off substantially, and refinements continue to increase the benefits. In the late 1950s the company was achieving an 80 percent customer service level, (that is, 80 percent of the orders were being delivered according to original customer requests—with no delays or adjusting of dates). The sales inventory ratio was a respectable 4.2. However, the production cost variance averaged 16.3 percent. Clerical expenses ran 3.6 percent of sales.

This was not good enough in a highly competitive business. Since the primary asset a company has (in addition to high quality, reliable products) is customer service, an improvement in customer service was given top priority.

In addition to the top-priority project of enhancing the competitive position through improved customer service, three areas of cost control also were given top priority.

1. Production costs must be controlled within tight tolerances. This is especially true in a business where prices are negotiable at field sales level.

2. Distribution costs, especially the costs associated with a nationwide disbursement of inventory, must be controlled within reasonable limits relative to needs for customer service.

3. Clerical costs in a growing business must be contained and, if possible, reduced.

A computerized integrated management information and control system was instituted. By the late 1970s performance in the four areas of high priority was greatly improved.

1. Customer service. Fully 97 percent of orders were filled as requested, a substantial improvement.

2. Inventory turnover. The sales inventory ratio was 6.2, a 50 percent increase over the previous performance. More improvement is expected.

3. Production cost variance. This category has all but disappeared, being controlled within a 1 percent tolerance. This is possible because timely, accurate information is now available when it is needed.

4. Clerical expense. The ratio of clerical expenses has dropped to 2.8 percent, an unusual achievement in a rapidly growing business that must face the increasing rates of clerical labor.

Development of the system took imagination, perspective, planning, and time, but the benefits were there.

Business and Personnel Services

The business and personnel services category covers a broad range of companies. It includes computer service centers (accounting for a large number of installed computers), consulting firms, certified public accountants, credit agencies, personnel companies, and the like. The applications in this industry segment cover a wide spectrum, ranging from such basic service bureau applications as payroll and order processing to the preparation of tax returns, accounting, and the maintenance of client records (in the case of service companies). The advanced applications include complex econometric input-output models, online processing and time sharing (such as the on-line credit checking system described in this section), computer-aided engineering design performed by architects, and various central data base applications, such as legal and medical information retrieval.

The case histories that follow describe a computer service

center and an on-line, communications-oriented credit card company.

APPLICATIONS AT A COMPUTER SERVICE CENTER

**Company
Background**

One of the many growing service centers in the New York City area provides a virtually unlimited range of data-processing services and support to an equally wide range of small, medium, and large businesses. The company's most important product, data-processing expertise, is manifest in the broad scope of data-processing services offered—hardware, software, applications, and systems support. A large number of the customers are computer users who require overload computer time, operations assistance, and specialized systems and programming support.

**Emergency EDP
Assistance**

Typical of businesses that offer a service, the company receives panic calls for help. It must be prepared for these situations and must be able to accommodate the inevitable pressures.

One emergency involved a customer whose computer installation was destroyed by fire. The service center incorporated the customer's processing activities into its schedule and assumed full responsibility for production while the customer was arranging for the replacement of the computer installation. The entire processing job was performed without loss in time or money to the customer. Reports were produced on schedule, and the customer's data-processing needs were fulfilled to complete satisfaction.

**Standard
Application
Development**

Some of the functions a service center offers to its customers are developing new systems, writing programs, providing computer time for processing, and providing the support inevitably required for these services. This company has a history of success in the development and support of such standard accounting applications as accounts payable, accounts receivable, general ledger, billing, and inventory.

It offers a complete inventory management system that is processed daily for many customers. This system generates the daily invoices and exception reports. Produced on a weekly and monthly basis are complete sales and inventory reports that are tailored specifically to the customer's requirements. The invoices produced on the daily runs are posted automatically to the accounts receivable ledger, and monthly statements and reports are printed for management use. Significantly, the service center inventory system permits a customer to process enormous fluctuations in volume with a minimum of internal changes.

Specialized Application Development

The service center provides its wide range of services to over one hundred different customers. In addition to the standard accounting applications, it maintains programs for cost analysis, sales analysis, list maintenance, and market research. As an innovative and growing young company, however, it is not afraid to assume responsibility for writing specialized programs for customers with unique needs.

One example of the customized services available is research data-processing services. The center processes market research data and produces special reports for a research company. In another instance, the center provided a management consultant with complete data-processing services. By employing the center to develop and implement systems and to perform the actual computer processing of data, the consultant has transferred the tedious and time-consuming data-handling operations that are an inevitable part of his work.

REAL-TIME PROCESSING FOR REAL-LIFE SITUATIONS

This country's expanded use of credit cards for purchasing all kinds of goods and services has put a new strain on data-processing capabilities. For the credit card companies what was needed were new approaches to the credit card business—new ways to authorize charges, pay establishments, and collect from cardholders.

The critical area for an authorization system is the point of sale: the airline, restaurant, motel, or car rental clerk writing up the sale and trying to handle two or more urgent customers; and the customers themselves, on a hurried lunch hour, tired after a long trip, trying to catch a plane. If the authorization process isn't fast enough to satisfy these people, the system breaks down.

The real-time system at one company responds to these real-life situations through a communications network covering all points in the United States, plus lines to handle queries from foreign countries.

At the point of sale, the person seeking authorization calls the credit card company's central computing center. Within seconds the system retrieves all data necessary for authorization. The advanced software permits the data to be stored on "shared files"; two computer systems can access these files simultaneously. As soon as a record is updated through either computer, the data are available to on-line inquiry.

On the basis of these up-to-date data, the computer determines whether to grant authorization. If it approves credit, the computer itself generates a voice response back to the caller at the establishment, saying that the sale is approved and giving an authorization number.

If there is a problem, however, the computer sends a different voice message: "Please stand by for the credit manager." In the authorization room, a light flashes. The call is switched to a credit manager's video display terminal. The cardholder's file appears on the screen. The nature of the problem flashes on and off in the upper left-hand corner . . . "amount exceeds credit limit" . . . "card reported stolen" . . . or any of several dozen other conditions.

The credit manager then makes a judgment on the authorization. In cases of lost or stolen cards, he can ask the person at the establishment to confiscate the card. In other cases the credit manager may ask to speak to the cardholder to verify identity or to resolve a question about the account. Though the vast majority of authorization queries are handled entirely by the computer, the problem situations are handled by human judgment.

Banking and Finance

Banks and financial institutions are major users of computers. Much of their work centers around paper, an area where data processing finds its greatest utility. For many years banks have been using a special reader that interprets magnetic ink identifiers on each check. The checks then are sorted by individual and bank before demand deposit or savings account records are updated. Proof and transit and other accounting and cost control operations are common computer applications in most banks.

On-line savings systems, such as the one about to be described, have been implemented by many banks. Centralized file systems combine savings, checking, personal loan, and mortgage files for an individual into a single integrated file. Banks and financial institutions also use such computer-aided techniques as portfolio analysis and cash flow analysis to invest and control the funds essential for efficient operation. The following examples show how a savings bank and a full-service bank each use computers.

TODAY'S BANK MUST SERVE
TOMORROW'S NEEDS

With this philosophy in mind, one mutual savings bank has replaced an outdated computer with a new, advanced, on-line, high-performance system that provides the growth potential essential to fulfill tomorrow's needs.

Company Background

In the century since it opened its doors to serve the community, this bank has come a long way. Quill pens have given way to high-speed computerized accounting methods. Two men are no longer able to handle the complicated and specialized business affairs. Deposits and depositors have increased enormously, and a multitude of new services are offered.

The savings bank has nineteen branches scattered strategically throughout the metropolitan area where it is based. The president still adheres to the beliefs of the bank's founders: "An important part of our growth depends on locating new branches in areas convenient to our present and potential depositors."

The affairs of the bank are directed by its board of managers, 25 men prominent in the business, professional, and educational life of the community. The daily routines are carried out by over 400 employees. All records are maintained by a computer that provides immediate access to all information.

Decision to Go On-Line

The decision to go on-line was made in November 1975. For conversion ease, the savings bank built its system using a two-phased program:

Phase I was initiated in April 1976. A medium-speed central processor was installed to convert all of the Christmas club and vacation club files. Programs to be implemented during Phase II were also developed and tested during this period.

Phase II was initiated in September 1977 with the substitution of a larger central processor and disk pack drives. In May 1979 teller terminals were added. The central processor is now linked to forty-nine teller terminals.

The Application System

The on-line application system is one of the most advanced in banking. With it, any bank employee can communicate within seconds with the computer. Each teller's window is linked directly to the computer at the bank's data-processing center. Customers can make payments, deposits, or withdrawals from any branch and have the transactions recorded immediately by the computer.

Using a teller terminal, a teller enters the customer's bank book number on the keyboard. The computer then selects the proper account, matches the balances on the record and in the book, and instructs the teller to proceed with the next transaction. A typical operation takes less than ten seconds.

Since there are nine different types of accounts (individual; joint; in trust; corporate; fiduciary; automatic income; society, club, and lodge; special purpose; and Christmas and vacation clubs) this feature alone enables the bank to give better and faster service to depositors and customers.

Since "the teller machines . . . are totally electronic, . . . in effect, they will place the unlimited power of the computer at each teller's fingertips," stated the vice-president in charge of EDP operations. As the teller completes each transaction, the computer automatically updates the customer's bank book with interest (when applicable) and with any deposits or withdrawals that were made previously without the book. The customer's individual record is also updated in the computer. At that point, the latest account information is available to any teller at any location.

The teller's messages to the computer are transmitted over telephone lines.

Future Plans

This modern communications network accepts more than 260,000 regular savings depositors, 45,000 home owners with mortgages, and 53,000 special-type savings accounts. Future plans will allow even greater numbers. In addition to deposit and withdrawal transactions, the application will eventually be handling mortgage loan accounting and such peripheral operations as compiling daily settlement sheets and printing checks and money orders. Future refinements include sophisticated applications for investment analysis and a central information file.

The dynamic management information analysis system will permit such investment activities as bond trade analysis, stock analysis, resources allocation, and mortgage loan rating. Using stored data, video display units, or audio response equipment can supply management personnel with answers to a vast number of questions. These techniques guarantee that long-term management policies and decisions will be made faster and with a high degree of reliability.

A BANK PLANS A MANAGEMENT
INFORMATION SYSTEM

**Current
Applications**

Since the initial installation of its first computer, a New York bank has added two additional computers and a wide array of peripheral devices for both on-line and off-line processing. With the capacity to process over 90,000 items daily and the facility to accommodate the needs of more than thirty branches, the bank today puts its emphasis on communications. It has developed an on-line system that transmits customer information accurately and quickly to all branches. With a system of cathode ray tubes, audio response devices, and teleprinters, a bank employee can communicate directly with a central processor and receive instantaneous responses on account balances and credit information.

As soon as the second computer was installed, the bank was able to add all the applications designed for the previous system (integrated internal accounting, branch profit and loss accounting, and a payroll deposit plan). Although the personnel workload diminished and the number of items processed daily increased from 35,000 to 60,000, the bank was able to implement several applications previously considered impossible. Some of these included automatic proof and transit, general ledger accounting, and responsibility reporting.

Future Plans

Currently under development in the bank is a totally integrated management information system that will allow full utilization of all file data. Designed to facilitate the organization, storage, and retrieval of data, the central information file system is based on the concept of a centralized data base. Files are structured on a hierarchical level so that when one file is interrogated, the computer will automatically access related files and generate all relevant information. This system will allow the bank to eliminate redundant information and establish relationships between accounts and between customers so that information can be retrieved through the customer's name or any of the customer's account numbers.

**Federal
Government**

The use of computers in the federal government is a microcosm of the use of computers in the rest of the business community. The federal government operates manufacturing plants, financial institutions, service operations, hospitals, education facilities, transportation, distribution outlets, and the like. Basic applications include accounting and administration, processing and auditing tax returns, maintaining and analyzing census data, and order processing and billing for the services the government performs for individuals and businesses.

The government uses such advanced applications as information retrieval functions like the one described in the first example for various functions of intelligence work, for command and control systems for the armed services (see the submarine simulator described in the second example), as well as for analyzing a variety of ecological statistics and data to help curb the spread of pollution.

A MANAGEMENT INFORMATION SYSTEM
DESIGNED BY MANAGERS

[Reprinted in part from an article appearing in **Datamation** magazine by Walter M. Carlson, then director of technical information for the Department of Defense.]

Information Retrieval

The Department of Defense, in coordination with the National Aeronautics and Space Administration, has installed a technical management information system that has been and continues to be designed by the management users of the system. The system provides current status data on research and exploratory development program expenditures of more than $1.5 billion annually. Successful and satisfactory experience with the system within DoD and NASA during the first year of operation has led toward adoption by other federal agencies and, possibly, by some allied defense organizations.

In addition to the direct and continuing involvement of research and development management at all echelons in the evolving design, the system has major features that are both unique and contrary to previous practices in information systems. A large measure of management's acceptance of the system can be credited to use of a computer to serve individual requests; no printouts are prepared from a data bank containing more than 50 million digits of information until and unless a specific request is made.

System's Purpose

The purpose of the system is to provide prompt DoD management access to the current status of research and technology efforts being performed in-house and under contract or grant. The goal of the system is to have the information on significant changes in status available in a central data bank within 15 days after the change occurs. A "significant change" may range from an important technical result or assignment of new people all the way to termination of the work.

The scope provides complete coverage of the DoD program in the Research and Exploratory Development categories and selected activities in the other program categories of the R&D budget. For each "work unit" a total of 35 data elements are recorded near or at their point of generation, if possible, and entered into the system in carefully standardized formats. More than 20,000 separate work units have been reported on, and updating of the reports is continuous, as changes occur, rather than periodic.

[The middle section of the article explains the system and how it was implemented. Mr. Carlson concludes the discussion as follows:]

Top Management Tool

Perhaps the most significant aspect of the future will be the change in management methodology. Top management have already found, to their great satisfaction, that they can find out directly what is happening now by going to the data bank rather than through a complex organization. To the extent that top management continues to design the system by reacting to organization and middle management performance rather than to technical detail on individual work unit decisions, the system will grow and prosper. If management's design is to do "project engineering" at all levels, the cover-up reactions at lower levels will try to thwart the necessary visibility, and the system will fail.

SAILORS FIGHT REALISTIC BATTLES IN COMPUTERIZED SIMULATED SUBS

Simulated Battles

The air in the submarine attack center fairly crackles with the tension of men in combat.

One sailor, his forehead beaded with nervous perspiration, launches a torpedo to destroy an enemy ship.

Other men are absorbed in other tasks in the cramped, dimly lit heart of the nuclear sub—navigating, manning communications equipment, operating sonar and radar systems. Bulkheads are lined with control panels bristling with dials, knobs, and levers.

When the battle is over, nobody has been injured or killed. Every member of the crew remains unscathed. The reason for the crew's safety is demonstrated when its members walk out, not of a submarine hatch, but through a doorway in a three-story building at the U.S. Naval Submarine School at New London, Connecticut.

These men are trainees. They have just emerged from several nerve-jangling hours of a maneuver so realistic that it temporarily transported them into another world, a world at war. They come out more seasoned naval fighters than they were when they went in. They have gained invaluable experience in anticipation of the day when war games might cease to be games.

The myriad knobs, levers, and dials are exact duplicates of their counterparts on an actual submarine. Much of the equipment is operational. The rest is a painstakingly accurate facsimile.

For all this electronic realism the taxpayer spends relatively little money. Without the simulator, the only way to conduct such exercises would be under vastly more expensive operational conditions at sea.

The New London Simulation Facility

Three attack centers, each a copy of a center aboard one of the three classes of U.S. nuclear submarines, are housed in one wing of the building at New London. The centers are the key sections of a device called the submarine attack center trainer.

In another section of the trainer are its "brains" —a huge, complex digital computer. The computer makes possible the simulation of virtually all the jobs performed by the attack center equipment.

Beyond its primary goal of seasoning attack center crews in offensive and defensive submarine tactics, the trainer serves a vital secondary purpose. It trains naval officers in directing and coordinating sub task force groups with supporting aircraft and surface ships.

The place where the war games are controlled and observed is a separate, auditoriumlike room known as the tactical display room. From this part of the building, officers can coordinate the overall action of the three attack centers. As many as twenty-four submarines, surface ships, and planes may be brought into the maneuvers. The maneuvers may be conducted in real or compressed time.

Movements of the various vehicles are recorded on a projection screen with colored tracks. The screen represents the hundreds of square miles of ocean where the battle is fought.

At the back of the room is the control panel—the master instructor's console—where the outlines of the battle are sent to all three attack centers.

Unseen by the trainees during an exercise, other instructors sit at similar panels in areas adjoining each attack center and direct that center's part in the battle. On smaller projection screens the story of the battle's progress unfolds. Elsewhere in the building are command centers equipped with status boards and communications facilities. There, command and staff officers take part in advanced tactical maneuvers.

When the war games are over, all the participants gather in the tactical display room for a critique of their performance.

How large a role does this intricate electronic hookup play in maintaining the defense readiness of the U.S. Navy? One high-ranking officer has called the new facility "dramatic evidence of the advance in the art of naval warfare."

Education

Education has become one of the fastest-growing users of computers. Machines handle the attendance, grading, and scoring of students, as well as other administrative functions of a school. The advanced computer applications include student scheduling, a serious problem in large schools with a varied curriculum. Computers maintain indexes and cross-indexes to enable students and teachers to make better use of school library facilities. Computer-aided instruction also is a growing field (see the following discussion). In addition, computers are being used to combine student records and personal data in order to correlate interests and suggest courses of study and career paths that the student might not have considered.

ONE COMPUTER—SEVEN COLLEGES

The Cooperative Computer System

A group of small colleges, with a total student population of 18,500 is linked (via leased telephone lines) in a data-processing network. Computers are used for applications in administration, programming instruction, and scholarly research.

Amid the whirring of magnetic tapes and disks and the muffled tapping of a high-speed printer, a staff of experienced professionals uses a computer on one campus to perform data-processing tasks for the seven colleges.

At each of the participating colleges, as well as in the office of the state Department of Education, a smaller computer has been installed for computer-to-computer communications that give access to the extensive centralized computing facilities. In this cooperative system, student records, administrative reports, and instructional compilations can be processed for all schools with the speed and flexibility of a powerful computer. Such a powerful machine could not have been justified for just one college's use.

Centralization of Functions

The centralization of administrative functions for the participating colleges has led to uniformity in several areas. Automated budgetary accounting simplifies the management of state funds. For each principal department in each college a statement of conformance to budget is printed monthly. Common formats for reporting to state agencies are used. Computer applications in this area include a variety of statistical and financial reports.

The computerized maintenance of course schedules and student record files further facilitates administrative and clerical procedures. For any given semester, the three student record files—admissions file, inactive student file, and active student history file—correspond, respectively, to information concerning all students admitted, all admitted students who did not matriculate, and all admitted students who did matriculate. The records for active students are cumulative, beginning with data gathered from the student's application for admission.

Better administration of all departments is now possible. With the completion of an impressive list of programming accomplishments for the registrars' offices, each administrator and faculty member can give more time to decision making and instruction.

Accuracy and high speed characterize the grade reporting system. For example, 8,000 grade reports for students on one campus are printed overnight. Data from remote colleges enter the network via the communication lines. Grade reports are then transmitted back to the colleges for printing. Also included in this system are the analysis of grades and the printing of the dean's list, the honor roll, and permanent record labels.

Previous EDP experience at one college has motivated the development of scheduling and instructional applications. Scheduling of students there is now a routine computer function. At the beginning of each semester, students' course requests are sent to the computer and processed for the assignment of students to class sections and for the creation of individual course cards. Each course request is analyzed according to a series of priorities. Preference in course selections can be determined using class year and degree requirements as criteria.

EDP is also used in the classroom. A student enrolled in a FORTRAN course submits a coded program to the instructor in punched-card form during the class session. At 4:00 P.M., the program is communicated to the computer across state. By 7:00 A.M., the next day the classroom printer is tapping away, and the printed compilation is available for the morning's first class session.

"At this point, we are providing the basic processing necessities for the colleges," says the director of data processing. "Our aggregate goal is to fulfill the needs of seven different organizations and to standardize divergent areas that lend themselves to greater efficiency through uniformity."

Future Applications

Efforts to refine and extend existing programming applications will focus on three main areas: programming instruction, course scheduling, and accounting and administrative processing. In addition to the FORTRAN compilations now processed, software will be developed for on-line transmissions and subsequent scheduled compilations of students' programs in other languages, such as COBOL. In the area of financial administration, cost projections and more comprehensive budgetary accounting will assist the colleges' administrators in planning more accurately and in conforming more consistently to budgetary allocations.

Computerized circulation control for the colleges' libraries is planned. Within minutes the computer would print a catalog by subject, title, or author. Look-up information for all publications stored at the individual libraries would be recorded in the computer system to permit the printing of a common catalog for the group of seven libraries. If a book were not available at one library, it could be requested from another college's library via the computer network. The system could maintain statistics of borrowing habits to coordinate book purchases with current interests and projected quantity requirements.

Insurance

The insurance industry was an early user of computing equipment to simplify the handling of administrative paperwork. The volume and repetition of such activities as the calculation of customer premiums or the billing of policyholders make them ideal computer applications. In addition, computers produce a variety of external reports and handle such statistical jobs as calculating insurance reserves. The advanced applications move the computer into calculating actuarial statistics, approving policies, analyzing historical patterns, and predicating future actions on projected probabilities. In addition, the computer is being used in investment and cash flow analysis: two areas vital to insurance company operations.

COMPUTERS
AT AN INSURANCE COMPANY

It was apparent that manual methods and punched-card records at one large insurance company were no longer adequate to provide the fast service that policyholders expect. With future growth and the need for a strong user-supplier relationship in mind, the company decided to install a computer. The anticipated move to EDP was complicated by the burdens of rapid expansion and the need to maintain existing operations without interruption.

Installing a computer was the first step in a plan to implement an operating system that would perform the essential business functions of the company. This system stores and processes all data pertinent to a given insurance contract. The tape-oriented system performs premium billing, general accounting, and actuarial valuation processing.

The master policy record produced for each new policy is the backbone of the system. The record stores client data, agent data, and policy details, as well as billing, commission, deposit, and loan statistics. On a bimonthly basis the master file is processed through four production subsystems: billing, commission, dividend, and loan processing.

In addition to the accounting functions for each of the production applications, the system also prints a variety of documentation. Bills, payment checks, fiscal statistics, control listing, activity registers—the output provides the insurance company with the crucial information required for successful operation. From returnable collection cards to new issue declaration sheets, the system provides a total capability that turns the wheels of efficiency and growth.

MAJOR INSURANCE COMPANY INSTALLS
ON-LINE COMMUNICATIONS

Three major insurance information processing tasks—premium collections, account business transactions, and agent recordkeeping—were described at the demonstration of a prominent life insurance company's new nationwide computer communication system. A description of how the computer handles one of these jobs—premium collection—will serve to illustrate the benefits of the system.

Premium notices, prepared in a single pass on a high-speed printer at the home office, are printed with conventional policyholder information and also with a special bar code, called Orthocode. The Orthocode contains such fixed customer data as policyholder account number and premium due.

The notices are sent to customers, who return one section, with payments, to their local office. Local personnel batch and insert the notices into the communications console. The console scans the bar code and prints the coded data in English on the teleprinter and punches it on the punched-tape unit associated with the teleprinter. Additional information may be typed in at this time.

The printed copy serves as the local office record. The punched tape record is read over telephone lines through the multiple communications control unit and into the computer's memory. From there it will be routed to a magnetic tape file for subsequent processing.

Thus, premium collections, the vast majority of data-handling transactions, can be accomplished quickly and easily. The system is used for monthly, quarterly, semiannual, and annual collections.

Utilities

The utilities industry includes the gas and electric companies as well as communications services, the teletype and telephone companies. With the volume of customers and variety of available services, the computer made early inroads into the basic applications of customer billing and accounting, as well as meter reading and inventory control for the variety of products and supplies handled by the utility companies. Advanced applications center around analysis of rate structures and facility scheduling and loading. In addition, simulation and financial models are used to determine the impact of population growth and other ecological factors on power and service demands.

The following case studies illustrate the use of communication-oriented systems by utilities. The first shows how a gas and electric company handles a portion of the customer service functions. The second example tells how a telephone company automatically calculates long-distance toll rates.

VISUAL DISPLAY TERMINALS IMPROVE CUSTOMER SERVICE FOR GAS AND ELECTRIC COMPANY

The gas and electric company's system is built around the concept of separating high-volume, relatively stable data from low-volume, rapidly changing data. The stable data—a year's billing data for each gas and electric service to each customer—change only once a month, at regular intervals. The record of accounts receivable and pending service orders for a particular customer changes daily. The current status is very significant in providing customer service. The utility company uses a combination of local microfilm records and on-line visual computer inquiry to satisfy its requirements.

This is the way it works. A customer enters the service office to inquire about the status of a service call and also the status of his account. The clerk goes to the file to obtain the microfilm record for the customer. The clerk then enters the customer's account number in the visual display unit on the desk. The depression of the transmit key sends the inquiry across a telephone line into the computer memory some miles away. The computer searches out the pertinent record from random-access storage and transmits back current information concerning the customer. The reply is displayed on the screen of the remote terminal on the clerk's desk within seconds. With the current transactions and the historical microfilm record at hand, the clerk knows the complete status of the customer's account and can answer the inquiry. This is an example of a practical and successful use of visual display units tied to a central computer.

TELEPHONE COMPANY SWITCHES TO VOICE ANSWER-BACK SERVICE—SPEEDS UP LONG-DISTANCE TOLL RATING

The Voice Answer-Back Approach

Talking computers are giving long-distance telephone operators split-second information on the cost of calling any of the more than 30,000 possible toll centers in the United States and Canada.

A matched pair of computers now makes it possible for one telephone company to give its customers much faster service in determining charges on intercity calls.

The new computerized telephone toll-rating system is designed primarily to calculate rates on the thousands of long-distance calls made each day from public telephones, motels, and hotels. It is expected to handle as many as 5,000 requests an hour.

The computer, whose "voice" is recorded on a small magnetic drum, "talks" by picking from the drum the words it needs to tell operators how much a call costs.

The Toll-rating Procedure

The toll-rating sequence might begin when a customer enters a telephone booth to place a long-distance call, for example. The operator asks for the area code and number being called and the area code and telephone number of the caller. The operator then keys in to the keyset a three-digit access code that connects to one of the computers—which may be hundreds of miles away.

The computer says that the operator has made the right connection by sending an acknowledgment tone. The operator then keys in thirteen more digits: The first six are the area and central office codes of the telephone where the call is being placed; the second six are the area and central office codes of the telephone being called. The final digit tells the computer the type of call, such as station-to-station or person-to-person.

The computer uses the geographical coordinates of 30,000 central office locations in the U.S. and Canada to calculate the distances, and the resulting charge, by referring to rate tables. The system makes use of the computer memory and auxiliary random-access drum storage.

Less than a tenth of a second after the last digit is transmitted, the computer gives the operator a "voice" reply. For example, the operator might hear "One-five-five, station-one-five-five." This would tell that the charge for the initial period of the call (normally three minutes) is $1.55. The operator would add to this any applicable tax and ask the customer to deposit the total amount.

Prerecorded in the audio response unit are the phrases necessary for intelligent replies. The computer automatically selects the phrases it needs from the appropriate audio response tracks.

State and Local Government   The applications in state and local government range from the basics of utility billing, city and state payrolls, tax records, and school administration to the advanced applications of analyzing traffic patterns and assigning traffic lights accordingly, budget preparation and administration, and as an aid in city planning (see the second example). In addition, some cities and states have police systems that maintain data banks on criminals, suspected criminals, stolen cars, and the like, to improve law enforcement. The following are two examples of the use of computers by state and local government.

COMPUTERS SERVE HEALTH SERVICES
AND EDUCATION

Faced with burgeoning administrative and reporting tasks, one state's department of health and education turned to electronic data processing.

In the fields of public education and public health, the state can boast success on four frontiers. The Department of Health is implementing an extensive medical assistance program with its computer, while the Department of Education is using its computer for the normal administrative and reporting functions. Perhaps more importantly, the state is providing computer services directly to local school districts. These services include test scoring and analysis, with plans for scheduling and data bank applications in the near future. The two state universities both have put their computers to work handling cumbersome administrative tasks, scheduling, scoring, and grade reporting. In addition, both schools are using their computers as teaching tools in a computer sciences curriculum.

A CITY GOES ON-LINE

The Key to Efficiency

Twenty-four hours ago, the city manager initiated a citywide study of the relation of crime to street lighting conditions. Today, with the results of that study, he is already taking action to bring light to poorly illuminated streets pinpointed by the study as having a high or rising crime rate.

The city manager's actions reflect the spirit and responsibility of one city's forward-looking government. It also reveals an efficiency uncommon in cities of any size. How can a major study such as the one undertaken by the city manager be accomplished overnight?

The city manager simply filled out a preprinted form stating the nature and the format of his study. His report request was added to report requests from various city departments, including the Assessor's Office, Public Works Department, and the City Planning Department, and was delivered to the city's data-processing center. There, with the aid of a computer, reports representing work-years of effort were produced in less than two hours. All reports were, as usual, delivered on time. All reports were accurate and up to date.

The City Data Bank

After a full systems feasibility study, the city council authorized the development of a comprehensive computer information storage and retrieval system designed to serve all departments and agencies of the city.

The system presently consists of two files, a street section file and a parcel file, containing over a million and a half information items. From these files, using the system's retrieval program and high-speed computer processing, almost any survey or analysis report that the city government desires can be produced in a matter of minutes.

The city manager states, "The city is pleased with our new system. Our new computer has added a finer touch and quicker action to the data-processing facilities. Reports and studies vital to the administration of this modern progressive community are produced faster and more accurately than was previously possible."

The stored information is playing an important role in urban renewal projects. Reports pinpointing areas of substandard housing and wasted space give the planning department the information it needs to schedule renovation.

Use of the data-processing center is shared by the Department of Education. This year, using a student scheduling system, educators citywide are looking forward to a smoother school year opening, with fewer course conflicts and fewer scheduling crises.

Reports on street and sanitation conditions, as well as complete tax information, are stored in the data bank's comprehensive files to be used in any reports these departments might require. In these public service departments, the data bank has streamlined the normal information flow and simplified the tax and public works projects while decreasing costs.

The computer system is a modern tool that saves the city time and money in hundreds of ways. Presently, the computer is used for the data bank, city payroll, real estate tax, city auto tags, personal property tax, library accounting, city shop (city vehicle cost accounting and performance), dog license listings, mailing lists for six departments, and student scheduling.

Distribution

The major function of a distributor is to maintain the flow of merchandise from manufacturer to retailer, and computers have aided materially in this process. Computers are used extensively for order processing, inventory control, purchasing, and warehouse control. Computers also aid in vehicle and load scheduling and in forecasting and merchandising, where the computer aids in spotting fast- and slow-moving items and in projecting the probable success of new items. Advanced systems can facilitate the development of ethnic and cultural models, which when combined with traffic patterns and competitive factors, can aid in the selection of successful store and sales outlet sites.

FOOD DISTRIBUTION
TURNS TO COMPUTERS

Company Background

One of the largest wholesale cooperative grocery companies in the nation started as a single neighborhood grocery store. Today its annual volume totals more than $300 million.

Today the company distributes nearly 18,000 grocery, delicatessen, frozen food and nonfood items to some 3,000 retail stores.

Servicing customers are six regional warehouses. This broad distribution capability is supplemented by thirty-eight terminal warehouses. These operate as cash and carry outlets servicing predominately nonmember customers.

Computer Service to Its Cooperative Members

As an early user of electronic data-processing equipment, the distributor has always placed very heavy emphasis on member reporting services. Today, with four regional data-processing centers, each fully equipped with third-generation computers and communication facilities, the emphasis has not changed.

More than 3,500 reports are prepared for members each month. These reports range from monthly recaps, profits and percentage reports to twelve-month item movement analysis. Each report provides an up-to-the-minute statistical analysis of the members' individual store activity. Additionally, customized private order guides are prepared for those members who desire this service.

The Inventory Control System

Another aspect of providing total service for members has been the recent installation of a system designed to meet the rigid requirements of inventory replenishment in the distribution industry. The system enables distributors to optimize inventory levels and purchase orders to maximize the return on inventory investment.

The system accomplished its results by combining dynamic forecasting of sales with advanced joint replenishment techniques. The best forecasting model for each item in inventory is selected automatically by the system and is then continually monitored and changed as market conditions vary. This dynamic approach assures accurately tailored forecasts to fit the changing needs of members and customers.

Order strategies are produced based on the concept of joint replenishment at the lowest total cost. The best order strategy for each stock item is used as the basis for calculating the reorder point, order quantity, and safety stock. These values enable the system to issue purchase orders for effective control of stocking levels. The system develops new order strategies as changing conditions dictate.

Transportation

Transportation includes motor carriers (trucks and auto leasing) as well as the airlines, ship lines, and railroads. Basic applications center on cost analysis and accounting, calculating tariff rates from rather complex formulas and regulations, and handling vehicle maintenance by projecting repair schedules based on historical patterns. Advanced applications include the complex reservation systems developed by the airlines and sophisticated analysis of traffic patterns to optimize routing and scheduling. In addition, computers are being used to analyze, update, and maintain tariff tables and to automatically calculate bills on the basis of individual loads, routes, and local conditions. The following illustrates this use of a computer.

A COMPUTER HELPS AUTOMATE RATE TARIFFS

Company Background

A nonprofit organization owned by the motor carriers serving a region provides a means for its members to arrive jointly at uniform rates and charges for their services. When these rates are proposed by the carriers, the association acts as the agent for obtaining Interstate Commerce Commission approval. The rates are published and distributed to the member carriers and to other subscribers in the motor carrier and shipping industry.

Because of the frequent rate adjustments and the need for rapid distribution of the latest rates, the association carries a big load. This load gets bigger all the time as competitive conditions and ICC regulations become more complex, and as the demand for accurate and up-to-date information increases.

When one association was founded more than thirty years ago it had five employees aided by a few simple business machines. But as the industry and its needs grew, so did the association. Today it employs an average of one hundred people, many of them specialists in their fields.

On-Line Tariff Maintenance

The association soon found that tabulating machines and manual processing methods could no longer keep pace with the increasing needs of the industry. A card-oriented computer system was installed, but it soon was outgrown. A new computer system was installed for payroll, billing, mailing, and freight traffic studies conducted by the association. It was gradually used for more sophisticated applications. The association could now see a far more important use for computer—on-line maintenance of the published tariffs.

Tariff 26, the Routing Guide, was selected as the first tariff to be maintained on-line. The Routing Guide lists all of the carriers, the cities in which they interchange, and the connecting carriers with whom they do business. The guide contains hundreds of pages and many thousands of entries. Due to the cross-reference nature of the listings, a single entry may appear on two different pages of the guide.

In the past, it was necessary for someone called the traffic compiler, on being informed of a routing change, to correct both pages individually. All corrections were made manually, just before the date of issue, so that the latest information could be incorporated. It was a scramble to meet each production date.

Today, a newly installed cathode ray tube terminal has eliminated the hectic activity that used to accompany the preparation of the Routing Guide. This video display terminal is located on the tariff compiler's desk. With it the compiler makes a routine change on-line to the computer, and the computer immediately updates all of the information affected by the change. The Routing Guide file is always up to date. At publication time the Routing Guide is printed by the computer, saving many hours of compiling, typing, and proofreading.

The executive vice-president of the association put it this way: "The ability of the compiler to update routing changes on a real-time basis will greatly eliminate delays in revising and reissuing this tariff. This breakthrough into real-time updating of our computer-stored Routing Guide is very significant. It has brought us closer to computerizing our more complex commodity rate tariffs and a step closer to the eventual goal of computer rate retrieval. We will continue to seek meaningful results from each dollar expended in the computer."

Health Care   Computers are becoming commonplace in the administrative functions of a hospital performing jobs like patient billing, inventory control of medical instruments and facilities, and also producing health care statistics and maintaining patient histories. Computers are beginning to cater to the more exciting advanced applications. Computers are scheduling lab tests and operations and scanning patient symptoms for preliminary diagnosis. Gradually the computer is being used to reduce the administrative load on nurses, giving them more time for other important nursing functions. In addition, the hospitals are using computers to monitor patients in intensive care wards, employing the principle of process control more familiar in process manufacturing. The following are examples of the use of computers in hospitals.

HOSPITAL OPENS COMPUTER POISON CONTROL CENTER

A fully computerized poison control center helps solve what the director of one hospital calls one of the greatest problems of today's emergency medical clinics—obtaining fast access to pertinent data on the variety of poisons commonly ingested by children.

The computer stores information on drugs, household products, and chemicals that children may find and swallow. The computer is linked to the hospital's emergency room by teleprinter.

The computer is programmed to accept an inquiry—for example, the name of a household cleaning product—and to respond within four seconds with detailed information. The information lists all chemicals in the product, identifies those that are poisonous, and supplies a grading code of 1 to 4, from mildly poisonous to fatal.

The computer also lists the symptoms experienced after swallowing the product and suggests treatment. When the project is complete, information on 5,000 products will be available.

"This computer system is used as a retrieval device and does not replace clinical judgment," the hospital director said. "But the inquiry program saves valuable time in locating the requested poison, and we consider it the first segment of the hospital's concept of comprehensive computer support to medicine."

The computer is used primarily for general data processing in the hospital's statistical and accounting departments. Inquiries to the poison control file are handled without interruption of the computer's regular data-processing jobs.

DIGITIZING HEART IS KEY TO DIAGNOSIS

A fully automated radiological diagnosis system has been demonstrated to perform as well as or better than trained radiologists using traditional techniques.

In a technical paper presented by researchers at the University of Missouri Medical Center and College of Engineering, the computer-based system's diagnostic accuracy was reported to be 73 percent, compared with 62 percent for a ten-member panel of experienced radiologists—one of whom was the principal research investigator. What is more, the scanner had only the frontal view of each patient, whereas the panelists had both front and side views.

Each physician examined some or all of the 135 cases, for a

total of 639 radiologist diagnoses available for comparison with the automated system.

The researchers are working on advancing the diagnosis techniques beyond heart ailments. Respiratory, digestive, and bone tumor diagnosis techniques are under development.

Such a technique might be expanded by locating scanners around rural areas, for example. General practitioners could enter their patients' X rays for computer processing. In effect, the best consultation in the state would be available around the clock to many people.

Retail   Retailing has been a slow industry to computerize. Computers now handle the basic paperwork procedures of customer billing, sales analysis, inventory reporting, and the other accounting functions within a retailing environment. Some retailers are moving into the more advanced applications of sales forecasting and merchandising, where a computer can be used to spot trends in item movement and discern the impact of advertising and special promotions. Retailers are turning to source data automation—recording the movement of goods from the store on machine-readable media that can then be used directly as basis for reordering, inventory control, sales analysis, and profitability accounting. Cash flow analysis is another example of the use of computers in an advanced application category. The following description shows how one retailing company is using computers.

INFORMATION FOR RETAIL MANAGEMENT

Entry into Data Processing

For a business to expand and remain profitable and competitive today requires accurate and timely operational information. At one chain of department stores expansion has occurred without loss of either inventory control or profitability accounting. This is evidence of sound information system planning and implementation.

All basic accounting functions are automated. These include payroll processing, accounts payable, accounts receivable, expense and profit and loss reporting, inventory and gross profit, and general accounting.

More Advanced Applications

A fashion sales analysis system using printed punch tickets provides daily reports to buyers and management on the movement of goods. Trends can be spotted quickly in a merchandising area noted for its uncertainties.

In another application a daily sales audit converts paper tapes from more than 400 cash registers to magnetic tape. After the computer processes this tape, the sales performance for every department, division, and branch is known by the start of business the following day. The chain is testing state-of-the-art, point-of-sale transaction registers that will allow immediate updating of the inventory and sales data base with every purchase.

The showcase application is the innovative inventory and gross profit system by classification and location. With this system the chain can determine the profitability of specific departments and lines of goods. Weekly, monthly, and yearly reports are generated from the inventory and sales reporting data base. The inventory and gross profit system provides store management with the kind of critical information required to make profitable business decisions, information that the still highly conceptual management information systems promise to deliver to American business in the future.

In addition to meeting its own needs, the store-owned information-processing center provides services to several other retailers in the surrounding area.

Printing and Publishing

In the printing and publishing industry, computers are used to automate newspaper and magazine circulation as well as to bill for advertising and other services. In addition, accounting functions and payroll are commonplace computer applications. At some installations a computer produces a paper tape that is fed into the controller of a typesetting machine to produce hyphenated and justified print copy. This approach can be extended so that the computer calculates an entire page layout. Computers can also be used to determine the optimum advertising space for maximizing revenue without reducing reader acceptance. Another application is maintaining a history of classified ads. For example, a subscriber could receive a listing of houses for sale in a particular price range, location, and size. The following example is a newspaper that employs computerized typesetting.

AN ON-LINE COMPOSING SYSTEM

One of the nation's largest daily newspapers, publishing six daily editions and 600,000 copies of its Sunday edition, uses a computer to set 95 percent of its total typesetting requirements. At peak load capacity it can set 20,000 lines per hour. The advanced computer communications system provides two-way response between operators and the hardware system. This improves accuracy and ease of operation.

The paper supplements its composing system with administrative applications on a second computer, but in all cases, typesetting has priority.

The paper's on-line composing system employs computers, remote operating consoles, input keyboard devices, and various linecasters with tape control. Copy is entered directly into the computer through the keyboards. The computer verifies the copy and feeds punched paper tape to the linecasters. A linofilm tape station automatically produces type in the proper format for photocomposition paste-up. Additional facilities handle reworked copy and other special jobs.

Input to the system is the copy entered on the keyboard. Output is set type. Communication between keyboard operator and computer is two-way, insuring that errors are caught as made and that only usable output is produced. The keyboard becomes a teaching machine, accelerating training of new operators and reinforcing correct procedures as they are learned and used.

Communications facilities in the output area permit the newspaper to use more reliable tape punches that are matched to the speed of the linecaster. All output devices can operate simultaneously, providing increased overall speed, flexibility, and a better balanced work-load distribution.

The use of communications for data input has eliminated 75 percent of all errors normally occurring in the paper tape system. System input usually averages 4,000 newspaper lines per hour, but the computer, taking copy from all input stations simultaneously, can handle 19,200 lines per hour for short periods of time. While the system presently handles news, classified ads, and ad copy for photocomposition paste-up, it has the potential for ultrahigh-speed photocomposition as well. The communications capabilities of the system will permit remote entry of copy into the system when the wire services, for instance, use computers in copy preparation. Then computer-to-computer data transfer can be implemented to high speed, without intervening steps.

Miscellaneous Application Areas

To conclude the survey of computer applications I have selected examples of some interesting applications being performed by computers outside the specified industry spectrum. These include areas I think will be of interest to the reader.

COMPUTER USED IN WAR ON CRIME

In a court case Ontario Attorney General's Laboratory presented evidence evaluated by a computer.

A wide variety of organic materials can be identified by use of neutron activation analysis. A hair, a piece of cloth, mud, grease smudges, a sliver of glass, even the tiniest piece of material found on a suspect or at the scene of a crime is taken to the nuclear reactor at McMaster University in Hamilton. The object is bombarded with neutrons and returned to the laboratory, where the radioactivity induced by the neutron bombardment is counted. The counting equipment produces a perforated tape. The tape is fed into a card-punching machine and the cards are fed to a computer.

At least twenty materials can be identified. For example, this method could prove that a mud sample from someone's clothing is exactly the same as mud at the scene of a crime. With the aid of computer analysis, a few strands of hair (the odds of finding two alike are more than a million to one) can be as conclusive as fingerprints.

GLOBAL PROBLEMS PUT TO COMPUTER

The Club of Rome

An extraordinary organization known as the Club of Rome, but with worldwide connections, believes that the world's problems have become too complex and interrelated for resolution by the human mind.

The club therefore commissioned a systems analysis group at the Massachusetts Institute of Technology to program the world's problems and their interactions into a computer.

According to Aurelio Peccei, the Italian business leader and management specialist who is a central figure of Club of Rome, the goal of the computer experiments is not to predict the future or to solve work problems. Instead, the purpose is to identify what factors in the world situation are most critical in the evolution of civilization.

The Computer's Role in the Project

The computer study at MIT was under the direction of Jay W. Forrester, a professor of management. In the past Forrester has sought to use computer methods to attack the extremely complex problems faced by cities and large corporations.

"As our business organizations and social systems have grown," he wrote recently, "they have become too complex for human judgement and intuition."

60

The thesis of the study is that modern technology has made the world a single, extremely complex system with all its elements interdependent. No problem within that system—political, economic, or technological—can be solved by analyzing that problem alone.

At this point in history, Mr. Peccei said, "every nation and people therefore has acquired a vested interest in the solution of the principal problems of the others, lest their degeneration contaminate the world system, and their own life." Some problems are of such complexity, he added, that "no nation or conventional group of nations, however powerful, can single-handedly resolve them."

The MIT group was asked to express the many problems of the world mathematically so that their interactions could be described by mathematical equations. Then a computer analyzed the equations.

The five prime variables are world population, capital investment in industry, capital investment in food production, the world inventory of natural resources, and the level of man's interference with nature (notably by pollution).

The interactions and feedback influences of these variables on one another were described by the group in some forty equations. Plans exist for an expanded analysis, using more variables, in the future.

GAMBLING AND THE COMPUTER

An electronic whiz has a job in Las Vegas for one of the giant hotel casinos. He uses a computer to simplify complex operations, even those as individualistic as dealing blackjack.

RELIGION CONVERTS TO COMPUTERS

A Methodist minister in partnership with an EDP services company formed a company that specializes in managing church financial records.

COMPUTERS DOWN ON THE FARM

Some of the most bizarre-sounding uses of computers are in farm management and agricultural planning.

Along with more ordinary applications such as farm management information systems and recordkeeping, computers are simulating fruit trees to determine how much force is needed to shake ripe fruit from the branches. Computers plan breeding schedules for dairy herds, predict crop output, and develop new high-quality feed mixtures.

PROGRAM FINGERS PRISONERS LIKELY TO ESCAPE

Fewer than half the number of inmates escaped this year compared with five years ago from the prisons of a large eastern state as a result of a computerized program that indicates prisoner escape risks.

Since it costs between $5,000 and $70,000 to search for each escaped prisoner, depending on whether helicopters are used, the system has saved the prisons a possible $1 million per year, according to the developer of the program.

The system analyzes the results of several standard psychological tests that measure achievement, intelligence, personality, motivation, and psychopathology. Although the tests were given to entering prison inmates before the program's inception, the results were filed away and never used for such things as predicting escape risks. The system flags certain items of information and prints out four lists for quick reference. The lists indicate escape risks, inmates needing psychological attention, suicide risks, and inmates who lied about themselves on the tests.

The system, which has analyzed 35,000 inmates since its inception, tests prisoners as they enter prison. In some situations, the program developer states, "we work in the community prior to sentencing." The system can indicate to a judge what risks would be involved if an offender were put on probation rather than sentenced to jail. It can tell a judge what community services and resources—psychiatric, supervisory, educational—would be needed and how to access them.

COMPUTER IN THE KITCHEN

People who design computers sat up and listened when a housewife told how she used a computer to help keep the family checking account, to figure recipes, to calculate the price of draperies, and even to entertain.

Mrs. Smith was reporting on a pioneering research program in which she and nineteen other housewives in Phoenix each used a remote data terminal for a year. The experiment aimed to see if laymen could use a computer to lessen some home-front drudgery.

The terminal, a teleprinter, was connected to a computer specially programmed to help with household chores. When Mrs. Smith wanted an answer, she'd simply step up to the teletype and write a command. The machine figured the answer in microseconds and typed it out at the rate of 100 words a minute.

In cooking, the computer adjusted the quantity of ingredients if a recipe meant for six was supposed to serve nine. Presto, out came the measurements for a batch big enough to serve nine.

Mrs. Smith's husband, manager of the group in charge of the experiment, put a few remarks into the program designed to help with the checking account. "When too many checks were written in a row," he said, "the computer would comment, 'Gawd, but you're spending a lot.' "

And about the entertaining? "The computer could play blackjack very well," Mrs. Smith reported. "We greatly enjoyed showing this to friends, and we found that almost anyone can get hooked on playing blackjack with a machine.

"When they took away my remote data terminal—my lifeline to the computer—I felt as though I had lost an old friend," she said. Mrs. Smith said in an interview that she hopes someday every household can have one.

SUMMARY

Chapter 2 has described the types of applications implemented and planned in various industries. The types of applications were categorized as administrative, operational, and strategic. The various ways to communicate with a computer, ranging from the batch or sequential approach to communication-oriented transaction processing, were reviewed. The chapter looked at management attitudes, reflecting a practical perspective on selecting applications for computerization and a realistic view toward controlling their implementation. A series of case histories from various industries described the variety and scope of both basic and advanced types of applications.

There is no question that computers and computer applications have grown and proliferated. This chapter reinforces with many examples the fact that computers are deeply embedded in the operations of business and government. Computers and electronic data processing have become a way of life—and are as commonplace as production machinery or typewriters in most companies. We have the computing power to bombard management and business with all kinds of data and analyses; the key question now is *what* we do with the data.

The president of a foreign automobile manufacturer puts it this way: "We think that the jet aircraft with its high-speed comfort has made our life easier. Instead, we now find we spend more time traveling—not less. We go greater distances, but in doing so may accomplish less.

"Thirty years ago, a trip from London to Frankfurt was carefully planned. It was not an easy trip and, therefore, was made only after proper preparations. Today, the trip is so quick, so easy, that we tend to do it without planning.

"As a result, we often come back without accomplishment. And because the trip was so easy and so quick, we are less disappointed when it is not productive. Many times a thoughtful letter or an intelligent and well-prepared telephone conversation could have accomplished more.

"My greatest problem is not lack of information, but rather a surplus of it. There is no surplus of what I need to know, but there is a surplus of what others think I should know. We must return to concise and economical communications."

Selecting and Implementing
3 Computer Applications

Chapter 2 delved into the "what" of computers, describing the variety of uses and applications to which computers are applied. This chapter will discuss the important "why" of computers—the cost/benefit justification.

Surprisingly, there are few treatments of the dollars and cents aspects of computers. The real payback on computer investment has been illusive to measure. Survey after survey indicates management's disillusionment with the overall cost effectiveness of electronic data processing. Many companies indicated outright that the returns from their computer investment were not positive, while others stated they did not possess the measurement tools to know one way or the other. A surprising number of companies maintain no historical cost records for their computer operation. Even more companies have no way to determine how much it is going to cost to computerize an application (or series of applications).

A company can assess its own effectiveness in this area by asking the following questions:

- Do I have historical records of computer costs?
- Are the costs broken down by specific applications?
- Do I have a cost justification procedure for computer applications?

- Does the EDP department work under a budgetary or cost-control system?
- Do I have a method for estimating future EDP costs?
- Is there a follow-up audit or review to indicate whether the computer applications did what we thought they would?

If the answer to most of these is no, a company might well be negligent in a very important area—maybe *the* important area of computer operation. What else is a computer supposed to do if it is not to provide cost benefits to its users? This basic fact of computer usage is often overlooked or underemphasized: The common denominator of computer usage is dollars. Computers must return more dollars to a company's coffers than it took to install and operate the machine. A company must avoid the so-called computer mystique, installing one just for the image or to keep up with the Joneses. Management must ask the simple computer question—why?

COMPUTER FEASIBILITY CRITERIA

There are certain things that computers can do effectively and efficiently, and there are things that a computer cannot do effectively and efficiently. A starting point in this determination for each application is to apply some basic computer feasibility criteria. Generally speaking, computers can be of benefit when several of the following elements are present:

- *High volume of transactions.* For example, sales orders, inventory issues, customer claims, student course enrollments, hospital lab tests.
- *Repetitive nature of transaction types.* A repetition of the same type of operation, not one-of-a-kind transactions.
- *Common source documents.* Information from the same source document used for several purposes. As an example, a sales order is the basis for shipping the item, setting up an account receivable, paying the sales commission, and scheduling production of the item.
- *Mathematical processing.* A considerable amount of mathematical computation is required. For example, a sales forecast is determined by statistically analyzing past demands, calculating a trend, and projecting that trend into subsequent time periods.

- *Demand for quick turnaround time.* Information is required much quicker than is currently possible. For example, a bank may desire to show the current balance and interest within seconds after a customer asks for it.
- *Accuracy and validity of information.* The data to be processed must be free of clerical errors. They must be correctly entered, validated, checked for reasonableness, and processed consistently each time.
- *Application by-product.* Often a particular application can be a simple by-product of another application, although none of the foregoing conditions are met.

Figure 3-1 evaluates several examples of possible applications using the foregoing criteria.

Payroll and order-processing applications, for example, each have volume and repetitiveness and emanate from a common source document (the payroll time card and the sales order). Payroll normally doesn't require quick turnaround, although it must meet a predetermined schedule. Order processing may or may not require quick turnaround depending on the nature of the order cycle. Both applications require accuracy. The applications should computerize well.

A monthly labor summary or a yearly tax report does not have the same characteristics. They probably would not be good computer applications, except that they are by-products: The labor summary from the payroll processing, and the tax report from the accounting system.

In scientific processing and student scheduling there is

FIGURE 3-1

Computer Feasibility Criteria

	Payroll	Order Processing	Monthly Labor Summary	Yearly Tax Reports	Scientific Processing	Student Scheduling	Long-Range Strategic Planning
Volume	X	X					
Repetitiveness	X	X					
Common source document	X	X	X				
Mathematical processing					X	X	
Quick turnaround		X				X	
Accuracy	X	X			X	X	
By product			X	X			

scant volume and repetitiveness when compared with payroll and order processing. Scientific processing may be required weekly or monthly, while student scheduling may be required only twice a year.

The development of a long-range strategic plan does not possess any of the computer feasibility criteria and therefore would probably not benefit from computerization, although companies have attempted to use a computer in this area. However, the financial expression of the long-range plan, with its iterative mathematics, is a candidate for computerization.

These criteria are merely guidelines, and obviously there are exceptions. However, for the most part, potential computer applications should fill at least two of the criteria or else cost justification will not be reached. The ultimate criterion for computerization is benefits or savings greater than the costs, or investment in computerization that yields a return that satisfies a company's financial standards (for example, 30 percent before taxes). In addition, the elements of risk must be considered carefully, particularly for an inexperienced company. Not only should the risks of success be evaluated, the risks of failure should be considered. For example, if a company is installing an on-line credit checking system or an on-line savings system, it should evaluate the risks of the system being out of operation. In both cases the impact on customer service would be significant. This risk must be weighed in determining feasibility.

The would-be computer user must consider the basic but often overlooked premise that it is often possible to obtain many of the projected benefits by developing an improved manual or semiautomatic system. A common fallacy in measuring benefits is to give the computer system credit for all the benefits when, in fact, most benefits might have been accrued by resystemization alone, without a computer. The other side of the coin is true as well—the computer usually takes the rap for everything that goes wrong, even though faulty execution may have been the cause. Often a company is shocked by the increase in error rate when a computerized system is put into operation. However, what may be happening is that the computer system is picking up so-called quiet errors that went undetected before.

The computer frequently acts as the catalyst for much-needed system and operation reevaluation. As such, the credit for improvement quite possibly belongs to the computer, even if the benefits could have been obtained without it.

I remember one instance where a company allowed its

clerical force to diminish through attrition in preparation for the installation of a computer. The installation subsequently was delayed, then delayed further, and finally the whole computer project was dropped. Significantly, the company found it could handle the workload with 15 percent fewer people by a change in work methods. The computer, though not the cause of the savings, was the catalyst for the change.

There are two basic elements in computer justification: the benefits or savings resulting from the new approach and the costs or investment necessary to produce the benefits. Management must weigh both sides of the formula in order to determine feasibility.

ESTIMATING COMPUTER COSTS

Estimating computer costs can be quite illusive, but it usually is a more exact process than estimating computer benefits. Costs as well as benefits must be viewed from a time perspective. The cost of eight work-years has a different perspective if it implies four people for two years rather than two people for four years. In the one case the full benefits of the manpower effort will be felt in only two years, while in the other case the benefits may begin after a year or so but the full impact will not occur for four years.

Life-cycle costing is being used increasingly as a justification technique by government and commercial evaluators comparing contractor proposals. The major concept of life-cycle costing is value—it may be desirable to pay more initially for a product that can be shown to be cheaper over its expected life. This imposes the need to project and justify a product over a longer range than just a year or two. Examples of this method can be seen in any industry in which the original manufacturer has a maintenance responsibility for the product. It is generally agreed that improved quality-control methods have had a great deal to do with the long-term warranties in the automotive industry. The car manufacturer puts more money into the cost of manufacturing the product because he calculates that it more than offsets the added maintenance costs. It makes sense to spend a little more to ensure the quality of a transmission if you must pay the high labor cost to rebuild one. Life-cycle costing in this case necessitated a long-term cost projection in order to determine the true effect of a long-term warranty.

Life-cycle costing is equally appropriate in evaluating a computer installation. A one-year or two-year projection does not tell the entire story. This is particularly true, for example, with a system that is directed at improving business operations rather than a system directed at reducing costs. The latter shows a higher short-term return, but the former may not be significant until the later years of the project. It is wise to look at computer justification over at least a five-year period.

Data-Processing Costs

International Data Corporation projects the data-processing costs for U.S. companies from a survey they make each year. Figure 3-2 indicates budgets by category for the year 1980. The statistics were compiled from 200 users, segmented by budget size and cross-checked with known industry parameters. The costs can be broken down into three general categories, hardware, personnel, and supplies and services. In looking at the costs of acquiring a first computer system or in converting to a new system, there is another category of front-end, or nonrecurring, costs that are encountered in getting the new system up and running.

FIGURE 3-2
1980 EDP Budgets

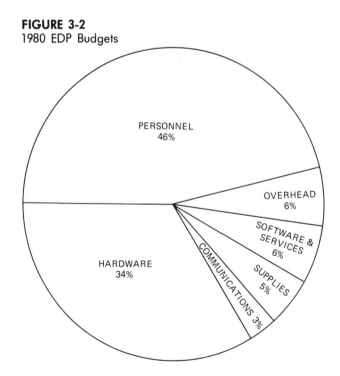

Hardware Costs   The hardware costs include rental or lease payments and depreciation charges for equipment that is purchased. Also included are data entry, data communication equipment, and remote equipment as well as maintenance charges on all of the hardware. Because of the continued cost reduction as a result of micro-miniaturization, hardware costs as a percentage of total EDP costs have gone down over the years, though the absolute value is up. The reason for the latter is that companies are adding more and more applications. Management may argue that increased productivity from lower-priced hardware should offset this absolute value increase, but this is a difficult issue to resolve.

The IDC survey indicates a 9-percent rise in hardware costs over 1979, which is lower than the overall EDP budget increase of 14 percent. Thus hardware continues to follow the trend of increasing in dollars, but representing a diminishing portion of total EDP costs.

Personnel Costs   The largest element of data-processing cost is the salaries and related salary support costs of the systems analysts, programmers, and operations staff who comprise the department. The overhead costs of 6 percent are predominately salary-related so that when combined with the personnel cost, people-related expenses are 52 percent. Salary expense has shown a steady growth over the years, and the 1980 figure is 17 percent over the corresponding number in 1979.

The growth in personnel expense is a result of several factors. Inflationary pressures are at work here, unlike in the hardware arena, where costs have dropped despite inflation. Another factor is the increasing application work load that has been added to most computer systems throughout the country, fueled by such developments as distributed data processing and data base technology. Also, the application saturation level, the measure of computerized applications versus total potential applications, is relatively low in many industries. However, as in hardware, a key question is productivity. Advances in software development have not kept pace with hardware development. The developments of higher-level languages and improved data base construction and inquiry have increased user productivity, but there is still a long way to go in the area of application development tools. On the user side, advances have been made in the control and management of application development. People productivity should be a top priority in data-processing departments.

Supplies and Services

This expense category includes business forms, cards, and other media supplies. While a combination of exception reporting, integrated data files, and terminal screen interaction have been expected to reduce the heavy paper output of computer systems, this just hasn't happened. Supplies continue to rise and are up 14 percent over 1979. Communication line costs are also included in this expense category with 1980 costs 20 percent over 1979. The amount of communications is increasing but is partially offset by the declining per-unit cost. Software outside services, the remaining portion of the supplies and services expense, is the fastest-growing element of them all. This category includes software packages acquired from third parties, custom software and consulting, and time-sharing services. Costs in 1980 show a 27-percent increase over 1979.

International Data Corporation estimates total U.S. expenditure on data processing of $54 billion in 1980, up 14 percent over 1979. Data processing is taking a healthy portion of a company's revenue dollar, emphasizing the importance of measuring and improving EDP productivity.

Method of Acquiring Computers

There are a number of ways to acquire computer power. Distribution channels will be discussed at more length in the next chapter, centering on acquisition either direct from a computer vendor or indirect through a variety of third-party participants.

Generally speaking, computer systems can be rented or purchased. There has been a definite trend toward purchase tempered somewhat by the high interest rates of recent times. This may prove only a temporary condition because as users become more sophisticated and have realized that a computer decision is really a three-to-five-year commitment (or longer), they have felt more security in purchase. There are other available financial avenues, such as the third-party leasing company. The leasing company or agent procures machines from the manufacturer or in the open marketplace and leases them on the basis that the actual life of a computer is longer than the usual five years over which the manufacturer figures depreciation. A third-party lessor can offer equipment at a 10 to 20 percent reduction from purchase price and still earn money over the life of the machine.

With the advent of common or standard interfaces, a user can buy or lease equipment from several manufacturers or can lease some equipment from a third party while buying or leasing other equipment direct from the manufacturer. The multiple options available and the third-party participants make mixing and matching a common practice. Another force in the marketplace is the so-called plug compatibles. These are third parties who concentrate on high-volume peripherals and central processors that can be added and plugged into another vendor's system. Since IBM has about 60 percent of the equipment installed, these plug compatible vendors have concentrated on the IBM user base, though there are plug compatibles for other mainframe equipment as well.

Sales Volume and Computer Expenditure

Surveys made of computer installation have brought out the correlation of sales volume and expenditure for EDP. One of the first such surveys in the 1960s, by McKinsey & Company, found that expenditures average $5,600 per every $1 million of sales. A more recent survey made by IDC in the late 1970s indicates an expenditure of $7,000 per $1 million of sales. The higher figure seems reasonable in light of the discussion of the countervailing trends in computer costs, with hardware costs dropping in relation to performance and functionality while people costs have shown a steady increase.

By simple calculation a company could multiply its sales volume by 7,000 and compare the result with its actual EDP expenditure. However, remember this is only a crude rule of thumb, since there are many other significant variables, among them being that the $7,000 will vary depending upon the particular industry, the size of the company, and the particular position of a company in the industry. Also the level of application saturation is obviously crucial. At any rate, it is human nature to look for a shortcut, a simple yardstick or a rule of thumb, and in this $7,000 figure, we have such a device. The ultimate measurement of the return on computer investment (ROI) rests in the resultant savings and benefits. Companies may be wise in expending twice the industry average or half of it, depending on their internal situation. In the long run the formula is

$$\frac{\text{savings and benefits}}{\text{computer investment}} = \underline{\qquad} \% \text{ ROI}$$

Companies should place the highest priority on an increased understanding of this equation.

COMPUTER SAVINGS AND BENEFITS

It is even more difficult to estimate potential savings and benefits accruing from the computer than it is to ascertain the costs. There are some guidelines, but judgment is still a significant ingredient.

Two general categories of computer benefits can be distinguished. A *tangible benefit* can be measured and can be directly related to the introduction of a computer system. An example is a clerical cost reduction, where work formerly accomplished by clerical staff is now handled by computer. An example of an *intangible benefit* is an improvement in customer service brought on by a more responsive order-processing system. Although it is often clear that the improvement is a result of the computer, it is difficult to place a monetary value on the effect this has on overall company profitability. There are degrees of intangibility in computer benefits—certainly an improved company image is less tangible than improved customer service.

Major Benefit Areas

In order of significance, the major benefit areas experienced by companies that have installed computers are as follows:

1. Ability to obtain reports and information previously unavailable.
2. Availability of reports and information on a more timely basis.
3. Improvement in a basic operating area.
4. Increased ability to perform computations that were not practical before.
5. Reduction in clerical cost.
6. Maintenance of competitive position.
7. Aid in management decision making.
8. Intangibles, such as customer image, leadership in the industry and community, increased customer morale, and management confidence.

It is significant to note that clerical cost reduction falls well down the list of principal benefits. Most companies entering data processing overemphasize this element and only later discover that major benefits were in the first four categories.

Estimating Dollar Benefits

Placing a dollar value on anticipated computer benefits is a difficult task. An example in a specific area may serve to illustrate the type of analysis that can be used for this purpose. Many companies have inventory problems—overstocking certain items and understocking others. The key consideration in inventory control is maintaining a balanced inventory that provides the required level of customer service. How much can inventory be reduced by automating the inventory control operation? Most business managers would say "plenty," but this is hardly a quantified statement of fact.

One might look at other companies with similar operations that have computer-based inventory control systems to determine what reductions they have achieved. Another way is to use a computer to analyze past demand and prior levels of inventory. Through a process called simulation, the computer can use mathematical inventory decision rules to indicate what levels of inventory would have been required to meet the desired customer service level. Comparing these simulated levels with actual levels gives a company an idea of potential inventory reductions. This could be done on a service bureau machine or at some other facility if the company is conducting an initial feasibility study.

Although simulation gives a solid indication of what is possible, it still may not be convincing. An alternate approach is to work backward through break-even analysis. After the projected computer costs have been accumulated, the amount of inventory reduction necessary to cover these costs can be calculated. Maintaining inventory results in such carrying costs as taxes, insurance, investment on the capital, spoilage, obsolescence, and space. These costs typically amount to between 15 and 20 percent of the inventory value, not including the value of money, which of course varies with interest rates. If the total computer costs (hardware, systems, and operating costs) are $60,000 per year, an inventory reduction of $400,000 is necessary to offset these costs (15% × $400,000 = $60,000). Management can now focus on the question of how likely is it that an automatic inventory control system can reduce inventory to that extent. This type of break-even approach can be used in assessing computer benefits in other operating areas as well.

It is much more difficult to estimate benefits in the profit-producing areas of a business than it is in the cost-cutting areas. Estimating profit improvement involves an analysis of the marginal value or utility of information. For example, how valuable is the ability to forecast business activity ± 10 percent versus ± 20 percent? This, of course, depends on the type of business and the type of product. In some cases, a 10 percent margin of error has little leverage on the business, and it would be unwise to spend $100,000 for a computer system to produce that margin of error. In other operations, a deviation of 1 or 2 percent can cause significant upheavals. The value of improved forecasting in this instance may be as high as $500,000 or more.

As in most activities, the law of diminishing returns operates. At a certain point information glut occurs—the extra level of detail hinders rather than helps a situation. In evaluating computer feasibility the idea that a particular application will give management more information on which to base decisions must be quantified. Management must look beyond the often-times grandiose claims of optimistic, but possibly idealistic, systems designers who say that they can do twice as much work in half the time that company XYZ took.

Return on Investment Analysis

The decision to acquire a computer requires a long-term commitment by a company. The costs incurred and the benefits realized should be related to each other in such a way as to take account of the time periods in which each is realized.

The discounted cash flow method provides such an approach because it recognizes the time value of money: Dollars spent or earned in earlier years are of greater value to the company than dollars earned or spent in later years. This is so because those same dollars could be invested elsewhere in the company to produce a profitable return.

Figures 3-3 and 3-4 illustrate the costs and savings from initial computer investment by a company. The same investment principles apply as well to a company replacing an existing computer, upgrading capability, or adding a new application.

Figure 3-5 indicates that over the four-year period $797,000 of net positive savings are realized from the computer investment. Figure 3-6 indicates a net positive savings of $242,000, using tangible savings only.

The ROI (return on investment) technique provides a better measurement for management because it translates the dollar into a common percentage format. This is accomplished by use of financial tables that discount both the positive and negative flows until they equal one another. In the foregoing examples, the ROI is 97.8 percent based on measuring full savings, and

FIGURE 3-3
Cost Summary (in dollars)

| Cost | Year of Installation | | | | |
	0	1	2	3	4
Initial systems and programming	60,000	20,000			
Site preparation	6,000				
File conversion	3,000	3,000			
Parallel operation		4,000			
Other	1,000	1,000			
Total one-time costs	70,000	28,000			
Hardware rental		62,000	70,000	75,000	75,000
Personnel costs		90,000	100,000	105,000	115,000
Supplies and services	12,000	22,000	30,000	30,000	35,000
Other	1,000	1,000			
Total recurring costs	13,000	175,000	200,000	210,000	225,000
Total cost	83,000	203,000	200,000	210,000	225,000

FIGURE 3-4
Savings Summary (in dollars)

| Savings | Year of Installation | | | | |
	0	1	2	3	4
Reduction in current data-processing costs		50,000	110,000	115,000	125,000
Clerical costs outside data processing		10,000	20,000	30,000	50,000
Inventory reduction (carrying cost)		40,000	125,000	150,000	160,000
Overtime reduction		5,000	20,000	22,000	32,000
Production variances			5,000	40,000	50,000
Other		1,000	1,000	1,000	1,000
Total tangible savings		106,000	281,000	358,000	418,000
Profit on sales (increased customer service)		5,000	50,000	100,000	100,000
Improved sales analysis			100,000	100,000	100,000
Increased management control					
More meaningful data					
Other					
Total intangible savings		5,000	150,000	200,000	200,000
Total savings		111,000	431,000	558,000	618,000

FIGURE 3-5

Net Cash Flows from Computer Investment (in $ thousands)

| | Year of Installation | | | | | |
	0	1	2	3	4	Total
Costs	83	203	200	210	225	921
Savings		111	431	558	618	1,718
Net savings	(83)	(92)	231	348	393	797

FIGURE 3-6

Net Cash Flows from Computer Investment—Tangible Savings Only (in $ thousands)

| | Year of Installation | | | | | |
	0	1	2	3	4	Total
Costs	83	203	200	210	225	921
Savings		106	281	358	418	1,163
Net savings	(83)	(97)	81	148	193	242

37.6 percent when measured on tangible savings only. This return can now be related to the company's cost of borrowing or other investment yardsticks.

GETTING AN APPLICATION ON THE AIR

Figure 3-7 divides the process of selecting and implementing computer applications into phases: analysis, synthesis, and implementation. Analysis is defined as the separation of anything into its constituent parts. Applied to computer acquisition, analysis is the review of company operation and the division of the total operation into workable units for measurement and evaluation. The purpose of analysis is to see if there are better ways to accomplish the objectives of the business.

Synthesis, the opposite of analysis, combines the parts into a whole. The analysis stage dissected business operations to show up areas in need of improvement (particularly information analysis and its effect on the control of operations). The synthesis phase combines these elements in such a way as to improve the original operation.

FIGURE 3-7

Steps in Selecting and Implementing Computer Applications

Activities	Subphase	Phase
Establish study objectives Analyze cost vs. benefits Determine potential of further study	Feasibility study	Analysis
Determine business objectives Determine systems objectives Analyze data input-output-processing and develop system specification	Systems study	
Evaluate various vendors Calculate return on investment Present final computer analysis	Justification	Synthesis
Develop alternate solutions Explore computer solutions Determine best solution	Systems design	
Develop installation plan Select and train computer staff Design and program applications	Programming	Implementation
Test computer applications Initiate productive operations Review resulting benefits	Operating	
Evaluate operational performance Fine-tune application running Plan for future growth	Maintenance-modification	

Implementation is the proof of the pudding. At this point the synthesis—or improved solution—is designed, programmed, and put into operation. The concluding phase is the maintenance and modification of operational applications to ensure that they remain free of errors and discrepancies.

A further breakdown of the computer selection process indicates that analysis consists of subphases, the feasibility study and the systems study. The feasibility study begins with the establishment of objectives—the time and cost of the study, the people who will conduct the study, and the general manner in which the study will be conducted. The feasibility study should answer the question: "Does a computer (or a computer application) offer sufficient benefits to a company to warrant further investigation?" An effective systems study requires a considerable investment in time and money. It should be undertaken only if a preliminary study indicates that a computer may be a feasible solution. Further systems study might indicate that a computer is not justified, but a company should be reasonably sure that it is justified before embarking on a comprehensive systems study.

The systems study begins with an analysis of overall business objectives, focusing on the information and control system. This enables a company to better plan, schedule, and control operations. The total information system will be broken down into progressively smaller and smaller units until the focus is on manageable subsystems. The input, output, and processing steps of these subsystems will be analyzed carefully to form the foundation for the synthesis phase of the computer selection cycle.

The synthesis phase consists of justification and systems-design subphases. The justification subphase evaluates the responses of vendors to the specifications submitted to them. Various methods of competitive comparison are used to select a vendor or vendors. With the cost of the computer system in hand, the company next justifies the cost by measuring it against the expected benefits. The various methods of cost justification usually include some analysis of return on investment. After justification, the final presentation is prepared and presented to those responsible for making the computer decision. The systems study looks at what is being done and compares that with what should be done. Systems design compares how it should be done with how it is being done. The detail produced during the systems study is used to develop several alternate computer solutions.

The installation plan developed at the outset of the implementation phase outlines the resources necessary to get the system operating. The implementation staff transforms the design specification into progressively greater and greater detail, in preparation for computer processing. The resulting programs are tested and put into operation. The programs then are reviewed to determine whether they meet the objectives. The resultant improvements and benefits of the system are measured against the projection.

Implementation does not end at this point but includes maintenance and modification. Overall operational performance must be evaluated before the running applications are fine-tuned. A plan must be instituted to resolve and correct the inevitable operational errors and program discrepancies that will surface. With the fine-tuning accomplished, both short- and long-range plans for future growth are refined.

MANAGEMENT INVOLVEMENT

Management must play a key role throughout the process of selecting and implementing computer applications. The lack of proper management involvement has been a major cause of mediocre results. Management has a role to play whether the company is selecting its first computer, adding a single application, or implementing an interlocking network of advanced applications.

Figure 3-8 outlines the involvement of management in the phases of the computer application process. In the chart top management is defined to include the president, vice-presidents, and major division heads (such as marketing and engineering within a manufacturing company). Middle or operating management includes the department heads, the manager of production scheduling, and the manager of sales, for example. Administrative management is those lower-level supervisors who implement the policies and directives of top and middle management. They are implementors and doers—their jobs have sparse planning content.

Figure 3-8 indicates generally that higher levels of management have more concern with the initial phases of the process and less with the more detailed implementation phases. On the other hand, the lower levels of management are more concerned with the detailed phases. Data-processing management is involved with all phases of the cycle. They must provide the continuity on management decisions regarding application selection, design, and implementation. If the resultant application does not meet the original specifications and produce the dollar and cents results projected for it, then management may have no one to blame but themselves.

Top Management Role

Top management must provide the overall direction of the feasibility study and indicate the scope and objectives of the study. This level should hold exclusive authority for the final decision as to whether the particular application(s) under study have the potential to justify further analysis. This point applies only if the applications under study warrant such a high level of management involvement. A decision to refine an existing payroll system would not need top management attention. A new standard cost accounting system throughout the entire company operation, however, does require top management awareness and direction.

FIGURE 3-8
Management Involvement in Computer Application Process

	Feasibility	Systems Study	Justification	Systems Design	Programming and Operating	Maintenance and Modification
Top management	• Overall direction • Final go/no-go decision	• Approve priorities • Establish guidelines	• Review alternatives • Approve recommendations			
Middle or operating management	• Steering committee, if department is affected • Validate benefits	• Final approval on specifications • Decide key system trade-offs	• Review recommendations, if department is affected • Validate benefits	• As required for system trade-off decisions	• Approve and review schedules	• Validate original justification
Administrative management		• Work with systems analysts to develop specs	• Validate benefits	• Assign personnel, if department is affected • Work alongside systems analysts	• Participate in test running • Approve procedures and operating documentation	• Audit system effectiveness • Define areas for alteration and improvement

Top management should establish guidelines and approve priorities for the systems study phase. The feasibility study may show multiple operational areas where computerization can be effective. Since all areas can't be tackled simultaneously, management must determine the priority. In the final justification phase, top management must review the various alternatives, assessing relative benefits, costs, and risks and then approve or disapprove the recommendation of the computer application evaluation team.

Middle or Operating Management Role

Middle management is the pivotal group involved in every phase of the cycle. Middle management people should participate as members of the steering committee for applications affecting their department. This level should validate the benefits prior to the presentation to top management.

Middle management determine the "what" of the application, since the system's objective is to aid their departments' performance. It is wrong for the EDP staff to determine system specifications—this vital concern is the prerogative of middle management.

Though not responsible for the systems design, middle management must be available to make specific systems trade-off decisions. An example of such a trade-off is whether to go on-line with a system or to rely on conventional on-site batch operation. If middle management is not able to make such decisions, impasses can cause delay and procrastination.

Middle management should approve the schedule for the programming and operating phase and should validate the original justification and system specification after the application is in operation.

Administrative Management Role

Administrative management bows to middle and upper management in determining feasibility, provided the applications are broad in scope and beyond the concern of an individual supervisor. However, administrative management works very closely with the systems analysts to determine system specifications and also to validate benefits during the justification phase. Administrative management assumes a prime role in systems design, assigning people and working alongside the systems analysts. They continue to play a strong role in the programming and operating phases. They must ensure that the test running and the operating procedures and documentation are both effective and comprehensible. These are the people who must operate the system once it is checked out, so they must participate in the testing and phasing-in of the system. Administrative management must audit the effectiveness of the system (once in operation) and be able to point out areas of improvement and enhancement.

BASIC MANAGEMENT GUIDELINES

There are five particular areas where the correct management decision has significant leverage on the success or failure of computer operation.

1. *Place EDP in the right spot in the organization.* Responsibility for EDP has traditionally fallen to the controller or the chief financial officer of the company. This was a natural development because early computers were primarily in the accounting and administrative areas. However, the mix of computer usage has been changing with the introduction of the computer in such areas as inventory control, production scheduling, forecasting, and investment analysis. In many companies, the computer is devoted more to operational problems than to administrative ones. Top management should take another look at the place of EDP in the organizational structure in light of the broadening scope of computer application. In more and more cases, the EDP function is being removed from the financial arm of the company and is being placed on the same status with the other major departments. The EDP department must still serve the financial department, however, it must serve the other departments as well. (As previous discussion has pointed out, the most profit-making computer applications are outside the accounting and administrative area.) Placing the EDP function outside any single operating department emphasizes the concept of the computer as an information utility serving the needs of all operating groups. It also serves to give EDP the status it needs to implement information systems that affect operating management.

2. *Select the right people for EDP.* What are the qualifications of the new breed of computer professionals who are becoming so important in managing today's electronic world? First of all, these people must process the qualities required by successful managers charged with the responsibility of running other major functions of the business. Such a manager must be motivated to get a job done—motivated enough to bounce back time and time again after meeting discouraging and frustrating roadblocks. An EDP manager must have broad human relations skills in order to sell ideas and concepts to a skeptical customer.

Another necessary prerequisite of the computer manager is a thorough grasp of the overall business activities of the company. It is not enough to know computer programming and operation. A manager at this level must possess the perspective to distinguish the things that are important to the profitability of the company. It is important to be able to see the impact of introducing the right products at the right time, or the need to control mounting production costs. The EDP manager must be able to see these things as clearly as the significance of cutting the running time of a computer program.

The computer professional also must be technically qualified, acquainted with the principles of computer operation from hardware to software to advanced systems. Such a person must have a mind that likes to explore and to learn new things. This is no place for a status quo person who likes to feel secure in acquired knowledge—there is just too much to learn in the rapidly changing EDP field. This is one of the reasons you do not see much white hair in the computer profession. Although there are older managers who are doing an excellent job, the rapidity of change generally makes the computer field a young person's profession.

Probably the single most important characteristic of the computer person, systems and programming analysts as well as management, is awareness, motivation, and interest in the business side of the company. The computer person is a professional, and a technologist, but one who recognizes that technology is only of value if it operates within the existing business environment.

3. *Stress the management steering committee.* This chapter has stressed the proper involvement of management throughout the computer cycle. A key vehicle to ensure this involvement is the management steering committee. Depending upon the scope of the system under analysis, the steering committee should be headed by a top management official of the company who has the authority and the overall business perspective to make key trade-off decisions. In addition to the steering committee leader, those managers whose departments are affected by the particular computer application under study should be members of the group. EDP people also should be members of the steering group. The group should meet regularly to review progress, handle trade-offs or bottlenecks, anticipate potential problem areas, and initiate action. The steering committee is a vital step in ensuring that the proper communications and interaction takes place between EDP people and the users of EDP throughout a company. As was previously pointed out, the communications barrier has been a prime deterrent to progress in the business world.

4. *Embed EDP in the basic fabric of business operation.* Too often, the computer is viewed either as an isolated operation area, working apart from the mainline business operation, or as a control tool, imposing constraints and making more rigid the way of doing business. Neither philosophy is conducive to getting the most from your computer investment. A computer system should be flexible and modular and adjust to the way the company operates—not the other way around. The computer should be a tool of management, aimed at improving operations. It is true that early limitations (hardware, software, and application) caused EDP management to impose quite rigid ground rules both in the way input was prepared for the system and in the type of output users received. Technology and know-how have reached a stage, however, where report formats can easily be altered to suit the users, even after the system goes into operation. Good systems design takes into account that business and business management are dynamic entities where change is a normal fact of life. Good systems design incorporates change.

EDP planning must be consistent with business planning. The fact that a company expects to expand its product line over the next several years, or to acquire a new line of business, or to open a new facility is a vital concern of EDP planning. Plans in one area cannot be developed without knowledge of the other. In the past, EDP long-range planning was an ignored field. Now, however, with greater maturity and stability, EDP planning has increased. A company should ensure that the EDP planning does not occur in an information vacuum.

5. *Take top control of EDP operation.* This is the principal message of the chapter. Top management must take over the top-level direction of EDP. Top management must insist that EDP is not immune to the procedures and controls that govern the other parts of the company. Such phrases as *return on investment, cost control, profit and loss,* and *implementation schedules* must become commonplace to EDP operation. The EDP manager must be made to feel that the job is more that of a business manager than a technical manager. Top management must show by their direction and involvement that they are seeking an entrepreneurial environment rather than a research environment. EDP should be run as a utility that benefits the rest of the company, and run on a cost-profit incentive basis. Top management must spend the time to see that this responsibility is carried out. They must spend the time—on steering committees, in special review sessions, or in individual meetings with EDP management—to indicate that they indeed have taken over the EDP reins. Purely technical decisions should remain in the hands of EDP. Certainly top management doesn't want to make systems design choices or individual hardware selection decisions—but they should make it quite clear that they hold EDP responsible to top management and to the company.

Management Checklist

Figure 3-9 provides a convenient checklist of questions that a top executive might ask his EDP manager and users of EDP services. It breaks down the questions into eight categories, starting with overall effectiveness (what is being done) and efficiency (how it is being done) and ending with management involvement. This is not exclusively aimed at EDP management because the top executives of a company are as responsible or in some instances more responsible than EDP personnel for the state of EDP services. The message here is to open up communications between EDP management and the users. It may come as a brutal shock to EDP management to discover that the perception of the users of services is quite at odds with that of the providers of services. The sooner this is on the table, the quicker the resolution.

SUMMARY

This chapter probed the economic considerations of EDP. Basic computer feasibility criteria were followed by a discussion of how computer costs relate to computer benefits. The discounted cash flow method illustrated how a computer investment can be justified. The steps to selecting and implementing computer applications were outlined, along with management's involvement in each step. Finally, basic management guidelines and a management checklist aimed at maximizing computer benefits were presented.

The chapter used such words as *business, profit,* and *cost control* throughout, and this is the message of the chapter: EDP

HOW WELL IS DATA PROCESSING SERVING YOUR COMPANY?

A. Effectiveness (What is being done?)
1. What functions are computerized? Administrative applications (payroll, order processing), logistical applications (inventory control, scheduling), Strategic applications (planning models, simulation)
2. Who sets priorities on application development?
3. What are the feasibility criteria for new applications?
4. What is the application backlog?
5. How useful is the information coming from data processing applications?
6. What new applications have been computerized in the past several years?

B. Efficiency (How is it being done?)
1. What is the user satisfaction level?
2. How timely and accurate is the information received?
3. What is the ability to recover in cases of unforeseen delays and minor calamities?
4. Are periodic equipment utilization studies conducted?
5. Do users generally have a positive attitude toward DP?

C. Financial Operation
1. How much is being spent on DP?
2. How does this compare to industry averages?
3. What has been the growth rate in DP over the past several years?
4. What is the split between hardware, software, supplies and services?
5. What type of financial justification is there for DP and DP applications?
6. Does your DP department operate as a profit or cost center, charging for its services?

D. Organization
1. To whom does the DP function report?
2. Is DP organization consistent with overall company organization? (i.e., centralized vs. decentralized)
3. What is the pay rate, salary structure compared to the industry?
4. Does DP control clerical, word processing, office automation activities?
5. How is the DP overall operating milieu and morale?
6. Are there training/education programs for DP personnel?
7. Are there good career opportunities and an exchange of personnel between DP and other business operations?

E. Management Techniques Employed
1. Does the DP department use project control techniques to control application development?
2. Are ROI or benefit/cost analyses employed?
3. Does the DP department have periodic audits or reviews?
4. What type of evaluation technique is used for acquiring additional facilities?
5. Is there a set of internal working standards and procedures?

F. Planning
1. Is there a short range DP operational plan?
2. Is there a long range plan?
3. Do the plans tie into the objectives/goals of the organization?
4. Who reviews and authorizes the plan?

G. Technology and Status of DP Function
1. Is the equipment state-of-the-art?
2. Does it have expansion potential without major conversion effort?
3. Is it modular and open ended?
4. Are industry standards/practices employed?
5. Is the technology level consistent with company philosophy? (i.e., pioneer, innovator or follower)

H. Management Involvement
1. Is there a Management Steering Committee?
2. Are users involved in the design and implementation of systems?
3. Are user education programs provided?
4. What is the interaction level with DP personnel?

FIGURE 3-9

must be viewed in light of its contribution to the overall operation of a company or business. Although this may seem a truism, EDP experience does not show that this principle has been heeded. Non-EDP management must work closely with EDP management to see that EDP becomes a powerful and expansive new source of profit. Only then will computers fulfill the prophecies that were made when they first appeared on the commercial scene in the early 1950s.

4 Mini/Micro Mania

One of the prevailing trends that have characterized the data-processing field since its inception is product proliferation. This aspect of the industry has been confusing for those providing the products, not to mention the turmoil to those procuring and using the products. Nowhere is this proliferation more frustrating than at the level of the small-business person or manager contemplating the purchase of his or her first computer system. The emerging low-end products are aimed at this person, who, however, is not often equipped with a knowledge base to comprehend this product cornucopia and to select the best course of action for his or her company.

The heart of the problem centers on the mini and micro computer mania that exists today. An almost endless stream of mini- and micro-based small computer systems and terminal products is coming off the production line. These systems are all billed as the solution to the growing paperwork burden of the small business, the key selling point being that they are so inexpensive that a business manager would be grossly remiss in not having one in his or her shop. The marketplace for small-business computers is estimated at 250,000 for companies in the $1- to $10-million sales range, with the figure burgeoning to over a million when companies under $1 million in sales are included. It is no wonder that computer companies are concentrating on this growing and seemingly attractive market.

The small-business person soon finds himself or herself thoroughly confused, confronting not only the vast array of products, but a myriad of distribution channels, all proclaiming the ability to deliver the product to him. These channels range from the computer retail store, the small-business system distributor, to the major mini and mainframe companies. Without some basic knowledge of the products and the industry selling channels, the businessperson is at the mercy of a plethora of computer salespeople and computer products.

This chapter focuses on an understanding of minis and micros and where they fit into the overall information-system business. The previous chapter dealt with computer feasibility. It is an important premise of this book that an understanding of a company's unique business environment and information requirements are mandatory before looking at specific computer systems or solutions.

THE MAINFRAME ERA

The brief computer history of Chapter 2 describes the genesis of mainframes from vacuum tubes and $3-million-plus purchase prices. As costs were reduced with transistors and integrated circuits, the market broadened. However, there was a limit to the cost-effectiveness of the new machines. First of all, the inherent design had a top-down focus—that is, the basic architecture was optimized for large-scale computing. It is difficult to subset a system whose design point is at the upper end of the power curve. Also, the architecture was geared to batch processing, the principal operation mode in the 1960s and early 1970s. Mainframe manufacturers did introduce new families of small machines, but these remained batch-oriented and carried over a good deal of large-machine mentality, including complex systems software, which required excessive amounts of memory. It has only been in recent years that mainframers have incorporated a transaction-oriented design philosophy to handle individual transactions in an on-line mode with quick turnaround to the waiting user, a requirement of most small business systems.

Mainframe companies built up large user bases where the inherent software lock-in and consumer loyalty (close to 80 percent of all mainframe consumers each year make decisions to upgrade or replace their systems with another model from their current vendor) motivate the mainframe manufacturer to provide compatibility and ease of upgrade to its existing base. This constrains, to a certain degree, the innovation and cost effectiveness that could be obtained without the compatibility requirement. Another important element is that a good portion of the mainframe business is rental versus outright purchase. Because of this, cash flow, especially early in the product life cycle, does not allow for both reasonable levels of development funds and maintaining acceptable profit rates.

To summarize, the evolution of the mainframe vendors with emphasis on large-scale computing power, product line compatibility, batch application orientation, and protection of their customer base left a niche for a new breed of computer vendor. This new breed, the minicomputer vendor, came on the scene with a high-technology product optimized around transaction processing and an interrupt-driven architecture. The minicomputer era consists of two phases—first, the special-purpose phase, corresponding roughly to the period from 1965 to 1973, and second, the general-purpose/commercial phase, starting in 1973.

THE MINICOMPUTER ERA

In the late 1960s there were few who could see the inroads that minis would make in the information-processing business in the decade to come. Indicative of this mini growth is that by 1980 both Digital Equipment Corporation (DEC) and Hewlett Packard had become $1-billion companies. International Data Corporation states that "small has become beautiful" and refers to the "magic minis, those centurions of EDP" and "the cottage industry in the 1960s that has become big business." Minis have been growing at a rate three times that of mainframes (33 percent per year compared with 12 percent) over the past decade. The key question is, What is the reason for this growth and what does it mean for the businessman/manager? The explanation comes from dividing the minicomputer period into two phases.

In the early days minis could be characterized as follows:

- Selling price under $25,000
- Maximum 16-bit architecture
- Limited input-output capability
- Limited general-purpose software

- Limited storage capability
- Specialized software, mostly scientific
- Special-purpose usage
- Architecture optimized for interrupt-driven applications

The market for minis was primarily in the industrial OEM (original equipment manufacturer) marketplace. A paper or chemical company requires computer-based control of production operations. A third party buys a minicomputer, adds special hardware-software, and develops a packaged system for a specific task. The industrial OEM then sells the package to the end user, who is usually not even aware of the embedded computer's brand name. It is a solution sell. Thus, during Phase I, the minis served a specialized industrial use. Other uses included communication message switching, laboratory statistical number crunching, computerized simulation models, and the like. The minis at this juncture were not employed in the commercial business marketplace dominated by IBM and the group that was referred to then as the seven dwarfs (Honeywell, Sperry Univac, Burroughs, RCA, NCR, GE, and Control Data).

During Phase I the mini companies were able to concentrate on technology (for the reasons already stated) and indeed succeeded in implementing cost-effective solutions for specific problems. It was only a matter of time until the mini vendors began to see the growing market potential if their product could be adapted to commercial business data processing. The hardware was there; what was lacking were the important ancillary peripheral and software capabilities. It was fortuitous for the mini vendor that the data-processing world was changing from a batch orientation to a transaction-processing environment (the architecture of minis). The same type of real-time response required in industrial process-control applications was carried over to the business data-processing arena. This became the focus of Phase II of the minicomputer era.

During Phase II minis were complemented with an expanded array of peripheral equipment. Business data processing requires a wide range of storage devices for applications such as inventory control and order processing. Storage capacity from low-cost removable diskettes (1 million characters) to large fixed disk devices in the billions-of-character range are commonplace in business applications. Likewise, line and serial printers are required and the scope of terminal and communications equipment broadened. From a hardware sense, it becomes difficult to tell a mini from a small or medium mainframe, and some of the large superminis even begin to compare with large mainframes.

But, as many users are beginning to realize, the name of the data-processing game has shifted from hardware to software. Here, too, the mini vendors have been diligent in producing the requisite small-business commercial software—the programming languages, operating systems, data-base software, and query languages. Application software is also in evidence, many developed by third-party software-system houses and marketed as a package along with the hardware. The question at this point might be, What's the difference between a business system emanating from a mini vendor and a business system emanating from a mainframe vendor? The answer is—very little. The products must be evaluated in the perspective of a company's individual needs and the overall cost effectiveness of the system solution (note the word *system* solution and not *hardware* solution). The elements of software, applications, service, support, and maintainability become increasingly important decision criteria as the system choices multiply at an almost exponential rate.

Because of the inherent interrupt-driven architecture of minis, they have also become extremely relevant as satellites in the exploding distributed data-processing field. International Data Corporation projects that 45 percent of the estimated $18 billion worth of distributed data-processing equipment installed in 1985 will be mini-based. Thus, the two major growth areas for minis are in general-purpose business use, particularly small business, and in distributed data processing. IDC predicts a shift to commercial markets for minis from 24 to 61 percent of total mini business between 1975 and 1984.

INTRODUCTION OF MICROCOMPUTERS

The appearance of microcomputers began in the mid 1970s with the development paralleling that of the minis. At first, the micro was a limited, special-purpose device aimed at specific functions and with limited peripheral and software capability. The uses were similar to those of the early minis, and in fact, micros replaced minis in many process- and industrial-control applications. However, by adding peripheral connections and enriching the software, the micro has become at home in the small-business world and also in the distributed processing world.

As minis have moved up to encroach on the mainframes, so

the micros have captured market territory that previously was the province of minis. The distinction between mainframe, mini, and micro has become blurred.

The micro vendors are typified by Texas Instruments, Motorola, National Semiconductor, Tandy, and Apple. The micro-based small-business computer is a natural offshoot. Micros appeared in this market in several ways. The first is via companies who incorporate their own micro or build a system around someone else's micro and market via the traditional sales channels. The second route is typified by Tandy and Apple. Their micros started out as home or hobby computers, used primarily by the technically bent engineer or professional. However, with added capabilities, these machines began to find their way into small business, sold through the retail store, the same channel used for the hobby computer.

The major influence of the micro in the distributed processing world has been via the growth of the intelligent terminal (or its more sophisticated big brother, the brilliant terminal). A simple cathode ray tube (CRT) terminal can be enhanced by microcomputer intelligence, or expanded into a cluster of terminal work stations replete with disk storage and printing capabilities. This now becomes an intelligent or brilliant terminal subsystem or satellite similar to the mini-based satellite.

THE MAJOR FORCE BEHIND
THE MINI/MICRO MANIA

Having traced the development, it is appropriate at this point to pause for a minute to define a mini and a micro and to explore the forces behind their development. Figure 4-1 indicates the phenomenon that has been occurring in the data-processing industry. It is not a precise statistical representation, but it does point out a most significant trend.

In our inflationary economy, the costs of people, paper, and power—three major elements of data-processing cost—have all risen substantially. However, the cost of semiconductor technology has dropped dramatically, an accepted industry figure being 20 percent per year over the past decade. The major driving force has been the development of large and very large scale integration (LSI and VLSI, as the industry terms it). LSI is the ability to fabricate a large number of electronic elements on a silicon die or chip, maybe a quarter of an inch square. The state

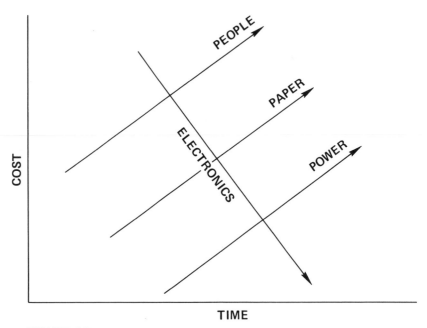

FIGURE 4-1
DP Cost Trends

of the art is that the equivalent power of 60,000 to 100,000 transistors can be placed on a single chip. Technologists predict that chips exceeding 1 million transistors will be commonplace before the end of the century. The result of this density is that complete computer logic units or processors can be placed on a single chip. Likewise, chip memories with densities of 64,000 bits per chip are commonplace, with 256,000-bit chips also on the scene. In concert with advanced mass-production techniques, LSI has reduced the cost of memory and logic units dramatically, as illustrated in the preceding chart.

The computer gurus refer to the development of LSI as the "new crude oil" powering the information revolution just as fossil fuels powered the Industrial Revolution. Along with the reduction in cost, LSI circuits are more reliable and require far less power than their predecessors. The expanded use of information systems with remote-access communication links allows more work to be performed at home, brings interactive television and a variety of education and entertainment modules into the home, thus reducing the need for travel and replacing crude oil power with LSI semiconductor power—so say the technological seers.

A minicomputer has been defined earlier. There is no simple definition, but for the most part, the mini has incorporated the evolving stages of LSI to produce an extremely cost-performant computer system. The micro can be defined a bit more concretely.

A microprocessor is a chip that has the capabilities of performing the logic functions of a computer processor. The next definition is a microcomputer, which utilizes a higher degree of LSI and in addition to the processor, has memory, input-output interfaces, and communication links located on chips. This array of chips is fabricated on a printed circuit board about 8 inches by 12 inches. Thus, the microcomputer utilizes LSI on a single board for all of the electronic elements of the system.

Consider, however, that a computer system is comprised of peripheral and terminal devices as well as a central processing unit. While LSI has helped reduce the cost of these devices, the mechanical nature of print mechanisms, paper feeds, disk read heads, and the like make them less sensitive to LSI breakthroughs. Peripherals and terminals comprise over 60 percent of the value of the hardware, so that while a 20-percent reduction in electronics brought on by LSI is quite significant, its impact on overall hardware cost is only 8 percent.

As electronic costs drop, the value of software, support, and maintenance of computer systems become increasingly significant, for they are labor-intensive elements. The message here is that while recognizing the role of LSI in reducing computer costs and lowering the threshold for computer entry, management should not conduct a computer feasibility study or a comparison of competitive computer systems without giving the necessary weight to the nonhardware elements.

A WORD ABOUT SOFTWARE

As mentioned, the application mode of information systems has switched from basically batch to a transaction-processing orientation. Remembering that software is written by people and that people costs are most assuredly rising, it is a great advantage to the user to buy a system where the vendor's hardware and software do as much of his job as possible.

The trend in computer architecture is to place what heretofore were software functions into the hardware. This is an attractive trade-off from a cost standpoint, and manufacturers are moving in this direction. Software, implemented in this manner, is placed on chips and the term used to describe the resulting product is *firmware*. Languages, segments of operating systems, and portions of applications are candidates for firmware. However, a prerequisite is that the process to be incorporated within the firmware be known well enough so that it is not subject to frequent change. Firmware lies somewhere between software and hardware; it is not as flexible and easy to change as software, but it is not hard-wired or as permanent as hardware.

DISTRIBUTION CHANNELS

As minis and micros have proliferated, so have the distribution channels, or delivery systems. I believe the period of the 1970s was as significant for the change in selling channels as it was for the change in product direction. The 1970s saw the entry of the third party into the computer business. While users could still purchase directly from the vendor, the emergence of the indirect channel was becoming more prevalent.

The emergence of the third party developed because of several reasons. As product cost dropped and the entry level to computing for small companies was lowered dramatically, the computer vendor saw a rising percentage of his cost devoted to marketing and support. Analysis of marketing costs encountered the option of a third-party sales force that specialized in sales to small companies, had low overhead costs, and could market computers more economically. This would allow the vendor to concentrate his efforts on his medium and large customers while still maintaining the volume at the low end to keep manufacturing costs down. On the other hand, third parties saw a business opportunity in the emerging mini and micro products for the small business and they realized the small company represented a lucrative and untapped computer source.

The third parties include the distributor who adds no value to the systems he buys from the manufacturer but provides the single contact point for purchase and service while packaging and documenting the system for the ultimate user. System integrators are another class of third party who provide added value to the system but not of their own production. They combine peripherals, terminals, a central processor, and software from a multiplicity of vendors, which they then integrate, package, and offer for resale. On the other hand, the system builder provides his own value added usually in the form of system software or application software. The trend is toward vertical industry or application specialization, where a particular system builder acquires knowledge and experience in providing systems to a specific industry segment, be it pharmacy accounting, real estate management, construction project control, or the like. This has advantages to the end user, who is really looking for a solution and not a bag of piece parts that he must assemble into a solution. The greater the specialization of the system builder, the closer he can usually come to providing a solution. However, there are pitfalls to a solution sell such that a user must make a careful analysis and match of his individual requirements against the capabilities of the proposed application solution.

Another growing distribution channel in the computer industry is mass marketing. Computer retail stores have sprung up, providing microcomputers for hobby/home use and also moving into the small-business arena. These stores are managed by a major computer manufacturer (DEC or IBM), a microcomputer manufacturer (Tandy or Apple), or by an independent store stocking products from a variety of vendors. Questions of support and maintenance are raised by these distribution channels. Factors to consider in analyzing the variety of selling channels are summarized in a later section. Suffice to state here, the retail store offers the least expensive method of distribution with the exception of direct mail or phone (used for supplies and add-on units, but not for systems), but there are trade-offs in product support, particularly on-site support.

MARKETS AND DISTRIBUTION CHANNELS

Figure 4-2 pulls together the various computer markets and distribution channels that have been discussed in this chapter. The various uses of computer systems comprise the bottom block of the figure. The market is divided into two broad segmentations: first, an industry segmentation, and second, a usage segmentation that cuts across industry lines.

The industry segmentation consists of the various industries (i.e. manufacturing, distribution, banking, finance and so on) where computer systems are employed. The usage segmentation is divided into four categories beginning with *freestanding*

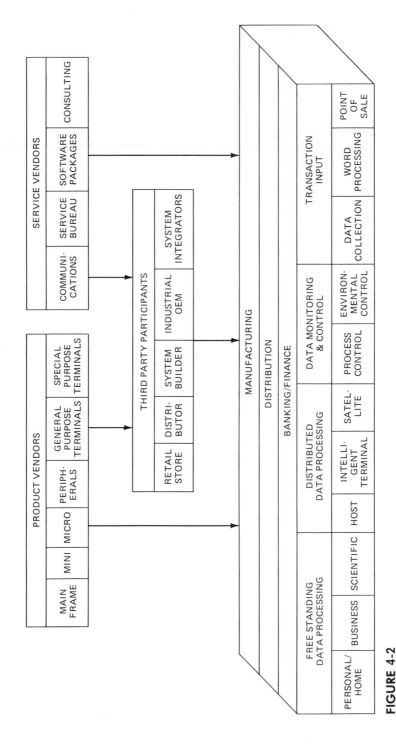

FIGURE 4-2
Data Processing Markets and Distribution Channels

100

data processing. This ranges from the use of micros in the home for personal hobby use to the largest segment in this category, the business computers used primarily by small-size and medium-size companies. (Most of the large companies fall into the next category, distributed data processing, since they have multiple remote sites that are linked by communications lines to a larger host computer.). Freestanding scientific computers are found in laboratories, research organizations, and educational institutions and range from micros to very large minis or even mainframes.

The second category, *distributed data processing*, has already been fairly well defined. The host machines in these communication networks can either be minis or mainframes, whereas the intelligent terminals and satellites are increasingly becoming mini or micro based.

Data monitoring and control, the third category, represents a more finite, definitive use of computers as opposed to commercial applications in the other categories. The focus of the book is not in this area, since the process control and CAD-CAM (computer aided design–computer aided manufacturing) areas continue to provide specialized use of computers as opposed to the general purpose application of business computers. This marketplace is satisfied exclusively by minis and micros. Computer aided design enables a designer or engineer to express specific design parameters which the computer program will transform into graphics on a screen display and ultimately reproduce on a hard-copy plotter.

Computer aided manufacturing uses computer control to provide the logic to operate a variety of machine tools or industrial processes. The computer program can automatically position a lathe or drive a drill press. An extension of CAM is robotics (from the word robot) where mechanical arms and extensions powered by computer logic can execute operations normally requiring manual involvement.

The fourth category, termed *transaction input*, covers the variety of systems specializing in data collection, both in the factory and in the office. These devices, which are either mini or micro driven, are dedicated to the collection of input transactions. The input is usually batched and the media carried physically or communicated over wire to a host computer for processing. Growing areas of mini and micro use are in word processing and point of sale. Word processing is built around the so-called intelligent typewriter, which is capable of capturing, storing, editing, and updating textual material and also communicating the output to remote locations. Word processing is a piece of the general-application area that is known as office automation. It is possible either to combine word processing and business processing on the same computer system or to treat them as separate dedicated entities. It is also possible to add other office applications, such as text and letter storage and retrieval, calendar and project scheduling, and mailing list maintenance, which are all part of office automation. Point-of-sale devices, like the optical character readers in grocery and department stores, represent yet another rapid growth area for minis and micros. Items identified by coded labels are scanned to provide access to a computerized inventory file, where pricing extensions and updates to inventory records occur simultaneously.

Moving to the top of Figure 4-2, the information vendors are divided into product vendors and service vendors. Product vendors have already been described. Service vendors include communication services such as AT&T and private carriers, for example, GTE, Telenet, and Tymnet, service bureaus that provide both on-line and on-site service, as well as the myriad of companies providing software packages, contract programming, and consulting. A word should be said about service bureaus because this is an additional source of computer power for the small businessman. The traditional sharing of computers, as provided by service bureaus, is decreasing because many small companies can now afford their own computers, but it still offers an alternative. A service bureau specializing in specific applications or specific industries may provide an attractive alternative. Currently service bureaus, in addition to their shared service, also offer on-site packaged systems. The service bureau then becomes similar to the system builder or system integrator except that the service bureau can offer a combination of on-site and communication-linked off-site service.

The product and service vendors market their offerings either directly to end users, as illustrated in the figure, or via the third parties, as explained earlier. This, then, completes the description of the various market and selling channels for mini and micro products. All of this is a bit awesome for the small-business person, but it is extremely important to understand the process. An added problem is that this structure is still in shakedown mode; that is, there is a fairly high mortality rate of third parties, with mergers and acquisitions quite common.

DECISION CRITERIA

This section attempts to tie together the proceeding discussion into an evaluation matrix that can serve the business person contemplating the purchase of a computer system. A mandatory base point before beginning such an analysis is for the company to review its own internal requirements and to conduct an initial feasibility study that shows there is a potential payoff in computerization. The approach described here is but one of several techniques for evaluating vendors, but it should serve to emphasize the necessity of a systematic method in making a decision as complex as selecting a computer system.

Note that Figure 4-3 is broken down into four general evaluation criteria with the particular weight that is placed on a particular criteria varying among companies. For example, a company with experienced computer personnel may place less weight on support. The first surprise in this analysis may be that hardware has the least weight, while support has the heaviest. Both systems software and application software are more significant than hardware in this particular weighting. I would venture to say that this scale is appropriate for the majority of small companies acquiring their first information system. An argument could be raised that support is insignificant if the user is promised a complete turnkey application software system that will accomplish the job. However, the user is cautioned that a truly turnkey system with the scope to do the total job for the user might well prove illusionary under more careful analysis.

The weights can be further subdivided among the factors in each of the general categories. For example, ease of use may be given 60 percent of the systems software weight of 25 percent and thus represent 15 percent of the overall evaluation. Again, these weightings depend on the particular company situation.

Note that price has not been mentioned as yet. This obviously is a key element and should be viewed as a total systems price, for it may be that some vendors include software in the price of hardware, have a packaged support plan, or whatever. Using a total system price will enable as close an apples-to-apples comparison as possible. It is a good idea to develop the scoring without pricing and to consider price after the other elements have been evaluated. There is judgment in all the elements listed in the matrix, but price represents a finite number.

The other side of the matrix lists the particular vendors

103

	WEIGHT	MAINFRAME A	MINI VENDOR B	DISTRIBUTOR A	SYSTEM BUILDER A	SYSTEM BUILDER B
HARDWARE	20					
Functionality						
Ease of Upgrade						
Reliability						
Peripherals						
Terminals						
Communications						
SYSTEMS SOFTWARE	25					
Ease of Use						
Languages						
Data Base						
Operating System						
Compatability						
APPLICATION SOFTWARE	25					
Applicability						
Ease of Use						
Functionality						
Documentation						
SUPPORT	30					
Education						
Maintenance						
Proximity						
Systems Assistance						
Stability of Vendor						

FIGURE 4-3
Decision Matrix

being considered. In this case, one mainframer, one mini vendor, one distributor, and two system builders are being evaluated. It is no small task in itself to reduce the potential vendor list to a half dozen or so, but this must be accomplished before more detailed evaluation is possible. The particular company situation, including past experience, reference data, and geographical location, will probably indicate the potential vendor list. As the

104

vendors are rated, it will become apparent where some fall short in what categories. For example, if systems assistance is required, it may not be available at all from the distributor. Also, the system builders may be lacking in the important maintenance support category. Machine failure and downtime in a transaction-driven system can materially hurt an operation. This is the type of issue that an evaluation methodology brings out. It focuses attention and thinking to high-priority questions and issues. If there were only one or two possible solutions for satisfying a company's information needs and only one or two possible sources of systems, a disciplined methodology might not be significant, but with the plethora of products and distribution channels described in this chapter, a methodology is mandatory.

SUMMARY

Though there should be items of interest in this chapter for the management of medium and large companies, the focus is on the manager of a small company. The mini-micro mania has been a major impact for the small-business person in that it has lowered the computer entry threshold and has made the small-business market a major target for product and service vendors selling through a multiplicity of third-party participants.

This chapter has traced the development of minis and micros from the mainframes. The minis and micros, whose genesis was in the process-control, special-purpose market, have found a niche in the commercial arena. Fortuitously, their basic architecture was optimized around transaction processing, and with the addition of a richer array of software, peripherals, and terminals, the stage was set for a successful penetration of the business market—and that is exactly what has happened.

All of this doesn't make it easier for the small-business person. The course is characterized by promises and pitfalls. Access to computer systems is an exciting possibility and indeed may in many instances be the only way to profitably grow and compete. However, pitfalls loom ahead because a wrong computer decision cannot only eliminate the potential benefits, it can make a company worse off than it was before the computer. The situation is far from bleak. By utilizing an evaluation methodology similar to that described in this chapter, a company can quantify the decision process and select the alternative where potential benefits outweigh the risks.

5 Understanding Software and Programming

There are a variety of teaching methods aimed at getting across the principles of computers and their applications. This book attacks the problem from a case-oriented viewpoint. It tackles the job from the outside in—that is, instead of discussing the principles of electronic data processing first and then seeing how these principles might apply to a typical business application, the sequence is reversed. A simple business application is presented and the discussion is confined to those computer principles pertinent in solving the problem. This method has several advantages for the executive. First, it starts on familiar ground. You do not get bogged down immediately in unfamiliar terrain but begin with a problem you can understand. Second, the case problem serves as a unifying force, giving meaning to the more advanced concepts that follow. Last, an immediate application of what is learned fits in the pieces of the puzzle as you go. In this way you can see the immediate relationship of one piece to another.

Some argue that executives or non-EDP business managers don't do the systems work and programming for a computer, so why should they be bothered with knowing anything about it? I think there is considerable merit in the manager understanding the entire process of putting a business application into productive operation on a computer. It presents a complete picture of the process. Taking a look at computer programming helps you better understand the role of the systems analyst and the programmer—and the complex, painstaking job they have in making things happen. I also think a "look under the hood" is useful if only to serve the curiosity factor. A businessperson has to discover just what it is that makes a computer tick. This chapter will define some computer terms such as flowcharting, software, COBOL, debugging, and the like. A manager who does not feel this type of curiosity or the need to delve a little into technical matters can scan this chapter and proceed with the next. However, I think that those who delve into the subject of programming will find the chapter rewarding. I suggest you take pencil and paper and sketch out the steps to programming a computer as you read the chapter.

CASE PROBLEM

The case problem is an inventory application. Most businesses maintain some type of inventory, whether it be baked beans, electric plugs, valves, gauges, paper, cement blocks, or steel sheeting. The primary purpose of this inventory is to provide customer service. Most businesses are concerned with producing and delivering a product to a customer, who may be an individual, a retail store, a wholesale distributor, or another manufacturer. Whoever the customer may be, he wants the item in his hand on time. Another reason for inventory is to balance the costs of obtaining the item against the costs involved in carrying an inventory. For example, it may be more economical for a manufacturer to produce one hundred of an item because the setup costs more than offset the cost of the additional inventory. Inventory also smooths out manufacturing cycles. It may be desirable to keep a production line going, even though it means producing for inventory, because the alternative is to lay off skilled workers.

Inventory control is a natural application for electronic data processing because of the volume and repetitive nature of inventory transactions. Maintaining an inventory of 20,000 items with some 2,000 different transactions handled each day requires a good deal of paperwork and recordkeeping. A computer system offers a fast, consistent, and reliable solution to the inventory control problem.

One type of inventory accounting serves as a scorekeeper,

adding receipts and subtracting issues from the inventory file to produce a status report of all inventory items. This is no small trick—relatively few companies can claim that transactions are being processed accurately and that their inventory records are current and correct.

Another type of inventory control is more sophisticated, using mathematical techniques to forecast product demand and calculate economic order point and economic order quantities.

Inventory accounting, in its basic form, is easy to understand. Inventory records are updated with receipts and depleted with orders for the item. Some type of inventory status report is produced periodically to indicate the level of each inventory item. This job can be performed manually, by semiautomatic equipment, by completely automatic equipment, or by any combination of the three methods. We will perform the job on a computer, although you will see that the basic input must still be prepared manually.

The inventory information will be kept on random-access disk storage, a common medium to maintain fixed information pertaining to either employee records or inventory records. Input could be via a variety of devices, but for this example, a common CRT display terminal will be employed.

STEPS IN COMPUTER PROGRAMMING

A prescribed methodology exists for preparing an application for computer processing. The steps in a larger, more complex job, would include additional steps—such functions as audit controls, documentation, and the like—but the steps described here are typical. The steps involved in preparing this job for a computer are as follows:

1. System description
2. System flowchart
3. Input-output format documents
4. File storage
5. Programmer's logic flowchart
6. Computer compilation
7. Computer programming
8. Program operation

System Description

We have already described the job as an inventory program that reads transactions from a CRT screen, finds the relevant master record on magnetic disk, updates the record, and prints out the new inventory status. This is the system description of the job.

System Flowchart

This step expresses the system description in flowchart form. The system flowchart is a symbolic overview of the entire operation. Figure 5-1, the system flowchart for this application, puts in symbolic form what we have already described in narrative form. A flowchart facilitates a quick analysis of the job being performed. Standard symbols enable programmers and systems analysts to understand each other's portrayal of the various input, output, and storage devices.

Input-Output Format Documents

Exactly how each input and output document will appear must now be determined. This step is necessary because a computer program is an exact and precise sequence of steps. A program operates correctly only when input data is located in prescribed positions on a CRT screen and in prescribed positions on magnetic disks. Furthermore, the program is designed to produce information fields in prescribed columns on a printed report.

The screen input document layout in Figure 5-2 will be used for the case problem. The item number is an eight-digit numeric field that identifies the item affected by the particular transaction. The next field is an eight-digit quantity indicating the amount of the particular transaction. The last field on the screen has a two-digit code that indicates the type of transaction. In this case, there will only be one type of transaction, a receipt. (There could be as many as one-hundred different types

FIGURE 5-1
System Flow Chart

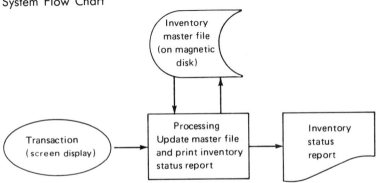

Contents of field	Item number	Quantity	Transaction code	not used
Column numbers	1-8	9-16	17-18	19-80

FIGURE 5-2
Screen Input Document

of transactions, but this would complicate the problem unnecessarily.) The remainder of the screen, columns 19-80, is not used in this example.

The printed output record is a very crucial part of electronic data processing, since it represents the purpose of the entire operation. Management is concerned almost exclusively with this document. The report layout will be a simple one (again for the purpose of understanding the problem.) The computer printer, in this example, is capable of printing 132 characters across a paper form. Figure 5-3 shows the printer format we will use for the case problem.

The job of laying out input-output format documents is now complete, and we can move to the next step of the job.

File Storage

As has been indicated, magnetic disk is the storage medium for the application. Disk storage devices come in a variety of sizes and capabilities, ranging from a 1-million-character diskette to billion-character disks, the kind of capacity that might be required by a medium to large insurance company or bank.

Data are represented on the disk surface by the presence or absence of ferrous oxide spots running sequentially along the

FIGURE 5-3
Printed Output Report

INVENTORY STATUS REPORT

Item number	Item description	Balance
Print positions 11-18	Positions 29-44	Positions 55-62

ory distinguishes the computer from other data-processing devices. Memory gives the computer the ability to store a lengthy series of instructions and to execute these instructions in a prescribed sequence.

Physically the memory unit in most computers consists of small chips, each capable of holding 4,000, 16,000, or 64,000 storage cells (bits of information). Each storage cell can be in one of two possible states (either a charge is present or it is absent). The presence or absence of the charge represents either a 1 or 0, respectively.

Since one storage cell can represent only two conditions, four cells are needed to represent the decimal digits 0 through 9. In the decimal numbering system, each position in a number represents a power of 10. The number 1,432 can be stated as $(1 \times 10^3) + (4 \times 10^2) + (3 \times 10^1) + (2 \times 10^0) = 1,432$. In the binary numbering system, each position represents a power of two. Thus, the binary number 1001 (keep in mind we can only use ones and zeros) is $(1 \times 2^3) + (0 \times 2^2) + (0 \times 2^1) + (1 \times 2^0) = 9$. The following table shows how the numbers from zero to nine are written in binary.

Decimal	Binary
0	0000
1	0001
2	0010
3	0011
4	0100
5	0101
6	0110
7	0111
8	1000
9	1001

In a computer, memory is made up of fixed units, each unit containing a certain number of storage cells. This arrangement is shown diagrammatically in Figure 5-6.

We want one unit to be able to represent either one of the ten decimal digits, an alphabetic character, or one of eleven special symbols (comma, asterisk, etc.). It would take six cells to represent these forty-seven different characters. Actually six cells can represent as many as sixty-four (2^6) different characters, but five cells can represent only thirty-two (2^5) characters. The number above each set of cells in Figure 5-6 is called the address of

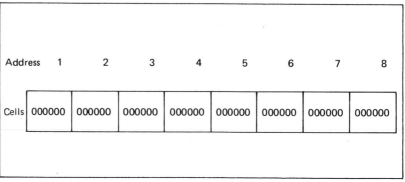

FIGURE 5-6
Memory Units

the data represented by the six cells. Each six-cell unit has a unique address. Addresses begin with 1 (or sometimes 0) and continue up to the capacity of the particular computer.

Computer Compilation

Compilation is translating programmer's language into actual (binary) computer language. Although chronologically the writing of the computer program precedes the compilation, discussing compilation first makes it easier to understand what a computer program does. We want to deliver the programmed instructions into computer memory so they can be used to process data and produce the report prescribed by the program. However, it would be very tedious to write the instructions in their binary form. Computer manufacturers have developed special programs called compiler programs that allow you to write the program in a format more similar to the English language. The compiler program then translates the program into binary notation and stores it in the computer.

Computer Programming

Let's now take a look at the instructions that make up the computer program. For this problem, we will use the COBOL programming language. COBOL (COmmon Business Oriented LAnguage) is the most widely used business programming language. All major computer manufacturers have COBOL compilers. COBOL aids a programmer by allowing the program to be written English-like statements. This makes it easier to learn how to program, easier to write programs, and easier to maintain and modify programs. In addition, COBOL is a standardized language so that programs written for one machine can be converted to run on another computer with minimal changes.

This no doubt is the briefest COBOL programming course ever attempted. The COBOL programming language consists of four major divisions:

1. Identification division
2. Environment division
3. Data division
4. Procedure division

The identification division simply identifies (names) the program to be written. The environment division lists the hardware elements (such as the CRT terminal, the disk unit, and the printer) that the program will use.

Figure 5-7 is an example of how a programmer would write the data division. It defines the input, output, and storage item layouts that will be used. In our problem we have previously described three such items: the transaction item, which we have called TRANS-RECORD; the disk file, which we have called DISK-RECORD; and the print file, which we have called PRINT-RECORD.

Note that the programming form is laid out with the header information and column headings across the top. Each line of the program must be keyed into a terminal device so that it can be read into the computer and translated into binary instruction code.

The files are described in accordance with the way the programmer has laid them out. For example, DISK-FILE indicates that the ITEM-NUM (this is the identifier that the programmer will use to access the item number on the disk file), the PICTURE IS (this is a particular phrase used in COBOL) eight digits in length. The 9 designates the field as numeric. The X on the next line indicates the item description field is alphanumeric. The programmer must indicate and describe the label records for both cards and disk. These labels are used to indicate such header information as name of file, creation date, reel number, and so on. For simplicity, we have omitted label records. The FILLER pictures in the PRINT-RECORD description indicate the spacing desired between fields—in this case, 10. The Z in the last line indicates that all leading 0s in the item balance field should be suppressed so that 00004328 will appear as 4328.

The procedure division contains the actual instructions to accomplish the job. It follows the programmer's flowchart. The program (Figure 5-8) begins by reading an item from the CRT display and checking to see if it's the last one. (Of course it

| PAGE NO. | PROGRAM | INVENTORY STATUS | | COBOL DIVISION | | PAGE | 1 | OF | 2 |
| | PROGRAMMER | H. JONES | | DATE | 11/7/79 | IDENT. | | 73 | I N S T A T U S |

```
DATA DIVISION.
FILE SECTION.

FD  TRANSACTION-SCREEN-LABEL RECORDS ARE OMITTED.
01  TRANS-RECORD.

    02  ITEM-NUMBER PICTURE IS 9(8).
    02  QUANTITY PICTURE IS 9(8).
    02  TRANS-CODE PICTURE IS 9(2).
    02  FILLER PICTURE IS X(62).

FD  DISK-FILE LABEL RECORDS ARE OMITTED.
01  DISK-RECORD.

    02  ITEM-NUM PICTURE IS 9(8).
    02  ITEM-DESCR PICTURE IS X(16).
    02  ITEM-BAL PICTURE IS 9(8).

FD  PRINT-FILE.
01  PRINT-RECORD

    02  FILLER PICTURE IS X(10), VALUE IS SPACES.
    02  P-ITEM-NUM PICTURE IS 9(8).
    02  FILLER PICTURE IS X(10), VALUE IS SPACES.
    02  P-ITEM-DESCR PICTURE IS X(20).
```

HIT 1523 'A K 152. PRINTED IN U.S.A.

Honeywell
COBOL PROGRAMMING FORM

| PAGE NO. | PROGRAM | INVENTORY STATUS | | COBOL DIVISION | | PAGE | 2 | OF | 2 |
| | PROGRAMMER | H. JONES | | DATE | 11/7/79 | IDENT. | | 73 | I N S T A T U S |

```
    02  FILLER PICTURE IS X(10), VALUE IS SPACES.
    02  P-ITEM-BAL PICTURE IS Z(8).
```

FIGURE 5-7
Sample COBOL Data Division

isn't—and won't be—until all the transactions are read and processed.) The next instruction is to read an inventory item from disk. In an actual program the programmer would have to indicate the technique to use to find the item on the disk from the item number on the screen. The instructions state that the quantity is to be subtracted from the ITEM-BAL. After this instruction is executed by the computer, ITEM-BAL will contain the new and updated inventory balance.

The print line is developed by use of the MOVE instructions as in Figure 5-8. The WRITE PRINT-RECORD instruction prints a line of the inventory status report, as shown on Figure 5-9, spacing two lines between print lines. The WRITE DISK-RECORD instruction places the updated data back on the disk.

After the disk is updated and the inventory status line printed, the program loops back to read another transaction item. Each transaction item is processed similarly. When the last item is sensed, the job is concluded.

This job has been simplified for ease of explanation, but the basic programming concepts should still be evident. Examples of added programming steps might be the handling of other transaction types. For instance, receipts. file changes, credit

FIGURE 5-8

Sample COBOL Procedure Division

Honeywell

COBOL PROGRAMMING FORM

```
PROGRAM: INVENTORY STATUS          COBOL DIVISION          PAGE 1 OF 1
PROGRAMMER: H. JONES               DATE 11/7/79    IDENT. INSTATUS

PROCEDURE DIVISION.

SCREEN READ.
    READ TRANSACTION-SCREEN AT END STOP RUN.
    READ DISK-FILE.
    IF ITEM-NUMBER EQUALS ITEM-NUM GO TO INV-STATUS.
    STOP RUN.

INV-STATUS.
    SUBTRACT QUANTITY FROM ITEM-BAL.
    MOVE ITEM-NUM TO P-ITEM-NUM.
    MOVE ITEM-DESCR TO P-ITEM-DESCR.
    MOVE ITEM-BAL TO P-ITEM-BAL.

    WRITE PRINT-RECORD BEFORE ADVANCING 2 LINES.
    WRITE DISK-RECORD.
    GO TO SCREEN READ.
```

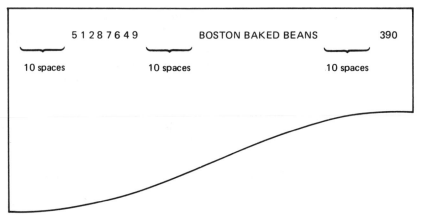

FIGURE 5-9
Inventory Status Report

transaction inventory adjustments, or many others might be included. Additional coding would be required, but the same program principles would apply.

Program Operation

After it has been compiled, the program is placed in memory in binary form. At this point it is ready to process transaction items—that is, to update the master file and print the report. The computer will execute one instruction after another in sequence until the program comes to a halt. In reality, testing (called debugging) is required to check out the operation of the program. For our purposes we will assume the program has been checked out and is ready to run.

HOW A COMPUTER OPERATES

Figure 5-10 summarizes in schematic form what we have been doing up to now. Transactions are keyed into the CRT and transferred into computer memory. In this instance the input is item 12345 and a quantity of two. Computer memory is illustrated in planes of A1 through A10, B1 through B10, and so on. The position A1 through A8 here represent the item number in binary (A1 through A5) and the quantity (A8).

Data are recorded along the tracks of the disk surface. Data enter memory via a prescribed channel and leave memory after processing via another prescribed channel. The data could be represented in any of the various memory planes. Assuming the balance in the disk file for item 12345 is four, the program (stored on memory planes allocated for this purpose) moves the transaction amount and balance amount into the arithmetic unit, subtracts the two amounts, and directs the answer to be printed. The required data are sent to the printer via the printer output channel. This process is repeated until all the transaction items are read and processed.

Each programmed instruction first goes to control memory, where it is interpreted and executed. For example, in the case of the "print" instruction, the control unit ensures that the memory area holding the line to be printed is delivered to the

FIGURE 5-10

How a Computer Operates

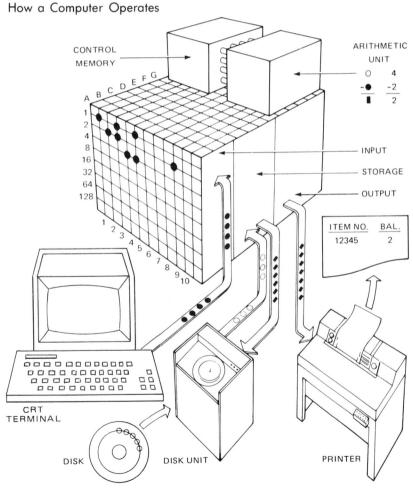

printer, the relevant print characters are activated, and the paper positioned for the next line.

We now have gone through the complete process of describing a computer application—flowcharting, coding, compiling, and operating it. The manager should now have some feeling of how information needs are translated into the language of the computer. The process may seem long, involved, and exacting, but once programmed, a computer can speedily and accurately update a large inventory file, producing inventory status reports with a wide variety of analytical information. For example, a small computer can update a 25,000-item inventory with 5,000 transactions and print out the items under a predetermined minimum or over a predetermined maximum in less than five minutes.

COMPUTER SOFTWARE

Electronic data processing can be viewed as having three dimensions: hardware, software, and application (see Figure 5-11).

Hardware is the physical computer devices that can be seen and touched. A CRT terminal, a central processing unit, and a line printer are hardware. When one thinks of a computer system, hardware more often than not is what comes to mind. Hardware by itself, however, does not accomplish anything for a business. The second side of the triangle, software, includes the programming languages and operating systems (explained in this chapter) that enable programming personnel to communicate with the hardware. This dimension is called software because it is a series of instructions that originate from paper documents (flowcharts, input-output format documents, programming forms, and the like). More and more, companies have

FIGURE 5-11
Three Dimensions of EDP

Hardware

awakened to the fact that the software is as important as (or even more important than) the hardware.

The computer programmer looks at the computer through its software. The systems analyst, business manager, and operating personnel look at the computer through its application. An application is an end product—order processing or inventory control, for example. Hardware and software are merely theoretical capabilities until they are applied to a problem. A computer's value is measured by how well it handles premium billings for a life insurance company or prints a production schedule for a manufacturing company. The application can be considered as software because it must be expressed by a series of instructions that originate from paper documents. However, it is relevant to make a distinction between the two. All three dimensions must be going for you—hardware, software, and application.

Assembly and Compiler Software

Early software developments centered primarily in assembly languages and compiler languages. Assembly languages allow the programmer to communicate with the computer in such simple mnemonics as ADD and MOVE. Compiler languages (COBOL, FORTRAN, PL/I, etc.) allow the use of structured programming language statements. The purpose of both assemblers and compilers is to allow the machine to go about its job in binary language, while the programmer can write in a more easily understood and remembered programming language. The programming language software translates from programming language to binary language.

The use of assembly languages has almost disappeared, being replaced by such higher-level languages as COBOL and other compiler languages. In the early days of COBOL the ratio of assembly language to compiler language usage was 9 to 1. This ratio has reversed. The ease of programming, ease of program update and change, and the ability to protect one's programming investment during change to a different computer are attributes of compiler languages.

An important event took place on June 23, 1969, when IBM announced a new pricing policy. Certain software systems and education and systems support services would be priced separately from hardware. This "unbundled" pricing structure enables independent software houses to compete for a user's software business. Separate pricing has become a fact of life in the computer industry, as the major vendors all have followed IBM's lead.

More Advanced Software

Another important software advance is the development of operating systems. The purpose of an operating system is to reduce and simplify the amount of manual intervention and gain as much productivity as possible from the machine. Such systems can be compared with the maintenance and setup crew for production-line machinery. The crew's duty is to perform routine housekeeping chores that ensure the equipment is as productive as possible during the work shift. Similarly, operating systems have evolved from the simple tasks, which were to clear memory, initialize the peripherals, handle routine error situations, load memory with the first program to be executed, and do the same with each program throughout the shift.

With the advent of communications-oriented processing, operating systems have taken on a new look. They now recognize demands from a host of remote terminals, allocate the necessary hardware resources to satisfy these demands, and at the same time run the daily production-line jobs at the central site. This complex monitoring and control capability represents the major challenge of today's operating systems.

The growth of scientific software reflects an expanding use of computers in advanced mathematical problem solving. This class of software had been the province of a small number of engineers and operations research analysts who used mathematical techniques to assist in engineering calculations and research projects. Now once-esoteric techniques such as linear programming and queueing theory are available for use in general business operations.

Data base management systems are a response to users' need to store large volumes of information in a central data base in order to provide integrated systems capability. This information must be indexed so that relevant pieces of the information base can be obtained as a unit—and in the time frame required by the business situation. Data management also must tie in closely with the operating system, as much of the inquiry and update activity takes place from remote locations over communication lines.

Because of the growing significance of data base, I would like to refer to an excellent manual described by William E. Bender of Westinghouse Tele-computer System Corporation. The manual is in the form of questions and answers which are abstracted below.

Q. What does data base management really mean?
A. Ambiguity surrounding its definition together with the misun-

derstanding of its purpose have been key factors contributing to the mystery which surrounds data base management.

The use and description of data base management systems have covered both ends of the spectrum: some describe them as the panacea for all data processing problems, others consider them little more than present-day file maintenance systems.

In its simplest form, a data base is a collection of data from which a company would like to establish and maintain certain relationships. A data base management system structures and maintains these relationships. Complex structures and relationships are not necessary and all corporate data need not be included in one data base. Through use of data base management systems, a company's data are now structured and related and therefore obtainable in a more orderly and logical fashion.

Q. How will a data base management system affect the role of the functional user?

A. Since the value of any system and data processing application is measured by its benefit to the functional user, the possibility of greatly increased capability in the data base systems environment brings a strong focus on the role of the functional user.

The principles of good systems design are equally applicable within the data base systems environment. The joint effort of users, systems analysts, and programmers to achieve optimum systems design is still a valid approach.

In addition to the traditional participation in the design and operation of a data processing application, a new perspective for the functional manager emerges. To fully benefit from the increased capabilities offered, user must be prepared to participate in the selecting of facilities and in designing a system that satisfies his requirements. Identifying the trade-offs and justifying the cost of implementation require a user to accurately assess the relative merits of the different possibilities. User acceptance and support during implementation are vital to ensure that transitional problems are minimized and adjustments to user interfaces are made as required. Without user support, an excellent system can fail; with total user commitment, even a mediocre system can at least partially succeed.

Q. What does a data base management system do?

A. A data base management system performs the following functions:

1. Organizes data. Data are organized or structured according to the specifications of the data definition language (DDL). These specifications are introduced by the data base administrator at the time the data base is established and may be reintroduced as the data base configuration changes. Data are organized in the manner most suitable to each application.

2. Integrates data. Data are interrelated or linked together at the element (named field of data) level and can, therefore, be assembled in many combinations during execution of a particular application program. The data base management system is the vehicle used to collect, combine, and return a portion of the available data to the user.

3. Separates data. A data base management system serves as a filter between application programs and their associated data. It separates application logic from the input/output logic needed to calculate addresses, follow chains or links, block/unblock data, locate records, and select data elements. In addition, it separates the logical description and relationships of data from the way in which the data are physically stored. The data base remains secure and intact even though it is processed by different programs which describe the data in different ways and which may be written in different programming languages.

4. Controls data. A data base management system appears to an application programmer to be an extension of the operating system software. As it receives data storage requests from host programs, it controls how and where data are physically stored. On data retrievals, it locates and returns requested elements of data to the programs.

5. Retrieves data. A record of data can be obtained via a data base management system: (1) serially (in its physically stored sequence), (2) sequentially according to the value of a user-specified key, (3) randomly by key, (4) randomly by address, and (5) by structural link. All or any portion of the data record can be returned to the user.

6. Protects data. A data base management system protects and secures both the content of a data base and the relationships of data elements. Data are protected against access by unauthorized users, physical damage, operating system failure, simultaneous updating, and certain interruptions initiated by a host program.

Q. What are some of the benefits of a data base management system?

A. There are many benefits to be derived from installing a data base management system. Some of the more tangible ones are:

1. Reduced programming costs. Because many of the input-output (file definition and file maintenance) routines normally coded by the programmers are now handled through the data base management system, the amount of time and money spent writing an application program is reduced.

2. Reduced development and implementation time. Because programmers spend less time writing applications, the amount of time required to implement new applications is reduced.

3. Reduced program and file maintenance costs. Nearly sixty percent of the programming dollar is spent on maintenance. Data base management systems reduce this expenditure by performing file maintenance in a more convenient and more efficient manner. Program maintenance is also reduced because the volatile areas of programs, input-output and file descriptions, are handled via the data base management system.

4. Reduced data redundancy. Redundant data items cost money in storage space, programmer time, and data maintenance. With a data base management system, data items need only be recorded once and are available for everyone to use. Programmers do not spend time coding file descriptions which contain the same data elements found in other files since each element of data is maintained by a single source.

5. Increased flexibility. Data base management systems will make the data processing organization more flexible and enable it to respond more quickly to the expanding needs of the business. Unique reporting requirements are more adequately met because special files do not have to be created or redesigned, and programming changes are minimized.

Application Software

Another significant EDP dimension (part of the software picture) is the application itself. It is apparent to those who have implemented applications that approximately 65 to 70 percent of the job is systems analysis, that is, in the phases of system description, system flowchart, input and output format documents, and determination of appropriate controls (omitted in the case problem). All this must be designed efficiently to reduce the amount of computer time necessary to execute the program. In addition, a feasibility analysis must be conducted to measure costs against projected savings and benefits. The other 30 to 35 percent of the job is the translation of the systems analysis into the programmer's logic flowchart and the actual program. This latter phase has been expedited by the developments in software.

Computer manufacturers and software houses now are beginning to tackle more effectively the larger part of the pie. The common name for this class of software is the application package. There is a danger in the use of the term *package* since this implies a ready-made solution to solving a company's problems without modification. This all-or-nothing philosophy ignores the basic tenet that operations of companies in the same industry may be similar, but they are not identical.

However, computer manufacturers are now supplying completely coded common portions of certain jobs. A package may include an order-processing system or an inventory control system. When these packages are designed in modular form, they can be tailored and modified to fit a particular company's needs. Computer users expect wider use of industry application packages that permit companies to build on the knowledge of others.

SUMMARY

At this point, you should better comprehend computer hardware and software and the role of the systems analyst or programmer. I have taken the time to describe a simple inventory accounting application through the steps on its ways to computerization. Although quite possibly this explanation was too detailed for the appetite of some, I feel a grasp of the material in this chapter will shed perspective on the role of a computer within a business. While I feel a manager should concentrate on the "what" of computers, a peek at the "how" will assist in this role.

The following points should be evident from this chapter.

- Computer programming is a precise and painstaking job.
- Programming steps are straightforward on an individual basis, but the extent and variety of the steps makes the total job highly complex.
- Programming investment, because of the time and money involved, should be taken very seriously.
- The nature of the programming effort makes standardization, formal procedures, and prescribed documentation essential.

- The significance of planning and control of the EDP function should not be underestimated.

- Computer hardware is useless without software and applications.

- Programming languages such as COBOL can help protect the resources a company invests in programs.

- Communication among programmers, systems analysts, and business managers is essential to ensure that the "how" is an accurate reflection of the "what."

- The value of a competent and imaginative systems and programming staff, properly managed, is immense.

With the programming behind us, we can take a look at some of the more advanced applications, applications centered around management science, communications, central data bases, and management information systems. This chapter provides a base point to view more sophisticated application and systems approach. Implementation of the systems to be discussed in chapters 6, 7 and 8 involves more complex interconnection and interaction of the programming elements described in this chapter.

6 Computer-aided Decision Making

Referring back to Chapter 2 and specifically Figure 2-1, three levels of application usage are presented: administrative, operational, and strategic. Computers are capable of aiding the decision-making process at all three levels. However, as has been indicated, computer systems have had greater impact on the administrative and operational levels than on the strategic level. A broad definition of computer-aided decision making is the use of mathematical models and programmed decision logic to aid management in making decisions. The degree of mathematical sophistication varies between administrative applications and strategic applications. A principal reason is that job functions at the lower levels are more structured and thus easier to translate into programmed logic. Indeed, many lower-level decisions become automatic, with no management intervention required.

A simple example of computer-aided decision making at the administrative level is a sales order processing system that suggests substitutes of options if the item ordered is not in stock. For example, a grocery store manager may order ten cases of twelve-ounce cans of tomatoes. The system, finding that there are no items in inventory at the closest warehouse, might shift the order to another warehouse, another brand, or substitute the ten-ounce can. These substitutions could be made automatically by preprogrammed logic or could be suggested to a merchandising manager who would then select one of the options.

An example of computer-aided decision making at the operational level is the production-scheduling function in a manufacturing plant. Based on such factors as sales forecasts, setup costs, inventory levels, factory load, workload, and other elements, a balanced factory work schedule is produced. Again this can be automatic, based on a preprogrammed computer algorithm, or semiautomatic, with the intervention of the production manager, who may have knowledge of variables not part of the computer model.

Computer-aided decision making at the strategic level adds an additional term to the information system lexicon—*decision support systems* (DSS). An accepted definition of a DSS is a computer-based system that draws on the technology of information systems and the tools of management sciences to provide support for the semistructured and unstructured decision-making tasks of upper-level managers. This higher-level employment of computer-aided decision making often involves an interactive dialogue between user and computer via a terminal screen, frequently having graphic capability. Because top management is concerned with the impact of decisions across the entire organization, business models are optimized (or at least targeted so) at the corporate level. An example was described by the director of management information systems of Northwest Industries at the 1979 annual meeting of the Society of Management Information Systems. He indicated their DSS as providing a "comprehensive business analysis and planning system, not only in the financial sense, but for strategic planning and econometric modelling of our formal four year business plan. It is a mainstream system with 100 users and about 100 terminals."

The remainder of the chapter is devoted to the tools used in developing computer-aided decision systems, specifically the class of tools labeled management science or the more generic term, *operations research* (OR). After a brief description of the process and its evolution, a discussion of the tools, with examples of their use, will be presented. Finally a phased plan that is aimed at gaining top management involvement in computer-aided decision making will be reviewed.

**Management
Science**

Management science takes its roots from OR, which began in England during the late 1930s, when a group of scientists were asked to help the military use their then newly developed radar in locating enemy aircraft. It was called operations research because it originally involved scientific research on the operational problem of radar. This successful activity led to the establishment of OR sections in the Royal Air Force, Army, and Navy. In 1942 the United States introduced OR into the military, and the postwar years brought OR to industry.

The original concept of OR was to assemble a team of experts from diverse disciplines to integrate their expertise to solve a complex problem usually involving sophisticated mathematic models and simulation. As OR spread to business, the name *management science* gradually came into vogue in an attempt to make the activity less imposing to management. OR connotes a think-tank concept where a group of intellectuals get together to mull over abstruse problems. Management science is the business reincarnation of operations research.

The best way of understanding management science is to present examples of the tools and techniques employed. But even before this, a description of the process, or methodology, is in order.

Figure 6-1 flowcharts the necessary steps. The first step is to analyze the problem, whether it be the balancing of production machine centers, the location of a new warehouse, or the optimum sales mix of products. The next step is to isolate the key elements, those factors that are significant in increasing profits or reducing costs. Next, a mathematical model is constructed that expresses the interrelationship of the variables and simulates the effect of different combinations of them. The model is then tested and the results measured against desired standards or against previous simulations. If the results are not satisfactory, the model is modified. This continues until the model's performance is satisfactory. Then actual conditions and facilities can be changed to conform to the model. If the model was a good one, the actual results should be the same as those obtained by the simulation.

MANAGEMENT SCIENCE APPLICATIONS

Business and professional people make decisions every day. Facts and data are gathered, arranged, sorted out, sequenced, assigned relative weights, and evaluated to form the basis for decision making. At some point decisions become very hard to make because the factors and decision criteria have become too complex. This is to a large extent due to the highly efficient and interrelated industrial organization that business has created. Today's decisions generate countless more ripples than they

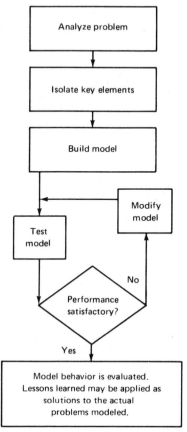

FIGURE 6-1
Steps in Management Science

used to. As a result, businesspeople pay more for incomplete, off-center, or "seat of the pants" decisions.

Companies on the leading edge of their industry are making effective use of management science methods. A prominent paper company has developed a computerized model of its timber and wood products division to gain the most efficient use of timberland and to plan site location for new plywood plants. The model consists of 8,000 equations and 15,000 variables. A major chemical company uses a computer model to simulate an industry segment and the company's potential for a share of market and profitability. A glass company has a corporate financial model that allows executives to test the impact of ideas and strategies on future profitability and to determine the needs for funds and physical resources.

Other examples described in business periodicals and trade publications indicate where companies, in addition to simulation, have used the computer-risk analysis, gaining a composite picture of the key factors involved in implementing a new policy, determining the probabilities of each event occurring on time, and determining the composite odds of success. Another area is sensitivity analysis, the measurement of the effect of the variation of individual factors on the final result. For example, in certain instances the leverage of an individual factor is high— a 5-percent increase in sales may trigger a 30-percent increase in inventory and may have a major impact on the overall result of a program. In another case a 50-percent fluctuation in one element has minimal effect on the final outcome.

The development of management science has led to a classification of different techniques that are applicable to particular classes of problems. These techniques include linear programming, queuing theory, simulation, and statistical analysis. Each of the four techniques will be described and illustrated. A more detailed treatment of the inventory control problem discussed in Chapter 5 will show how statistical analysis can be used.

Linear Programming

Linear programming (LP) is a mathematical technique to decide among competing demands for limited resources. A series of linear equations evaluates each factor in the problem in relation to the other factors. The classic example of a problem solved by LP is a number of warehouses throughout the country, a limited quantity of product, and a large number of distributors with a given demand. Knowing the cost of transporting goods from each warehouse to each distributor, the problem is to schedule shipments so as to minimize transportation costs. As the factors in problems of this type increase, manual procedures become inadequate.

A linear solution can be used for a product-mix problem, where a company wants to produce the maximum profit from a set of raw materials that can be combined in a number of different ways to satisfy finished-product specifications. Blending of gasoline is an example of this type of application.

Linear programming is used in a "cut-and-trim" situation to decide how to cut standard-size rolls of steel or paper into various widths and sizes to satisfy specified customer demands and to minimize trimming waste.

Another example of LP is its use by an advertising firm as illustrated by the following example adapted from a press release.

AUDIENCE BUYING HABITS AND MEDIA RATES ARE COMBINED IN A NEW MEDIA SERVICE

A computerized service that combines research data on the buying habits of media audiences with published media rates to provide advertising agencies with analyses of consumer audiences, rather than total audiences of various media, was demonstrated by a New York advertising firm.

The firm also unveiled a data communications system for the advertising industry. The system, which links a computer to a nation-wide teletype network, permits agencies anywhere in the U.S. to obtain immediate media market research and other information.

The service describes the audience characteristics of some 200 different media vehicles, including newspapers, magazines, and radio and television, in terms of the actual users and purchasers of any of 50 different product categories.

By defining media audiences in terms of their purchases, the system provides evidence of which media deliver the largest numbers of prospects for a given product. Through the combination of this information with current media rates, ad agencies can determine with greater accuracy the best media to use for advertising specific products, and the lowest cost for obtaining maximum coverage. A technique called linear programming combines these factors into the mathematical model necessary to produce the desired results.

During a press demonstration data from the New York market area in six product categories, combined in a four-step process with rate data from four local media, were shown. Within five minutes the computer analyzed the data and produced a two-medium combination that represents the best "media mix" for each of the six products based on the lowest cost to reach the largest unduplicated audience of prospective buyers for each product.

The product categories shown were dog food, cigarettes, cleansers, facial tissues, wines, and automatic washers. The media used were the **New York Times, New York News**, NBC-TV, and CBS-TV.

Although the New York market was used for the demonstration, every major market area in the nation, as well as the entire U.S. market, eventually will be included in the surveys.

Queuing Theory   This technique (less widely used than linear programming) is applicable to solving problems where it is desirable to minimize the costs or time associated with waiting lines, or queues. These problems occur, for example, at a checkout counter, at a receiving dock, or at a turnpike entrance. Given that on a Saturday 200 people randomly enter a supermarket every hour, and the average checkout time is five minutes, queuing theory can help schedule the number of checkout stations to minimize waiting time and labor cost.

The following example shows one practical application of queuing theory to a business problem.

DEPARTMENT STORE CHAIN USES COMPUTER TO CONSOLIDATE WAREHOUSES AND OPTIMIZE DOCK FACILITIES

A prominent Midwest department store chain has employed the concept of operations research and a high-speed digital computer to help it consolidate its warehousing activities. The chain formerly supplied its retail outlets from three warehouses located in the greater Chicago area. A series of changing conditions led management to consider that one warehouse could do the job in a more economical fashion and still maintain the desired delivery cycle.

An initial consideration was the addition of dock facilities necessary to handle the increased truck traffic. The additional dock facilities could be planned realistically if three factors were known— the number of trucks, their arrival time, and the time to service each truck. In addition there were economic considerations involved in the problem. The trucks were leased, so waiting time had a definite cost associated with it. However, additional dock facilities, while cutting down waiting time, necessitated a considerable monetary investment. The problem of cost factors in economic conflict with each other and the waiting-line principle is a classic case for the application of queuing theory. Here's the way the company went about solving the problem.

A study analyzed the existing traffic flow at the three warehouses, and the results were projected to that expected at a single warehouse. The study involved a sample seven-week period in the spring. The effect of seasonal variations was projected from the basic data using historical company records. It was discovered that the number of trucks increased only 5 percent during the Christmas rush but that the number of pieces handled increased 50 percent. In addition, truck servicing time was found to vary within certain bounds, depending on factors such as size of truck and type of merchandise. A service time pattern was found to be a combination of a fixed time interval and a variable time interval dependent on the number of pieces being handled.

While the number of truck arrivals had certain patterns and frequencies (for example, an average of 105 trucks arrived in the morning, while 65 arrived in the afternoon), there was a chance relationship that precluded a simple arithmetic solution. A new wrinkle was added to the classical queuing theory solution—the use of the "Monte Carlo" method. The name Monte Carlo implies the presence of chance. Using the frequency distributions produced by the studies as boundaries, the Monte Carlo technique randomly selected a time of arrival and a service time for each of the arriving trucks. This is where the power of the computer comes into play. The computer simulates a day's operation by totaling the waiting time and length of queue of each truck serviced that day. The computer runs through a full year's operation using random numbers to simulate actual conditions while assuming a varying number of docks. These iterations are repeated to the point where computer output indicates to management the trade-offs of waiting time and investment in new dock facilities. This then forms the basis for the most economical solution to the problem.

Problem solving is greatly enhanced by the processing power of the computer, running through massive simulations and arithmetic operations in a fraction of the time it would take to do them manually. In fact, the job would be so burdensome to do manually that it would never be attempted in the first place. Combining three warehouses into one and doing it in the most economical manner is a classic example of the use of advanced mathematical techniques and the power of modern computers.

Simulation

Simulation is used in business to determine the effects of decisions. Simulation reduces the risk and expense of decision making by using hypothetical or historical data instead of trying out decisions on live data, a risky and expensive method. This process is similar to using a wind tunnel to simulate wind velocities and pressures to find the effect of flight speeds on the fuselage of an airplane model. This is certainly far more expedient than building a full-scale plane to test a design. Likewise, businessmen can project the effects of their decisions through the use of mathematical models that react as the real world reacts.

An example of simulation is an inventory simulator that accepts product demand for particular items over prior sales periods, together with details concerning lead times, quantity discounts, and inventory and buying costs. Alternate inventory policies are simulated and measured against the resultant inventory levels, stockouts, and inventory and buying costs to determine which policy best meets management's objectives.

Business models are being used by a growing number of companies. These models enable management to view the impact of a variety of policies and decisions on the profitability of a company. Sometimes the result of a decision or policy goes against the intuitive expectation. A computer-based model can point this out by reflecting the mix of a variety of alternatives on profitability.

CORPORATE FINANCIAL MODEL DIRECTS COMPANY ACTIVITIES

An oil company has developed a corporate financial model that may be the largest and most complex corporate model yet. The computerized model takes into account the production, transportation, manufacturing, and marketing operations of the company. The working version required thirteen man-years to complete and an additional ten man-years to familiarize management with the operation of the model, to solicit comments and suggestions for improvement, and to incorporate some of the suggestions into the model. (Note that it took almost as much time to get the model into effect as to build and implement it in the first place.) The model puts pertinent information into an analytical framework that aids the management decision-making process. It performs the following functions:

- Forecasts net income for one year, accurate within 1 percent.
- Prepares short-term profit plans and long-range (ten-year) projections.
- Provides preplanning information in budget preparation.
- Calculates variances between budgeted and actual results.
- Triggers revised forecasts if not proceeding in accordance with plan.
- Acts as early-warning system for monitoring activities and signaling necessary reactive plans.
- Indicates effect on income and cash flow by following alternate investment strategies.
- Assists in planning the addition of new facilities and a host of special studies.

- Accomplishes all the preceding items with great speed (for example, the computer processing time to simulate one year of operation is fourteen seconds).

The corporate model is the core of the company's management system. The model can reflect the impact of a variety of company plans and actions on profitability. One of the major attributes of the system is the turnaround time for a simulation. Exploding a gross sales forecast into the components necessary to produce a particular volume and then to ascertain profit and loss from the mix formerly took ten days. With the computer model, this can be accomplished in less than a day. The previous methods discouraged changes or the testing of different forecast mixes on profitability; now management is encouraged to experiment and to innovate.

Statistical Analysis This technique is probably the most widely used of all the mathematical techniques available to businessmen. Statistical analysis covers a broad range of problems and is useful wherever large amounts of data or information must be evaluated. A typical application is sales forecasting, where the history of item movement is used to forecast future demand.

The following writeup of the computer studies performed by the Public Health Service illustrates typical applications of statistical analysis.

PUBLIC HEALTH SERVICE COLLECTS AND ANALYZES DATA TO MONITOR THE AIR AND WATER

The Public Health Service has installed a computer for use in a variety of radiation, water purification, air pollution, and other environmental studies. The computer is used in reducing large amounts of data in the study of environmental pollution to summaries. The summaries can be used to evaluate the hazards to health caused by the various pollutants. The computer also performs statistical analyses of data to support investigative research in areas such as water pollution, air pollution, radioactive contamination, and food sanitation. Data reduction and analysis are required for the many national sampling networks involved in the collection of information regarding pollution.

The source data in most cases is a reading of the density of bacteria, chemicals, and particles in air and water. These readings are taken at numerous locations throughout the United States on a 24-hour basis. This data is converted to digital form and sent to the center on paper tape.

The computer reads the paper tape, converts the raw data into usable units (e.g., parts per million), rejects data beyond pre-determined limits, and generates a report of the readings.

Applications of the computer in this area can be divided into the following categories:

Air Studies

A typical application involves the analysis of gaseous air pollution measurements in connection with the Public Health Service's National Air Sampling Network. At 10 different urban centers, measurements are automatically recorded around the clock at five-minute intervals for several different pollutants. Pollutants measured include carbon dioxide, nitric oxide, nitrogen dioxide, and sulfur dioxide. Over 150,000 readings per week are recorded on paper tape.

Along with the data are operator cards prepared from information received from operators of the data recording equipment in the field. These cards give information about periods when the recording equipment didn't work, when data was erroneous, when the equipment drifted in measurements, and when the equipment had to be recalibrated.

The data cards and operator cards are processed by a program which refines the raw data by adjusting it according to drift points, calibration, etc., and converts the data to units such as pollutant parts per million parts of air.

Every month the collected data is used to prepare a series of statistical summaries, for example, the daily average concentration for each pollutant for each city. Techniques of statistical analysis are used to calculate means and maximums for hourly and daily periods and to plot trends. By examining these reports, Public Health officials can spot areas in which pollutant readings are unusually high and can observe trends in different areas of the country. Reports on this subject are forwarded to Congress.

Water Studies

The water study programs receive data from laboratories doing analysis of water pollutants. For example, rivers are sampled to determine if industrial plants are discarding industrial chemicals. The data is then used in the same manner as the data on air. Statistical studies point out valuable trend information.

Radiological Studies

Radiological studies use another method of statistical analysis, called matrix algebra, to estimate radioactive pollutants. For example, an analysis of the feces of infants is made to determine how much radioactive material in various foods is absorbed by each child. In the area of animal physiology, experiments are made on guinea pigs to determine the effect of auto exhaust fumes. Statistical routines such as multiple regression, orthogonal polynomial curve fit, and confidence limits are also used to analyze data.

STATISTICAL INVENTORY CONTROL

The inventory application described in Chapter 5 is a very basic one. It takes transactions as input and processes each against an inventory master file to produce an updated inventory status report showing the current balance of each item. This is really nothing more than inventory accounting and hardly deserves the name *inventory control*. Let's now add the control dimension and see the practical application of Statistical Analysis to a familiar problem.

The major objective of inventory control is to buy for the least total cost consistent with customer service requirements. To do this, you must know when to buy and how much to buy. This is all that is required, but it takes certain mathematical calculations to answer these questions. The first calculation is a forecast, or the best estimate, of what we expect to sell of each item.

Forecasting Methods

There are various methods of forecasting. One is the "moving average" method, where you take an average of the last six months, each month adding the current month and deleting the oldest month. Another method is the "weighted moving average" where you give specific weight to particular months, normally to current months. This is an example of a weighted moving average:

Month		Demand	Weight		Weighted Demand
6	(current)	140	50%		70.0
5		130	25%		32.5
4		120	12%		14.4
3		110	10%		11.0
2		90	2%		1.8
1		80	1%		0.8
				Forecast	130.5

Both the foregoing forecasting techniques have shortcomings. The weighted-moving-average method is a little more sophisticated, but human judgment must still determine the relative weight for each month. A third technique is called "exponential smoothing." Exponential smoothing is a weighted-moving-average method that places the heaviest weighting on the most recent demand. It can be thought of as the learning curve representation of past demand. It continually measures actual demand against previous demands to determine the error and correct it. Exponential smoothing uses three factors to forecast demand.

$$\text{new forecast} = \text{forecast for last period} + \alpha \; (\text{forecast error for last period})$$

The first factor is the forecast for the last period. The second factor is the forecast error for the last period and the third factor, represented by the Greek letter alpha, is called the *smoothing constant*. This smoothing constant gives exponential smoothing its name. The smoothing constant gets its name because it "smoothes" out a demand curve projection by considering previous errors. The derivation of the term *exponential* comes from the fact that the weights assigned to the demands experienced in past periods vary exponentially with respect to the number of periods they are away from the current period. In the case of a smoothing constant of 0.5, a 50-percent weight is placed on the last period's demand, 25 percent on the previous period's demand, 12½ percent on the next previous period, and so on. Although not a panacea, exponential smoothing can automatically establish the best demand trend for an item based on prior experience and continue to evaluate its selection by measuring the error or distance away from the trend line of each succeeding period's demand. It can adjust the trend based on these errors and forecast probable demand for a wide range of items with varied demand patterns.

Forecast Error and Safety Stock

In discussing forecasting, the concept of forecast error was continually mentioned. It is obvious that forecasting depends on the theorems of probability, where there is no such thing as a sure bet. If we knew the forecast was accurate, knowing when to buy would be easy. The order point would be determined from knowing the quantity of the item we expect to sell over a lead time or procurement time. If it takes five days to procure the item and we sell at a rate of 50 per day, we should always order when our inventory balance shows 250. If we order 500 at a time, the order would arrive exactly as inventory hits a zero balance. This is shown graphically in Figure 6-2.

This, however, is an ideal situation. In reality, demand would not always be 50 per day. Safety stock is required to cover forecast errors and unforeseen situations. The level of safety stock can be determined statistically by knowing the forecast and forecast error of a given item and the desired customer service or percentage of stockouts that can be tolerated. A smaller safety stock is needed to ensure a 95-percent customer service level for an item with a stable demand pattern than is needed for an item with a fluctuating demand.

Figure 6-3 superimposes the safety stock requirement on the previous chart. We assume a need of 100 units as safety stock. The order point is now 350 units. The broken line indicates how safety stock is consumed when demand does not follow the forecast.

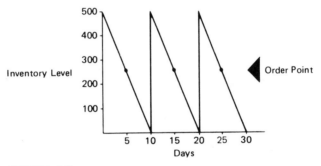

FIGURE 6-2
Ideal Reorder Curve

FIGURE 6-3
Reorder Curve with Safety Stock

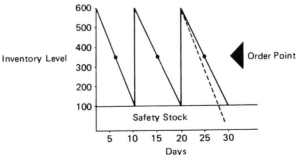

Calculating Economic Order Quantity

Let's now direct attention to the second major question of inventory control, "How much to buy?" In the foregoing example, the order quantity (or economic order quanity [EOQ], as it is called) was a ten-days' supply, or 500 units. This amount was determined arbitrarily and could be either too much or too little. Here is where the concept of economical order quantity comes into play. The problem is to minimize both inventory carrying costs (capital, taxes, insurance, storage, depreciation, etc.) and reorder costs (check writing, receiving, purchase order preparation, etc.). Inventory levels, and hence inventory carrying costs, can be reduced by a larger number of smaller purchases. But as the number of purchases increases, ordering costs increase. Likewise, any quantity discounts are lost. The EOQ formulation balances these opposing costs and defines the most economical quantity to purchase. The behavior of these two cost factors can be viewed graphically in Figure 6-4.

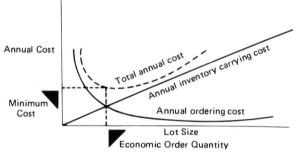

FIGURE 6-4
EOQ Determination

As the order quantity lot size increases, the cost of carrying inventory increases because greater inventory will be on hand at any given time. As the order quantity increases, the cost of ordering will decline because fewer purchases will be required throughout the year. The total cost line (broken line) is the sum of the carrying cost and ordering cost. The low point of the curve, where total costs are at a minimum, is the economic order quantity. This can be stated arithmetically by the following formula:

$$EOQ = \sqrt{\frac{2AO}{I}}$$

A is the annual demand of an item; O is the ordering cost; I is the inventory carrying cost.

In summary, we have considered the basic elements involved in inventory control and have illustrated the required statistical analysis. The technique of forecasting described is basic to inventory control. The question of when to buy led to a discussion of safety stock and the use of safety stock as a buffer to ensure a desired level of customer service. The question of how much to buy led to the economic order quantity and the statistical analysis involved in minimizing the opposing costs of ordering and carrying inventory.

IMPACT ON DECISION MAKING

There are three major reasons why management science has not had greater impact on decision making. The first reason is that the data required for the decisions faced by top management are external and unstructured. The second is that management science and operations research techniques are not well understood and have been slow to gain acceptance. The third reason is that much management decision making relies on intuition, executive sensitivity, "gut feel," and other unquantifiable data. Although more and more of the elements are being quantified, and more of the management process is becoming understood and programmed, there is still a factor of intuition with which the computer is incapable of dealing.

Unstructured Data

The data required by top management are unstructured, nonprogrammed, future oriented, inexact, and external. This information is the most difficult to acquire, update, and process. Therefore few computerized systems exist to handle problems in this area. Another factor restricting the development of management science for top management is the lack of definite cause-and-effect relationships among data. An example is a sales forecast for a planned item. In order to project a forecast, the company must know the market in which the product will compete, the market saturation for the product, and the impact on existing products in the line. Whether it is more reasonable to forecast by an extrapolation of how similar items have behaved in the past or by a competitive share of market analysis is open to question. The method selected is crucial to the forecast. Even if the necessary data are available (for example, sales history by item), there may be no logical basis by which to show the effect on sales of the introduction of a new item. There are many other situations where management decisions must be made in the absence of quantified cause-and-effect relationships. This is not to say that these relationships will never be known. However, the problem of obtaining the unquantified data required for top-management decisions, combined with the unstructured decision rules, presents a formidable obstacle for computerized management science systems directed at strategic planning.

Unfamiliarity of Management Science Techniques

Assuming that the proper management science technique has been selected for tackling a particular problem, there are still major barriers. A communication gap exists between management and the management science analyst responsible for preparing the linear equations (if, for example, the problem is one that can be handled by linear programming). Management may be skeptical of making a decision based on a set of poorly understood equations, and often the management science specialist is incapable of explaining in management terms just what the mathematical processing will accomplish. Furthermore, if a manager recognizes that the data used as input to the model do not have a high degree of accuracy, the results may appear suspicious. The manager may feel more secure with a complete "seat of the pants" decision than depending on the model. At least it is cheaper, he rationalizes. What management fails to realize is that although neither the management science solution nor the "seat of the pants" solution may prove to be wholly accurate, the odds on the management science solution (if the technique is properly used) are a good deal better.

Reliance on Intuition

Many top managers feel that good strategic decisions are made more by intuition than by a quantitative analysis of the available data. They do not ignore data when they exist but rely on intuition when little or no data are available. An article by Professor John Mihalasky of the Newark College of Engineering[1] points out that the higher a man is in an organization, the more incomplete are the data on which he bases decisions, and the more he relies on intuition, hunches, or instinct.

Professor Mihalasky feels that we may be putting too much faith on machines and data, on the logical decision maker versus the so-called nonlogical decision maker. He further points out that studies suggest that some managers have more precognitive ability than others. This ability gives these managers a better batting average in making decisions intuitively. The study divided twenty-five chief executives into two classes according to

[1] "Question: What Do Some Executives Have More of? Answer: Intuition, Maybe," *Think*, Nov.–Dec. 1969.

their proved performance, based on profitability. For one of the tests managers matched a series of numbers (0 to 9) printed out randomly by a computer. An average score is 10 percent. The successful executives outscored the nonperformers in 22 out of 27 tests. Statistically the chances of this happening by accident are fewer than 5 in 1,000.

Some people have extended the thesis suggested by Professor Mihalasky and used it as a rationale for ignoring quantitative and logical approaches to management decision making.

This study does not claim to justify the role of intuition in decision making, but it does raise some intriguing questions. If there is such a thing as intuitive ability and if the ability can be tested, to what degree should the intuitive decision be valued in contrast to the logical decision (based on advanced management science techniques)? Granted that the logical decision is the preferable one when the data are known and quantifiable, what degree of data reliability is the breakeven point, where the logical decision becomes preferred?

A Plan for Implementing Management Science

The old cliché of walking before you run is true in the EDP field. A three-phase plan to evolve a working relationship between EDP management and top management is presented. The objective is to move from a training mode slowly into a systems program that strikes at the highest-priority items of the executive's job, those on which his or her compensation package is based.

Your task before initiating the plan is to develop a strong training relationship between the EDP manager and this key operating executive. The theory is that success in training the key executive in the use of an on-line terminal that supports his or her specific job functions will have a top-down impact on the entire organization. The EDP manager should oversee and play a principal role in the training.

The next step is to develop a specific plan. An assessment of the EDP manager's skills and the information-processing capabilities of the company are necessary underpinnings. Look to a three-phased plan. Initially, ask the manager for an hour a week (any hour suited to his or her schedule) for the initiation of the personal training program. Explain the purpose and objectives of the program. The first stage is to develop jointly a simple program using BASIC or some other elementary interactive language that is available and can be run on a terminal. Any of a number of programs can be used, such as one that produces a report on selected common stocks held by the executive. The input for file preparation is the number of shares and cost per share of each stock. Then the current market price per share is keyed in while the program generates percentage gain or loss of each stock and its performance against the Dow Jones average or some other stock index. This is a good training example because it is personal and the executive can quickly envision how the program can be enhanced to produce more useful analysis. The analogy to the business situation is quickly made. So much for Phase I. Success will depend on the logical step-by-step explanation of the carefully preplanned programming exercise.

The second phase involves a review of the executive's individual goals or objectives. These are vital to an executive because they normally determine his or her compensation package for the year. The intent here is to strike directly at the area that has the manager's highest priority. The goals will include such quantifiable measurements as dollar profit, dollar sales, production volume, product margins and expense levels. Also included are such specific event goals as releases or first shipments of specified products or specific milestones for new product plans and specifications. In addition, the executive will have such facility goals as completing a plant extension, initiating a new production line, or opening a new sales office. Finally, there will be such people goals as maintaining a specified employee count, turnover rate, or minority percentage.

Establish Key Indicators

The objective during this second phase is to establish the key indicators or measurements for these top-level executive goals and to develop an information retrieval system so that the executive can ask the computer via his or her terminal for an updated status for any given time period. One can immediately conclude that this will require a degree of systems work; but, if kept simple, it should not be a major effort. The real benefit comes from a joint analysis of how the executive's goals are measured and the best way to gather the data to measure them. The measurement data usually come as a by-product of other computerized systems and can be incorporated manually, thus avoiding the effort and time of linking ongoing systems to the executive's data base.

Before entering Phase III, it is possible to enhance and add applications to Phase II to make that phase more meaningful. The same terminal can be used as a word processor and/or electronic mail medium by the executive's secretary if the company has sufficient capability and experience in this area. Another possibility is the use of the terminal as a time and meeting scheduler. The boss's schedule is filed in the computer along with those of his subordinates. As the need for a meeting arises, the secretary or even the executive can quickly determine the feasibility of a meeting at a specified time with a specified group. Though this may not be too promising an application if the executive acts in a reactive, quick, responsive manner, it is still a possible option.

Phase III starts when the executive begins to see the meaning of management information systems—as a top-management, decision-making aid. Still focusing on his or her personal goals and objectives, the executive is now able to ask "what if" questions. If the objective is a specified profit margin and he or she is the plant manager, the executive may want to know the year-end profit rate based on current product margins, overhead rates, and the latest volume forecast. He or she may then want to project year-end results based on reducing the overhead rate, increasing the product margin, increasing the volume, or some combination thereof. This moves the executive into the simulation and decision support arena. This phase will require closer working relationships and involvement than do the other two. But, by this time, the required management motivation should be established. This phase will take longer to implement because of the systems work that is required; however, the pressure and priority to complete will be present. The brevity of discussion here should in no way understate the effort that is needed in this phase. It is no mean task and the burden will be on the EDP manager.

This is the three-phase executive MIS program. There is risk in such a program. If the program falters in midstream, there can be a reverse impact and a worsening computer and MIS image in the eyes of the executive and, more damaging, a deterioration in the relationship between the EDP manager and the executive. The potential benefits of such an approach, however, are far-reaching and well worth the risk. A renaissance operating manager will have been created, and in so doing a renaissance EDP manager as well. The thrust of MIS will be focused in the real payoff area—in the strategic, decision-making arena. In establishing the framework for this arena, the goals and objectives passed down to middle-management levels will become a part of the analysis and measurement system and emphasize the value of the top-down philosophy.*

*The preceding section was reprinted from the author's article in *INFOSYSTEMS Magazine.* Copyright Hitchcock Publishing Co.

SUMMARY

This chapter has dealt with the applications of management science techniques to business problems—a leading trend in computer usage. Classes of management science problems were described and an example given to illustrate the major categories of linear programming, queuing theory, simulation, and statistical analysis. The inventory control application first defined in Chapter 5 was expanded to show how management science techniques can aid management decision making. Management considerations were reviewed to explain why these techniques have been relatively slow to become accepted within the business environment. A three-phase program was described that can lead to greater management involvement and a springboard to the use of management science.

There is no question in my mind that presidents of companies will still have to make the important business decisions and be the driving force in business success; they will not be replaced by computers and business models. More and more, however, their decisions will be tested and validated by the techniques described in this chapter. The rationale of decisions will be greatly enhanced. Computers and management science will not assure business success; however, these tools will improve one's odds.

7 Management Information Systems

A scan of the contents of any data-processing-oriented trade journal or a review of the agenda of any management seminar more often than not will uncover the general topic of management information systems (MIS). Although MIS is one of the most talked about areas confronting management today, there are few businesses that can claim to have an integrated management information system. And though results to date have often been frustrating or discouraging, few managers do not believe that this is the direction computer applications will follow. The spectacular success of MIS for the relative few point toward this trend.

DEFINITION OF MIS

Before determining where an inventory control system of the type described in Chapter 6 fits into an MIS, let's first define what is meant by a management information system. Let's approach the definition from the negative side and first indicate what such a system is not.

It is not some weird, automatic solution to the problems of management, whereby management planning and decision making are delegated to the computer and the systems priesthood that programs and runs the machine.

149

Neither is such a system a panacea whereby management may merely convert hitherto unsolved problems to some series of binary numbers, sit back, watch the lights flash, and receive an answer. This concept of "problems in—solutions out" often can result in "problems in—bigger problems out." Surveys have shown that management involvement is a major reason why some companies are successful in employing computers and others are not. Management of the successful companies recognized and took an active part in the determination of overall objectives and priorities and did not delegate these duties to subordinates.

Let's bring into focus that which we are talking about. An MIS is a system that aids management in making, carrying out, and controlling decisions. Decision making, including the process leading up to the decision, can be termed planning. Management can be defined as the planning and control of the physical and personnel resources of the company in order to reach company objectives. This definition of management differs from other descriptions (one of which is getting things done through people), but I feel it is more definitive. Getting things done through people, plus the selecting, training, and motivating of people, is assumed part of the control function. Implementing and controlling the decisions made will obviously require the motivation of people. Referring back to the MIS definition, we can simplify it by saying that MIS is a system that aids management in performing their job.

An MIS is not just a happenstance—a thing that just came to be. Many systems did just "come to be," but they are certainly not management information systems. They are more like badly worn inner tubes, patched and mended, sometimes with solutions not well thought out. In fact, in many frequently patched systems, a new patch will cause a blowout somewhere else. This type of crisis approach is a long way from an MIS.

CHARACTERISTICS OF MIS

It should be apparent that MIS is not an easy concept to deal with. It can be viewed and analyzed from many sides. MIS has been both used and abused. The first step in understanding its potential impact on business operation is to break through the semantic barriers. This section will summarize the pertinent characteristics of MIS.

**Management
Orientation**

This is the most significant characteristic of MIS. The system is designed from the top down. The top-down approach does not imply that the system will be geared to providing information directly to top management; rather, the system development starts from an appraisal of management needs and overall business objectives. It is possible that middle management or operating management is the focus of the system, and that their needs are the cornerstone on which the system is built. To illustrate the point, a payroll system designed to process employee time records and produce paychecks, deduction registers, payroll registers, and supporting material for government purposes is not a management-oriented system. It only satisfies administrative ends. However, a payroll system that supplies foremen with daily and weekly labor cost variance reports and production management with monthly labor summaries showing the amount of overtime, idle time, labor variances, and labor cost trends is management-oriented. It is geared to satisfy management needs—in this case, the need to optimize the use of the labor force.

**Management
Direction**

Because of the management orientation of MIS, management must actively direct the system development. In the preceding example, management must determine what labor standards should be established and what information is necessary to improve control of labor costs. It is rare to find an MIS where the manager, or a high-level representative, is not spending a good deal of time in systems design. This involvement is not a one-time effort. Continued review and participation are necessary to ensure that the implemented system meets the design specifications. Management, therefore, is responsible for setting systems specifications and must play a major role in the subsequent trade-off decisions that inevitably occur in systems development. An important element of effective systems planning is determining the priority of application development. Management must control this process if a management information system is to be effective. A company without a formal application approval cycle and a management steering committee to determine priorities will never develop an MIS.

Integration

Integration is a necessary characteristic of management information systems. Integration means taking a comprehensive view of the interlocking subsystems that operate within a company. One can start an MIS by attacking a specific subsystem, but unless that subsystem's proper place in the total system is reflected, serious shortcomings may result. An integrated system blends information from several operational areas.

For example, in order to develop an effective production scheduling system, it is necessary to balance such factors as setup costs, work force, overtime rates, production capacity, inventory levels, capital requirements, and customer service. A system that ignores one of these elements—inventory level, for example—is not providing management with an optimal schedule. The cost of carrying excess inventory may more than offset the benefits of the system.

Common Data Flows

Because of the integration concept of MIS, there is an opportunity to avoid duplication and redundancy in the gathering, storage, and dissemination of data. Systems designers are aware that a few key source documents account for much of the information flow and affect many functional areas. For example, customer orders are the basis for billing the customer for the goods ordered, setting up the accounts receivable, initiating production activity, forecasting sales, and so on. It is prudent to capture this data closest to the source and use them throughout. It is also prudent to avoid the duplicate entry of source data into several systems. This concept also applies to building and using master files and to providing reports. The common data flow concept avoids duplication, combines similar functions, and simplifies operations wherever possible. The development of common data flows is logical and economically sound, but it must be viewed in a pragmatic light—it may be better to live with a little duplication in order to make the system acceptable and workable. MIS is more important for its ability to relate several functional areas of a business and produce more meaningful management information than for producing that information more economically.

Given the track record of MIS to date, one should look closely at the amount of integration of common data flows. The degree of difficulty involved in producing common data flows is high. Many would-be implementers have failed because they underestimated the amount of time or did not possess the necessary systems design skills. I do not question the desirability of building common data flows into the system; rather, I am cautious about the degree to which the concept is emphasized. Building a system that cannot operate unless all data spring from a common path is usually an unwise design concept—as many companies have discovered to their detriment.

Heavy Planning Element

Management information systems are not built overnight; they take from three to five years—and longer—to get established within a company. A heavy planning element must be present in MIS development. Just as a civil engineer does not design a highway to handle today's traffic but to handle the traffic five to ten years from now, so the MIS designer must have the future needs of the company firmly in mind. The designer must avoid the possibility of early system obsolescence.

Subsystem Concept

In tackling a project as broad and complex in scope as a management information system, one must avoid losing sight of both the forest and the trees. Even though the system can be viewed as a single entity, it must be broken down into subsystems that can be implemented one at a time. A phasing plan must be developed. The breakdown of MIS into subsystems sets the stage for this phasing plan. This subsystem concept will be illustrated in the following section, when we begin constructing an integrated MIS. Subsystem analysis enables the designer to focus on manageable entities. Each subsystem can be assigned to a systems and programming team.

Central Data Base

The data base is the mortar that holds the functional systems together. Each system requires access to a master file of data covering inventory, personnel, vendors, customers, general ledger, work in process, and so on. If the data are stored efficiently and with common usage in mind, one master file can provide the data needed by any of the functional systems. It seems logical to gather data once, validate it, and place it on a central storage medium accessible to any system. It is not unusual, however, to find a company with several data files, one serving one functional system and another serving another. This is not an efficient way to operate.

Although it is possible to achieve the major objectives of MIS without a central data base (paying the price of duplicate storage and duplicate updating), more often than not the central data base is a characteristic of management information systems.

Computerization

It is possible to have an MIS without a computer, but most people would agree that the computer is an essential of medium- and large-scale information systems. The volume of throughput necessary to handle a wide variety of applications and the quick response required make it mandatory for the processing to be done by a computer. Accuracy, consistency, and the demand on the clerical staff make a computer the prime requirement in a management information system.

BUILDING AN MIS FRAMEWORK

The easiest way to understand the concept of an MIS is to use an example. The example could be a distributor of any type of product, a manufacturer, an insurance company, a bank, an educational or government operation, a hospital, or a service company. The general principles of system analysis and classification and the methodology of looking at a company's information requirements as a series of interlocking subsystems cross industry lines. The example we will use is a company in the food distribution business.

Order Processing, Accounting, and Stores Control Subsystems

Our information system model will begin with the sales subsystem. It is often stated that "nothing begins until something is sold." We will see that basic sales data are a primary information source for a host of useful management reports and analyses. Figure 7-1 is the starting point of the integrated system.

Satisfying customer demand is the principal reason for being in business. Management should continually strive to give the customer the best product at the best price and at the same time to realize a profit in line with the product. The cycle starts here because what goes out of the store must be replaced. As the shelves in the store are depleted, operations are put into play that result in the reorder of goods to replenish the shelves. The store will reorder goods on the basis of turnover and the lead time required to replenish the item. The store order is a basic source document that initiates a series of activities in many departments.

In Figure 7-1 this document enters the first of the subsystems, the order-processing subsystem. This subsystem will screen the orders for errors and determine that the order is valid before it proceeds farther into other subsystems. The connecting arrow to the accounting subsystem indicates that the store order is the basis for setting up accounts receivable and eventually reconciling the payment for the goods.

Another source document is the record of sales or the movement of items from the store. This document will eventually

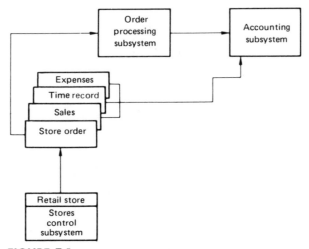

FIGURE 7-1
Order Processing, Stores Control, and Accounting Subsystems

produce sales statistics and analyses as output from the accounting and marketing subsystems.

In addition to the store order and record of sales, it takes people to run a store, and they must be paid. A time record indicates the hours worked and in Figure 7-1 is shown entering the accounting subsystem. Similarly, the expenses of store operation (heat, light, and maintenance) are recorded and entered into the accounting subsystem. (This would be the case only if the company controlled its own stores, as in a chain operation.)

The stores control subsystem has been little affected by automated information systems. Significant possibilities are now in the testing phase. Checkout counter devices can optically read imprinted prices and item numbers on products, automatically producing the customer sales total and at the same time recording the item and quantity sold as input into the order-processing subsystem. A simpler method is for the checkout clerk to key in the item number listed on the product for automatic entry into order processing. Another information system within the stores control subsystem is the scheduling of checkout personnel based on a simulation of activity through the store. Scheduling can be a reflection of historical sales patterns and other known conditions. For example, a study can indicate the staff requirements for a Thursday and Friday when Saturday is a holiday. Also, it is known that about 70 percent of the business for the week is done

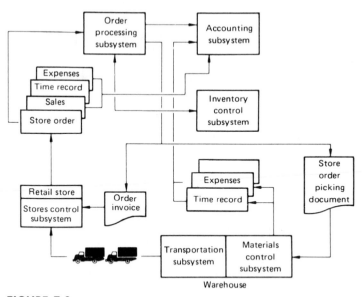

FIGURE 7-2
Addition of Inventory Control, Materials Control, and Transportation Subsystems

on Thursday, Friday, and Saturday. These factors can be reflected in a queuing model to assist in the scheduling of personnel.

Inventory Control, Materials Control, and Transportation Subsystems

Figure 7-2 adds the inventory control subsystem, the materials control subsystem, and transportation subsystem to the diagram in Figure 7-1. After a store order has been validated by the order-processing subsystem, it moves to the inventory control subsystem to be screened against the current inventory in the warehouse. This process is indicated by the two-way arrow connecting the order processing and inventory control subsystems. If sufficient inventory is on hand, the order-processing subsystem produces a store-order picking document for the warehouse and an order invoice for the retail store. Since employee labor and operating expenses were recorded at the store level, they must also be recorded at the warehouse level. These items can be seen entering the accounting system in Figure 7-2. The blank input form will be explained in Figure 7-3.

The materials control and transportation subsystems are excellent examples of how an integrated system operates. For example, basic information on orders and movement from the warehouse can be used to lay out warehouse space more effi-

156

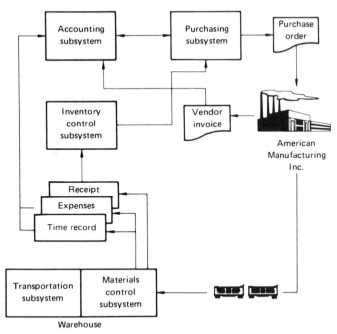

FIGURE 7-3
Addition of the Purchasing System

ciently. Similarly, the information on each order, such as the cubic content and weight of items, can be used to load and route trucks. These valuable by-products often can be real payoff applications. Thus, the same basic raw data are processed in a little different way to help handle another functional activity.

Purchasing Subsystem

Figure 7-3 adds another subsystem—the purchasing subsystem. This subsystem is dependent on the strength of the inventory control subsystem. A well-conceived inventory control system provides for automatic ordering based on customer service, economic order quantity, and lead time. Orders are screened against inventory records in Figure 7-2. When the inventory of particular items reaches a predetermined reorder point, the inventory control subsystem directs the purchasing system to write a purchase order (either by computer or by hand). The purchase order is sent to the vendor or manufacturer. The vendor in turn fills the order, ships the product to the warehouse, and submits an invoice for entry into the accounting subsystem. This process initiates accounts-payable activity and the eventual reconciliation of cash payments. The arrow indi-

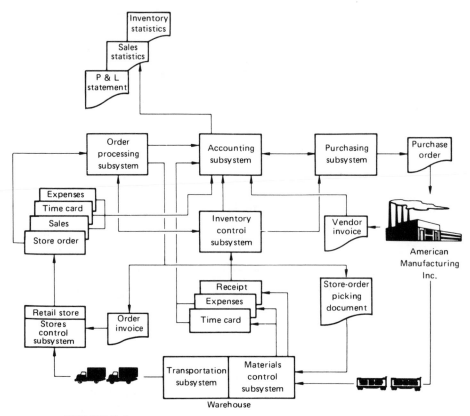

FIGURE 7-4
Basic Subsystems Summary

cates the connection of the accounting and purchasing subsystems. The blank input form in Figure 7-2 can now be identified—it is a receipt record. This record enters the inventory control subsystem to update pertinent inventory records. It also is passed through to the accounting subsystem to form the basis for vendor payment.

Basic Subsystems Summary

Figure 7-4 brings together the subsystems mentioned to this point. Two additional arrows have been added to the illustration. The first connects the inventory control and accounting subsystems. This step is necessary because inventory data is a requirement of accounting reports. The second arrow shows output of the accounting subsystem. Accounting acts as the scorekeeper for all the subsystems mentioned so far. It accumulates such data as store orders, cash sales, expenses, receipts, and

158

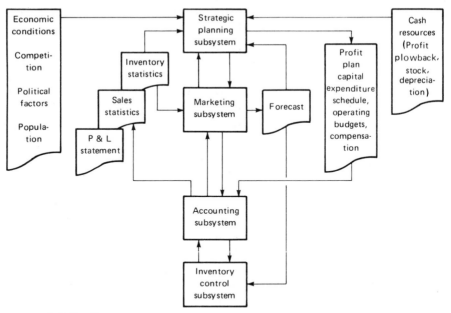

FIGURE 7-5
Addition of Marketing and Strategic Planning Subsystems

vendor invoices, and from this basic source information produces management reports. Three of these reports—profit-and-loss statement, inventory statistics, and sales statistics—are noted in Figure 7-4. These reports might show, for example, profitability by region, by store, or by department; or they might show sales by salesman or item grouping. They might indicate inventory turnover or return on inventory investment.

Marketing and Strategic Planning Subsystems

The subsystems discussed so far are basic ones common to most businesses. The computer applications are fairly routine, but it is still uncommon to find a computer system that has integrated all these subsystems and still has the capability of adding more sophisticated subsystems. Figure 7-5 shows advanced subsystems that can build on the basic ones already described.

Marketing and strategic planning are the subsystems that produce the greatest payoffs. The marketing subsystem uses the basic source data that have been collected and filed by the basic subsystems. However, the data are processed to answer specific management questions—questions such as the effect of promotion on sales, the effect of pricing changes and product mix, the comparative advantages of a limited as opposed to a full prod-

159

uct line, the significance of store layout and shelf allocation to profit, and the desirability of introducing new items or product lines.

Another key output of the marketing subsystem is the sales forecast. The forecast is based on historical sales movement (information from the accounting system) as well as on projected external events (buying trends, economic factors, and so on). The sales forecast is significant to all aspects of the business. It is shown in Figure 7-5 entering the inventory control system as a basis for establishing inventory policy and entering the strategic planning subsystem as a basis for influencing total company goals and objectives.

The marketing subsystem has been all but neglected by today's computer systems. There are several reasons for this situation. The first is the absence of the integrated concept. The subsystems described previously were not built to collect and store data for other uses; they were built only for the immediate job, whether order processing or payroll. The basic data needed for more sophisticated analysis are not available; they have been captured but not retained. A second reason why the marketing subsystem is not often attempted is that the payoffs are not as tangible as payoffs from the other subsystems. It is easy to see the clerical savings from computerizing order processing. It is more difficult to see how a change in advertising policy can improve profit margins. It is not that the potential benefits of the latter are insignificant; to the contrary, the benefits can far exceed those derived from computerizing order processing. The point is that conservative management is less convinced that the benefits can be attained.

The strategic planning subsystem is the core of the system model. It is here that major company decisions are made. Reports produced by the accounting subsystem are digested, reviewed, and analyzed. Overall company policies are determined and promulgated. Sophisticated integrated systems employ business models and simulation to determine the effect of different management policies on the profitability of the company. A mathematical model is constructed that indicates the effect of particular management decisions on such factors as sales, costs, and profits. The system can make it possible to build a paper world, where management can see the results of management decisions before they are actually made. The model is built from data captured by the basic subsystems, and the simulation uses the same historical data. In addition to the historical, or internal, data, the management planning subsystem uses external data gathered from outside sources. On one side are such economic factors as trends in gross national product, political factors, and population growth, while on the other side are the available cash resources, such as profit plowback, new stock issues, and depreciation. These factors are included in the mathematical model built to evaluate and determine management policy. The results of the strategic planning subsystem are marketing policies, as well as the profit plan, capital expenditure schedule, operating budget, and compensation. These figures enter the accounting subsystem to measure actual operation. They form the yardstick for measurement.

The Completed MIS Model

Figure 7-6 presents the complete integrated system that we have been building in stages. Nine subsystems were discussed, but the

FIGURE 7-6

Information System Model for a Distribution Company

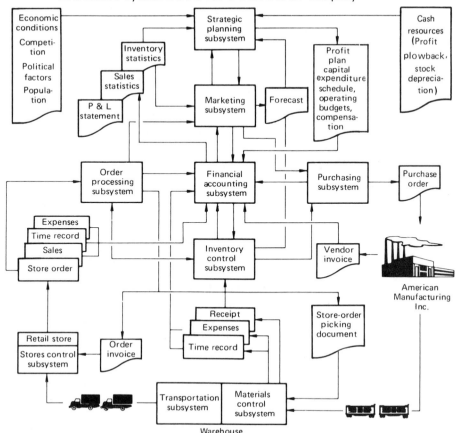

list probably could be fanned out to forty or fifty. The nine major subsystems can be further subdivided. For example, the financial and accounting subsystem includes subsystems for accounts receivable, accounts payable, general ledger, payroll, cost accounting, and the like.

A significant point to bear in mind in planning an MIS is to lay out the overall road map first. Developing an information system model for your company is an important first step in developing and gaining the benefits of MIS. The initial focus, for example, may be on improving the sales-order-processing subsystem. This should be undertaken, however, in light of where that particular system fits into the whole. Middle and top management need to begin with a framework similar to that illustrated in Figure 7-6. Too often the first thing they are shown is a detailed flowchart of the order-processing cycle. This does not allow easy comprehension of where order-processing fits into the overall information network, or show what part order-processing will play in a management information system. Although management is vitally concerned with improving the order cycle, and thereby improving inventory turnover and reducing capital requirements, they need to be able to see how the by-product data from this application can help them pinpoint unfavorable sales trends by product line and store location, or what action would improve the situation.

KEY IMPLEMENTATION ELEMENTS

Integrating the Subsystems

At the beginning of the Industrial Revolution, businesses were run by individual entrepreneurs who did the planning, selling, producing, and accounting. All information needed to carry out these duties was in the entrepreneur's head. The data-processing system was integrated—all policies, plans, and decisions sprang from a central source of information. The tasks, however, grew so complex that the entrepreneur could no longer handle all of them alone. Responsibilities such as accounting, production, and engineering were assigned to people hired to take over these various functions. Early in the process a good deal of overlap existed in the responsibilities of individuals for different functions; specialization would be a later development. But as business evolved, the entrepreneur could not train people on the job. Colleges and universities began to assist in the task. As curricula were developed, fences evolved (as a by-product) that became functional boundaries within a business—the accounting profession was formed, the advertising profession, and so on. This is not to say that these boundaries were based on logic; they just reflected the business organization.

The entrepreneur had a naturally integrated system, but the growth of functional boundaries tends to limit the scope of problems and the vision of individuals tackling these problems. This explains, to a great extent, why the majority of data-processing systems are performing only accounting applications. The computer is under the control of the accounting department, and the functional boundaries of accounting perpetuate only such applications as payroll, accounts receivable, and accounts payable.

This situation suggests a challenge for management. The top executive must somehow get the various functional heads to coordinate their activities to achieve the same effectiveness as the single entrepreneur. The integrated systems concept is a prime vehicle for accomplishing this step. I would like to emphasize that although the system is made up of parts, the parts must not be so specialized that their function as part of the whole is forgotten. Management cannot play a passive role in the design and development of an integrated system. Since the system crosses all functional boundaries, only top management can ensure that the computer will serve the overall needs of the company and not be used for parochial interests.

Using Common Data Flows

Figure 7-6 enables the systems analyst or business manager to see the interrelationships of subsystems. Tracing key source data will illustrate the necessity to design systems that avoid redundancy and take advantage of common data flows. The sales forecast is a prime example. The forecast is a key strategic tool in the operation of any company. First of all, a sales forecast is crucial to the planning process. It is the basis for determining whether a new item should be introduced or whether an entirely new product line should be developed. It forms the rationale for establishing plant capacity and long-range facility needs. It is a key determinant for budget preparation and profitability projection. In the operational and control area, the sales forecast determines purchasing policies (how much to order, when to order), manufacturing policies, work levels, hiring, training, quota setting, machine loading, inventory levels, and the like. These elements should be taken into account in designing a management information system. It is common to have a variety of forecasting systems, some of which are mutually inconsistent, within a single enterprise. The manufacturing manager may be formulating his production schedule on Forecast **A** while the materials control manager, who is responsible for supplying raw materials to production, may be ordering on the basis of Forecast **B**. This situation is a classic example of the lack of system integration.

The preceding discussion does not imply that the same forecast should be used in every instance. Indeed, there are logical reasons for using different forecasts. For example, from an inventory standpoint it may be wise to use a higher forecast and risk overstocking at a time when particular products are hard to procure. On the other hand, it may be logical to use a lower forecast in setting sales and quota goals for salespeople, lest their motivation and performance be adversely affected. The important point is that the concept of integration should be recognized; a single function should be dedicated to sales forecasting. The forecast should be made by the group with access to the most current data and with the ability to best process that data. All forecasts should be made from the same quantitative data. If adjustments are made to reflect various probabilities and risks, these adjustments should be made by the same group. A forecast could have three tracks: a most likely, most optimistic, and most pessimistic outlook. Each department could then select the forecast that represented the level of risk best for that department under the circumstances. However, in no case should the manufacturing manager and the material manager use different forecasts. They should jointly agree on a forecast and proceed to provide the necessary resources to meet the forecast.

Developing the Central Data Base

The development of the integrated system illustrates the need for gathering basic information from key source documents and using this information throughout the system. Likewise, it is equally important to develop basic master files that are used in common by the various subsystems. These common master files are normally referred to as a central data base.

The central data base holds all relevant information about a company's operation in one readily accessible file. Normally the central data base is subdivided into the major subsets needed to run a business. These subsets are:

1. Customer and sales file
2. Vendor file
3. Personnel file

4. Inventory file

5. General ledger accounting file

The subsystems use information from the same file. The key element in a data base is that each subsystem uses the same data base to satisfy its information needs. Duplicate files are eliminated.

The data-base concept is a logical approach to the paperwork explosion. Even so, management should not overlook some important considerations in developing the data base as part of an integrated system.

Erroneous data have an immediate influence on all subsystems and departments that use the data. At least this may mean that errors will be noticed more quickly. Feedback should help correct the data and devise appropriate input controls.

Another problem in building a single central file is the interdepartmental cooperation that is needed. One department may need an amount of detail that burdens the reporting source so heavily that the quality of all input suffers. Discussions, meetings, and eventual compromise are usually necessary if the implementation time frame is to be met.

An organizational phenomenon called the "geometric organizational syndrome" is often encountered during the development of the data base. The syndrome stems from the joint decisions needed to reach compromises. Compromise does not seem a formidable task until you recognize that the interaction pathways for four people are more than double that for two people. There is one communication path with two people, three with three people, six with four people, ten with five people. Complication comes with a geometric nature rather than an arithmetic nature. Thus, adding a fifth party to a discussion increases the communication pathways not by 25 but by 67 percent. The geometric organizational syndrome probably is accentuated by the psychological and political blocks that individuals bring with them into the situation.

Information security is a serious problem with a central data base. When departments maintain individual data files, file information security is not a problem. Other departments will not have access to confidential facts about an operation. In a highly centralized organization, the confidential nature of the central data base is not of primary concern, but in a highly decentralized organization the centralization of data in one central file can raise a serious obstacle. Divisions become skeptical about the information they submit to the central file because they wonder how it is going to be used. They do not want their performance figures known by other divisions. The suspicion generated by the security risks of the central data base can affect the validity of the information supplied by the users. Certainly, some quantitative data can be checked for obvious errors, but there is little or no check on the qualitative data. Qualitative data can take the form of how the customer is currently using the product or plans to use it. It also includes information on customer complaints and problems. The real measure of the success of the data-base concept is the input. The psychological considerations of submitting confidential data must be carefully considered.

Problems might also rise from the time dimension to information. For example, it might take two to three months from the time an order is placed to validate the terms of the order officially. From the viewpoint of the sales office, the sales effort for this order is completed. They would like to see the results reflected in the time period during which the customer placed the order. Their thinking is, that in 90 percent of the cases, contractual negotiations do not change the basic terms of the order. Production and accounting departments each have a different date when they would like to see the order become part of the customer and sales data base. Unless the new system satisfies the requirements of each department, that department is compelled to maintain a separate system. This, of course, defeats the purpose of the central data base. And the longer a department runs a system in parallel, the more difficult it is to get that department to supply accurate data to a system that does not serve its needs.

Building an integrated system around a central data base brings to light existing management problems—problems that would continue to grow if left unattended. These are the "quiet problems"—company communication, organization, and control. The development of the data base often acts as the catalyst in bringing the quiet problems to the surface.

PAYOFFS OF AN MIS

Despite the rather bleak record for MIS, the success achieved by a few indicates that management information systems will be employed by an increasing number of companies in the 1980s.

These companies prove that MIS can work and that considerable payoffs occur when it does. In one system a data base is being built to represent the marketplace, identifying existing and potential users to various products. This external data base enables the market to be broken down by product, type of customer, time period, geographical location, and other classifications. The proper modeling of this file of data enables management to gauge the potential effect of advertising programs, forecast sales for existing products and for products not yet introduced, and determine the most effective product distribution and sales coverage.

Another company concentrated on an MIS to control internal company operations. Initial concentration has been on the main operating areas of the business—inventory control, sales forecasting, and production scheduling—welding these systems into an integrated entity serving management at all levels. This approach reduced inventory over 30 percent during a period of rising sales volume, increased on-schedule deliveries from 80 to over 95 percent and reduced production cost variances from 16 to 1 percent. Both were directed to serve value creation first and cost reduction later. MIS emphasized profit-making applications over cost-cutting ones. Also, both companies are characterized by a management fully committed to EDP and heavily involved in system development.

ENVIRONMENT
FOR MIS DEVELOPMENT

It is enlightening to look at situations where MIS has achieved the strongest foothold. Both companies described above fall into the manufacturing category, but this is *not* the industry segment where MIS is strongest. The complexities and interaction of information subsystems within a manufacturing company make it difficult to design and install an MIS. For the most part, MIS has succeeded in manufacturing companies in those instances where management has studied the entire system but has concentrated on one major subsystem. For example, manufacturers of large durable goods, where the product value is high, need careful analysis of customer orders because of ongoing maintenance, modification, add-on business, and repeat sales. Management systems have been built around centralized data bases of customer status files. Many departments use this file and continually demand a variety of statistical and analytical reports. In many instances the management is by exception: The system itself triggers action and expedites reports when certain conditions are met. Many comprehensive MIS approaches have concentrated on a single vital area of business operation. There are not many examples of systems that attack the entire information base of the company and require a high level of integration before payoffs can be realized.

MIS is most prevalent in insurance and banking. Here the customer data base is vital to the entire operation. For example, the demand deposit file is a focal point for a major part of a bank's operation. Currently in many banks the savings account and loan account files are combined into a single file. However, even prior to this, the demand deposit file represented a prime source of management information. MIS has been built around this central data base.

Typical of the use of MIS is the approach of a large West Coast bank. This MIS was geared to changing the outputs of twenty-seven application areas already computerized. It covered demand deposit accounts, installment consumer loans, real estate loans, savings accounts, and so on, so that the bank could feed a new general ledger system, a summary of all business activity of the bank. Important management reports emanate from the general ledger system. This MIS takes into account the responsibility center concept employed by the bank and gears its reports to this breakdown. In a like manner an insurance company combines several types of policies into a central file. A policyholder may hold several different types of policies with the company, just as a bank customer holds several types of banking accounts.

Banks, insurance companies, and utility companies have much more in common with respect to MIS development than manufacturing companies do. Not all banks, insurance companies, and utility companies are similar in operation, but in light of MIS, they represent a distinct category. Elements in their method of operation make them more receptive to the employment of MIS than manufacturing companies. Besides the common use of a central file, banks and insurance companies are more structured in their way of doing business because of federal and state laws. They also use well-defined procedures. In addition, banks, insurance companies, and utilities have been in data processing longer than manufacturers (distributors and retailers are included in the same category as manufacturers for this discussion) and have tended to be more stable in organization and operation. These factors are important because of the three to five years it usually takes to design and install an MIS.

Another area where MIS has made headway is in the federal government. The National Institute of Health and the Department of Defense have installed what might be termed *technical management information systems*. For example, a system developed by the Department of Defense in coordination with the National Aeronautics and Space Administration provides timely access to various research and technology efforts. Each research effort is indexed, and a file of key elements concerning the effort is made a part of a central data base. The data base is responsive to a wide assortment of management requests for information. This type of system has many of the elements of a banking or insurance operation. Added similarities are a stable organizational structure and definite procedures and regulations. Another element facilitating the employment of MIS is an environment that can ensure adherence to strict rules regulating input and update procedures. Outside of government, older and better-established firms provide a more suitable environment for this required regimentation.

MIS has great potential for such industries as manufacturing, distribution, and retailing. Although they may be more difficult to achieve, in these areas the payoffs and benefits of MIS are significant.

MANAGEMENT CONSIDERATIONS IN IMPLEMENTATION

System Flexibility

Designers of a system (particularly an MIS) must have the foresight to build a system that will not be obsolete before it is installed. Management information systems are long-term projects that demand even more planning and foresight than conventional data-processing systems. Many future events and activities are difficult to foresee, of course. Even so, every effort should be made to allow for the unexpected. It is wise to develop a basic systems design that can incorporate added volume and adjust to the changing nature of operations.

An example will help clarify this point. A data base is a prime requisite of an MIS. Many systems are built on a data base that is very rigid. I have known cases where it cost a company thousands of dollars to revise files and programs that access the data base because the number of inventory items expanded beyond the original four-digit identification number. It is prudent, especially in MIS design, to allow for this kind of eventuality.

A payoff application might be precluded because of lack of system flexibility. In an MIS for a certain distributor an automatic dispatching system was developed that could aid substantially in truck loading and order deliveries. This system monitored the cubic volume of the order as well as the weight. It was decided to append a cubic volume field for each inventory item. Allowance must be made in the inventory record and in the system design to allow for this type of flexibility. If not, rework is required.

This is where the communications gap and credibility gap between operating and middle management and EDP management begin to widen. Such a seemingly trivial change can cause so much rework if the system was designed without the necessary flexibility. One of the principal ground rules of MIS is to design the system open-ended in order to incorporate the inevitable changes. Initially, this takes foresight and more planning time, but management must take a long-range view and be geared to life-cycle analysis.

Relationship of Physical Systems to Information Systems

It is very difficult to separate a physical system from an information system, but it is important for the systems designer to do so. The distribution information model brings to light several considerations in this regard. A store's shelf alignment and general layout are predicated on what is convenient for the customer, what promotes the sale of specific items (items either particularly profitable or overstocked), and what maximizes the amount of goods sold. This situation is true in almost every retail operation. The store layout should take into account the fact that buyers tend to pay more attention to the right aisle than the left, so impulse items should be on the right side.

The store manager reorders items by walking down the aisle and jotting down what items are short. The order catalog is in sequence by store layout. On the other hand, the warehouse supplying the items is organized in a different way. This fact is not surprising, for certain types of items lend themselves to particular storage facilities. Drugs and sundry items, for example, might be located where there already are small bin areas with the required shelving.

A systems designer determines that order-processing time and computer equipment cost can be reduced by laying out the warehouse in the same sequence as the store (assuming all stores are alike). This rearrangement precludes the need to sort orders into warehouse sequence prior to filling. Furthermore, orders can be unloaded from the truck directly onto the shelves, since the orders would be loaded by store location.

We have a situation here that shows the close interrelationship between a physical system and an information system. In many actual cases, the information system overrules the physical system, and physical layouts have been changed to facilitate systems design. This is the tail wagging the dog. Although the systems designer can point out areas where the two systems interact, plus the pros and cons of the alternatives, management must make the final decision. When management is not involved in systems design, the EDP staff exerts undue leverage on systems decisions. The decisions may be sound ones, but when the EDP staff is short on business perspective, a decision can have serious consequences for a company.

Another example of the relationship between physical and information systems is where a systems designer develops a strategy for serving the stores of two adjacent divisions with a common warehouse. There is nothing wrong in proposing the change and supporting it with a transportation and inventory model that shows the cost and customer service of one warehouse versus two. However, for the most part, physical facilities and operating strategies (e.g., profit centers) are the givens of systems design; the information system should build from these factors. It should not get bogged down in analyzing problems and considerations beyond the scope of EDP and MIS.

Priority Analysis in Selection of Subsystems

In Figure 7-6, it becomes clear that a distributor could not hope to accomplish the MIS in a short period of time. Starting points must be established as well as a priority and sequence of information subsystems implementation. The following list shows possible criteria to use in selecting subsystems for implementation.

- Degree of difficulty
- Time and cost
- Operational problem areas
- Potential high tangible payoff
- Potential high intangible payoff
- What other companies have done

- Potential competitive impact
- Where your capability lies
- Degree of stability of operational area
- User acceptance

The first two criteria are probably overused as a reason for not tackling certain applications. This may be because the EDP manager, who frequently makes the final selection, tends to steer away from areas that are difficult and time consuming. The potential impact (cost savings and benefits) on the organization is a more significant determinant of priorities. Sometimes it is appropriate to look for applications that can improve a problem area of a company. If, for example, it takes seventy-two hours to fill an order and even then a third of the items are out of stock, tangible and intangible benefits are very significant selection criteria. A computerized system can show tangible benefits, such as cutting clerical costs or reducing inventory, but it can also produce intangible benefits, such as improved customer service.

What other companies have done should be used only as a guide. Companies of about the same size in the same industry may be similar in operation, but they are not identical. What is good for your industry may not be good for your company. A system that can give a company a major competitive edge should be ranked high in the priority list.

The capabilities of the people responsible for systems development, the environment of the operational area, and the probability of acceptance by the end user should be taken into account. The initial thrust of MIS for a company might be steered away from the warehousing department if the personnel continually have resisted any form of automation. As in other systems decisions, there are competing and conflicting elements, and a relative weighing of the selection criteria is necessary.

Time Frame and Phasing Plan

The foregoing discussion leads quite naturally to the establishment of a time frame and phasing plan for MIS development. An initial question is: On what level of management should MIS be focused? Although it is essential to get top management's backing, support, and participation in the system, it is not wise to focus MIS initially at top management. The planning nature of the executive's job and the complexity of the decision process at that level make this a difficult area to computerize. Also, many of the strategic and planning decisions depend on data captured by other information subsystems. These subsystems are necessary prerequisites for planning and strategic subsystems.

The most realistic focus is on middle management—recognizing at the outset that the system will probably have greatest impact on administrative management and the people who work for administrative management. It is wise to focus the systems design at one level above the area of greatest impact. Doing so will ensure management participation and involvement and will also place pressure on system flexibility. A phasing plan suggested for a distributor follows:

Phase I	Order processing
	Inventory control
	Portions of accounting
Phase II	Transportation
	Materials control
	Purchasing
	Stores control
	Other portions of accounting
Phase III	Financial
	Marketing
	Strategic planning

This phasing plan is rather conservative, but it reflects the normal learning curve employed by companies just embarking on MIS. If the design is developed on an open-ended basis and reflects the eventual integration of information subsystems, the EDP staff can move into Phase II applications immediately after Phase I is complete. Practical MIS is built on a philosophy that is top-management-oriented, or top-down in design, but administrative management-oriented, or bottom up, in implementation. Problems in MIS have arisen from systems both designed and implemented from the bottom up.

For companies that want to move faster into MIS and are willing to make the necessary expenditure, a parallel effort can be directed at top management and the strategic planning information subsystems. A small team of management science, or operations research, experts can be exploring techniques for aiding management decision making while other applications are being designed. This activity should be dovetailed with the basic

MIS development to ensure that the necessary historical data will be available as a system by-product and in a form suitable for incorporating into the strategic systems. A management science group could, for example, be studying the warehouse locations with a view toward optimizing the number and location of warehouses. The management science group could also be developing a model that aids in the selection of store sites based on traffic patterns, population composition, shopping center locations, and the like. This parallel program of two groups concentrating on two levels of management is most desirable.

SUMMARY

Management information systems are an important application of computers to business. The discussion started with a definition of MIS and a listing of characteristics, since it is my belief that MIS has been maligned due to semantics in many instances. An MIS model showed the integration of subsystems constituting the total system. Two companies illustrated the payoffs from MIS employed with the full backing of top management. Finally management considerations in implementing an MIS emphasize the importance of management involvement, careful planning and time phasing, and above all, a practical and realistic approach to MIS design and implementation. The environment for MIS indicated the industries in which MIS is most prominent.

MIS has had a slow evolution; however, the successes of some MIS systems show the benefits of an MIS approach. There are benefits to be gained from the non-MIS approach, where management maintains functionally isolated operations and computerizes individual applications. The real benefits and payoffs from computerization will come, however, from systems that interconnect the subsystems, draw their input from a common data base, and produce meaningful and integrated reports to aid the management decision-making process.

8 Computer-based Teleprocessing Systems

Computer industry experts and industry forecasters agree: computer-based teleprocessing systems are the wave of the future. EDP research organizations, such as the International Data Corporation, predict that the greatest (IDC says "fantastic") growth in applications will be in teleprocessing. IDC states, "It's where users are headed ... inescapably. Interviews with large using organizations indicate that many are in the first phases of five- and ten-year development cycles aimed at implementing communications-oriented processing systems."

This chapter will describe just what a teleprocessing system is, present a brief history of teleprocessing, categorize the various types of teleprocessing, then give examples of how a teleprocessing system is developed, including considerations that management must employ in order to ensure its success.

To introduce teleprocessing systems we will return to the inventory application from Chapter 5. One of the objectives of inventory control is customer service. In some instances, an inventory report that lists inventory balances at the end of each business day is not adequate.

A teleprocessing order-processing and inventory control system might work like this: A customer enters a store to order a large number of an item. The customer wants to know immediately whether the item will be available by the day after tomorrow. If it won't, the customer will substitute something else. The item is a fast mover and the store manager is not sure the warehouse can supply the quantity desired. The manager directs the operator at the computer communications inquiry unit to place an order for 500 of item 8920. The operator keys the numbers 8920 and 500 into the keyboard and depresses the "end of message" key. Two seconds later the terminal screen indicates "order accepted." Additional data needed for billing purposes can then be keyed in. If sufficient inventory had not been on hand, the computer could have suggested an alternate.

The store is linked on-line to the computer, which may be many miles away—even across the country. The inventory record is interrogated directly to determine whether the item is available. This type of system also is called real-time response. The real-time response makes it possible to notify a waiting customer that the item can be shipped. *Real time* is a relative term—some time always passes between the moment the action is taken and when the result occurs. Flip a switch and a light goes on. This is real time as far as we are concerned, although there is a brief delay between action and result. The customer obtains a response in two seconds. This is also real time because it satisfies the time needs of the situation.

TYPES OF LONG-RANGE COMMUNICATION

Communication is defined in the *American College Dictionary* as "the imparting or interchange of thoughts, opinions or information by speech, writing or signs." Without the ability to transmit knowledge and ideas, there's no civilization. What we are concerned with here is how information in the form of "speech, writing or signs" can be communicated through time and space. This is the objective of computer-based teleprocessing systems— to send and receive information from one location to another (space) so that the activity can be carried out quickly (time).

The techniques of transmitting messages (see Figure 8-1) from one location to another can be seen as a key element in a civilization. Primitive societies developed long-distance communications using drums and smoke signals. We can begin to see trade-offs that must be considered in evaluating teleprocessing systems. A smoke signal has a much longer range than a drum, but it is ineffective where dense forests, mountains, or overcast

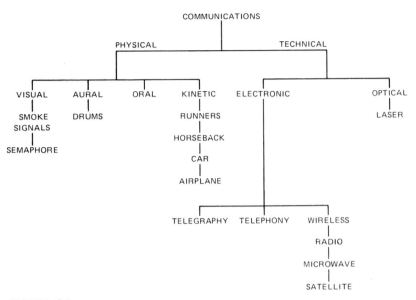

FIGURE 8-1
Methods of Communication

skies obscure vision. Every form of transmitting messages—runners, men on horseback, automobiles, and airplanes—had strengths and weaknesses.

Telegraphy

The era of electronic communications began in 1844, with the invention of the telegraph. In October 1832, Samuel F. B. Morse discussed a recent publication by Michael Faraday on electromagnetism with other passengers on a boat returning from Europe. Morse planned to make a telegraph recording instrument and devised a dot-dash code based on long and short duration electrical pulses.

In March 1838, after a successful demonstration before President Martin Van Buren and his cabinet, a bill was passed to appropriate funds for a practical test of the telegraph. Morse's transmission in 1844 of "what hath God wrought?" from the Supreme Court chamber in Washington to his partner in Baltimore over a forty-mile line was a landmark in communications.

A company was organized to extend the line to Philadelphia and New York City. By 1851 fifty companies using Morse patents were operating in the United States, and by 1861 Morse systems were operating in Europe.

The majority of the messages in the early days concerned train dispatching. The telegraph line shared the right-of-way with the rail line, and telegraphy and railroads supported each other's growth.

Automatic telegraphy, defined broadly to mean those systems where signals are transmitted by machine and recorded automatically, was the next major development. This development replaced the telegraph key and the dot-dash Morse code with the teleprinter and Baudot code. The Baudot code represents letters by a five-pulse code. With this code, it is possible to represent thirty-two different combinations: twenty-six for the alphabet and six for special functions. It is much more efficient than the dot-dash code. The pulses are delivered by a keyboard device to the telegraph line. The signals activate a teleprinter to print the message. Automated telegraphy introduced transmission and reception of messages punched on paper tape. These automatic methods were the forerunner of today's teleprocessing systems.

Telegraphy still provides low-cost data transmission where low speed is not a drawback, but its use has declined with the advances in telephony and microwave communication.

Telephony

Thirty years after the telegraph, another major development took place in Boston on June 2, 1875, when Alexander Graham Bell heard the twang of a steel spring over an electric wire. Earlier, Bell had described an apparatus that could transmit speech. It consisted of a strip of iron attached to a membrane. When activated by a voice the membrane vibrated before an electromagnet, inducing an electric current. Bell filed an application for a patent and in March 1876 transmitted the first complete sentence. It was not quite as grand as Morse's message. He called to his assistant at the other end of the line, "Mr. Watson, come here; I want you."

The first commercial telephone was put into operation in May 1877 and by 1879 there were more than 50,000 telephones within the United States. Today there are more than 175 million telephones.

Advanced technology has made it possible to conduct many conversations simultaneously over a single pair of wires. Coaxial cables and relays permit sharing hundreds of conversations. The first commercial manual telephone switchboard allowed the alternate switching of telegraph and voice communication over the same line. Dial systems were in use by 1892. Many other telephone innovations, such as automatic switching systems and direct distance dialing have been made.

Telephony advanced voice communication and provided the vital technology breakthrough for (nonverbal) data transmission. Telephone facilities are carrying data between computers and remote terminals and between computers in volumes that increase astronomically each year. The Bell System, currently with the capacity to handle a half a billion conversations daily, estimates that in the future more than half of the volume will be digital data going to and from computers as compared with voice communication.

Wireless Communications

The ability to communicate long distances without wires came in 1895, when Guglielmo Marconi developed the first wireless telegraph. Reginald Fessenden, an American physicist, demonstrated the first radio transmission of voices in 1900. Until then radio messages had been sent using the Morse's dot-dash code. In 1901 Marconi transmitted a radio message across the Atlantic. Commercial broadcasting began in the U.S. in 1920.

Television transmitting is similar in principle to radio, but it is modified to handle the very wide frequency bands required for the video signal.

Microwave is a short radio wave. Microwaves were noticed during World War II with their use in radar. Microwave networks can carry thousands of conversations simultaneously. Since microwaves travel in straight lines, relay towers must be constructed in the line of sight. Towers are usually no more than 30 miles apart because of the curvature of the earth.

Recently, communication satellites have assisted the communication of data within the United States and between continents. They serve as a microwave relay station. The satellite must be in a line-of-sight position from both relay points on the earth.

Independent companies have been formed whose objective is to provide communicative services via satellite links in competition with AT&T long lines. One such facility is XTEN, which is Xerox's entry into the national communications market, while another is Satellite Business Systems (SBS), a consortium put together by IBM, Aetna Insurance, and Comsat. Thus the company that has a large volume of data to be communicated between a variety of points within the United States will have a choice of using AT&T's long lines or satellite service provided by companies such as those just described.

Fiber Optics

Probably the most important advance in wired communication service is that of fiber optics. Fiber optics is a new process utilizing silicon as the base element for communication lines, as opposed to the use of copper wire today. Silicon, a nonmetallic chemical element, is more prevalent than any other element except oxygen, and one of the benefits of fiber optics is lower cost. Light-emitting diodes are employed to send signals via these fiber lines, which are no bigger than violin strings. Thus this medium offers the potential of lower cost, higher speed, and greater capacity. There is no question that fiber optics will play an important role in future communication systems.

The Future

Though I think this is a bit far out, the following quote, taken from "21st Century: A World of Artificial Men," in the *Washington Post*, might prove the ultimate in communication transmission.

It may be possible by 2067 for man to travel by "teleportation," that is, the cells of the human body, and even its personality and memories, will be transmitted from one place to another by radio. This could be done by feeding an individual's entire genetic code into a computer, and sending the information to another computer perhaps on the moon or Mars. The information then would be used to reconstruct the individual out of the essential materials in storage at the destination. This would amount to creation of exact replicas.

ELEMENTS OF A TELEPROCESSING SYSTEM

The best way to explain a teleprocessing system is to describe a typical system configuration and the elements that comprise it.

A schematic diagram of a typical teleprocessing module is shown in Figure 8-2. The terminal device at the remote outlet is linked to a communication line. Device intelligence and/or a multiplexor is used when several terminals share the same line. The modem device converts the keyed-in characters to electronic pulses for transmission over the communication line. At the receiving end another modem unscrambles the pulses from the different terminals. The host computer interface converts the pulses into binary code and delivers the data to the memory of the host computer. When the entire message—in our inventory control case study, for example—is delivered, the computer has

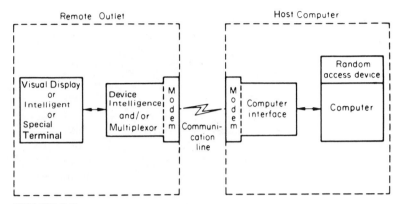

FIGURE 8-2
Typical Teleprocessing Communications Module

been instructed to seek out the appropriate inventory record (on the random-access device), determine whether the requested quantity can be filled, and send back an appropriate message. The computer must reduce the available amount of the item so that the correct response can be made for any subsequent orders.

The schematic diagram has six elements, which will now be discussed in more detail.

1. terminal device
2. device intelligence and/or multiplexor
3. modem
4. communication line
5. host computer interface
6. host computer

TERMINALS

The growth of the terminals segment of the information-processing industry in a word has been extraordinary. The overall trend of computer "extensibility," with the provision of computer power first to diverse locations within a building, then to remote locations in outlying plants and offices, and finally to service points and offices in industries such as retailing, banking, airlines, and the like, has accounted for this amazing terminal growth. A television screen or a CRT (cathode ray tube) has

181

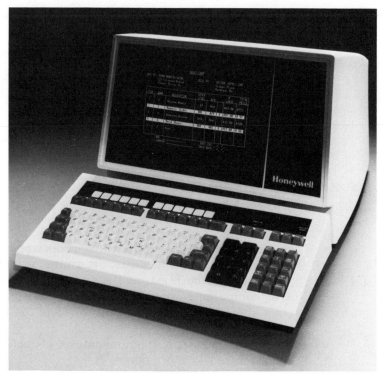

FIGURE 8-3
Typical CRT (Cathode Ray Tube) Terminal (Courtesy of Honeywell
Information Systems)

become almost as commonplace in the office as a telephone. The
proliferation of terminals along with the incorporation of low-
cost microprocessor-based intelligence represent one of the pro-
pelling forces in the industry. Terminals come in all sizes,
shapes, and functionality, but they can be grouped into several
types, as follows:

**CRT (Cathode
Ray Tube)
Terminal**

The basic building block or unit in any remote communication
subsystem is the CRT. It is the workhorse in today's communication field. Figure 8-3 is a picture of a typical CRT. Simply stated,
the unit has a twelve- or fifteen-inch screen that can display
alphanumeric characters. It has a keyboard to handle operator
input. The keyboard can range from a simple ten-key adding
machine type to a full alphanumeric set with a host of special-
purpose or function keys. Usually present is some local functional capability in the form of microprocessor-based logic and
memory that enables the operator to employ a variety of options

and facilitates ease-of-use features. This is usually a very low level of intelligence and thus this form of CRT is termed an "editing terminal". The word *terminal* implies that the device is not useful until it is linked to a computer, with the computer usually located some distance away from the terminal either within the building, in another facility, or in another city.

Intelligent Terminal

Though even the editing terminal has a degree of intelligence, it is not considered smart or intelligent unless it is equipped with enough memory and processing power to allow the user to write his own programs and specialize the unit for a specific use. There are obvious degrees of intelligence, and that is the reason for the terms *intelligent terminal* and *brilliant terminal*. The latter has enough processing power and memory to enable it to perform the functions of a small-scale computer system and sometimes even more. The brilliant terminal must have an array of peripheral devices to support it, and it follows that terminals are built with the capability of interfacing to printers and storage devices. When a terminal is so connected, it is more appropriate to call such a configuration a *terminal subsystem* or *work station*.

Graphic Terminal

In many applications, it is necessary to display graphic material in the form of charts, pictograms, design models, and the like, and some terminals are geared for handling just that type of application. There are two general types of graphic terminals—business graphics and design graphics. The latter is beyond the scope of business operations, since these are used primarily by design engineers and model builders in order to design automobiles, buildings, printed circuit board layouts, and the like. Business graphics become important to management users of information systems who want to see business results and projections in chart and graphic form (pie charts, bar charts, or regression curves). A color capability also becomes important in graphic terminals.

Optical and Voice Terminals

A point should be made that such special-function terminals as graphic, optical, or voice need not be treated as separate units, since these functions can often be provided as options to general-purpose terminals.

Optical terminals can sense special machine-readable numbers, letters, and special symbols, and can send these data to the computer. This bypasses the requirement for an operator to manually key the data. Utility bills, insurance premium invoices, or other turnaround documents produced by a computer are effective applications. Another version of the terminal senses magnetic ink that is recorded on the bottom of bank checks.

Voice synthesis employs devices that can comprehend a limited verbal vocabulary as input to a system. An individual voiceprint is established in order to allow for the idiosyncrasies of speech patterns. The individual is thus identified and is permitted to input commands and data to the system. Likewise, on the output side, a voice synthesizer facilitates verbal commands and data as system output. Credit checking is an example of an application using verbal output.

Special-Purpose Terminals

More and more, computer source data are being recorded at the point of the transaction. This so-called transaction-oriented approach updates the computer data base as the action occurs, speeds up the processing of the data, reduces errors, and eliminates redundancy in data recording. One example of this type of special-purpose (or application-specific) device is a factory transaction recorder, a station on the factory floor that serves as a remote input to a computer. A worker places his or her badge into a badge reader and sets the dials to the number corresponding to the job just worked on and the units completed. Time from an automatic time-of-day clock is added to the transaction, which is transmitted to the computer. These data are used for piecework payroll purposes, cost accounting, and other production analyses.

Banking terminals are another example of application-oriented terminal devices. A savings bank teller terminal allows a branch bank to verify a customer's savings account, compute the interest, and record the new deposit or withdrawal, all in a matter of seconds. Another device used in banking (and other industries) is the audio response unit. The computer selects and activates the proper track(s) on a voice record, combining the appropriate words into a message that is sent over the communication line, or the voice is synthesized electronically. The message "order accepted" might come across the line.

Likewise, point-of-sale devices are increasing in the retailing and distribution industries. An optical reader currently in use senses the special item code on a can or a bread label and, via a computer link, automatically calculates the price, tax, and any special allowances. When all purchases are made, the completed tape is ready for the consumer—without the need to key the amounts on a cash register manually. The grocery store has a continuous record of item movement (on an hour-by-hour basis, if required). It can initiate the reordering cycle automatically to ensure the availability of products.

An additional category of special-purpose terminals is the handheld terminal used in such applications as inventory audit or store ordering. A store supervisor can record via a ten-key adding machine the item number and quantity of either the inventory being audited or an order being taken. The device has a memory unit that can be used to transmit the data over a communication line to a host computer. It is conceivable that we will see wireless transmission such as is now found in walkie-talkies or citizens-band radios.

Device Intelligence and/or Multiplexor

As teleprocessing networks develop, the number and variety of terminal devices invariably increases. New applications are initiated, and transaction volume is expanded. One way to reduce communication costs is to provide a buffer between the terminals and the line to ensure that the best possible use is made of the line. So-called dumb controllers do not possess programmable logic and memory. They accomplish a specific task, such as collecting messages from low-speed terminals and preparing them for transmission over a communication line. Intelligent multiplexors actually contain a mini or micro computer. They have memory and can be programmed to accomplish such functions as error checking, data validation, message formating, simple processing, and so on. The trend is toward intelligent clusters of terminals linked to a host via an intelligent mini or micro computer.

Modem

The name *modem* stands for modulator-demodulator. On the transmission end the modulator converts the computer codes to tone signals for transmission over a telephone line. (Data signals are transmitted as tones.) On the receiving end the demodulator converts the tone signals back to computer code.

Communication Line

The job of selecting the proper balance of communication lines is very difficult. This section will merely describe some of the selection criteria that must be considered.

Bandwidth

Bandwidth determines the maximum transmission speed possible. Which bandwidth should be used depends on the volume and peak loads of the particular application. Narrow-band transmission uses the telegraph-grade line, while voice-grade uses the telephone line. Broad-band transmission depends on wireless types of transmission (such as microwaves) or special television-quality coaxial cable. In the past the common carriers (AT&T, Western Union, General Telephone, and the independent phone companies) have controlled the telegraph and voice-grade lines. However, the Federal Communications Commission has approved the requests of XTEN and SBS for development of private satellite communication. This has paved the way for added competition in the communication area.

Conditioning

Data communications techniques tend to distort signals in a variety of ways that can cause loss of transmission or loss of the message. A process called conditioning adjusts the frequency and response elements in order to remove these distortions. Conditioning amounts to tuning a specific communication line for peak performance. Various conditioning services are available to ensure higher validity of data transmission and fewer line losses.

One-Way/Two-Way Capability

Another consideration in selecting communication lines is whether you require simplex, half duplex, or full duplex capability. Simplex mode allows communication only in one direction; that is, a terminal may receive data, but it cannot transmit (or vice versa). Half duplex allows communications in both directions, but only one direction at a time. Full duplex allows simultaneous communication in both directions over the line.

Synchronous/Asynchronous Transmission

Two classes of timing schemes are used in transmitting data, asynchronous and synchronous. In the asynchronous mode special timing signals called start/stop bits are transmitted with each character. In the synchronous scheme timing signals are sent much less frequently, for example, once per hundred characters transmitted.

The asynchronous scheme is used most often with low-speed terminals (up to 1,200 bits per second) operating over voice-grade lines. The synchronous scheme is used with more sophisticated terminals on higher-speed lines (2,400–56,000 bits per second). The higher-quality line requires less timing information to keep it in step, permitting more message information to be transmitted per unit of time.

Dial-up or Private Service

Whether an application should employ a dial-up (switched) network or a private (leased) network is a function both of the volume of communications and the traffic patterns of the communication network. Most large companies find they require a combination of dial-up and private lines. The Bell System offers WATS (Wide Area Telephone Service), a flat-rate service for long-distance calls, and TWX (Teletypewriter Exchange Service) for teleprinters and low-speed messages. Data speed is offered for higher-speed transmission requirements. Western Union provides TELEX (similar to TWX) for low-speed communications and Broadband Exchange Service for higher speeds and more flexible service.

Another emerging service is that of VANS, or value-added networks. Such companies as GTE Telenet and Tymnet in addition to AT&T have established services for communicating digital data that provide data-processing services such as message store and forward, forms creation, and data storage in conjunction with communication handling.

Coding Systems   The two most significant transmission codes commonly in use are the Baudot five-level code and the American Standard Code for Information Interchange (ASCII) seven-level code. The selection of a code depends upon such requirements as compatibility, speed, error checking, validity, the software being used, and the terminal being used.

Host Computer Interface   Between the incoming data and the computer stands an interface device usually referred to as a front-end processor (FEP). It can be a minicomputer itself, in fact. The FEP acts as buffer for the computer. It receives and sends messages to the central processing unit. It preedits, formats, and arranges the messages prior to passing them along to the central computer for processing. It allows for a speed imbalance between the relatively slow communication line and the high-speed processing unit. The FEP also orders messages based on a preconceived priority scheme. Thus the FEP is able to offload the central computer, specializing in the preparation, editing, error checking, and formating of messages prior to their being sent or received.

Host Computer   The host computer is the nerve center of the entire communication network. It has processing power, stored programs to process the messages, and the data-base reference for the messages. In addition to the hardware required for a communication system, such as the necessary array of peripheral devices, high internal speed, program interrupt capability, and the required input/output speed and capacity, an advanced communication-oriented software operating system is essential.

Communication-oriented operating systems are needed to

implement advanced teleprocessing. A computer can be thought of as being similar to a production-line machine center in a manufacturing plant. The machine center is there to turn out a quality product in the most economic manner—and a computer center has the same goal. The input (raw material) consists of cassettes, diskettes, keyboard input, and the like. The product of the computer is useful printed or visual output. Tne computer center also has in-process inventory in the form of intermediate data tapes or transactions stored on disk.

To expand on the analogy, the computer operating system is similar to the production scheduling system, and the computer operating staff is similar to the machine tool operators who feed the machine and keep it in productive operation with minimal interjob interruption or downtime. Just as the production center operator is assisted by machine tools that automatically position and direct the machine's actions, so the computer operator is assisted by a computer operating system that automatically runs a series of programs without manual intervention. The computer operating system has two major functions: to schedule computer program operation based on the jobs to be run and the resources available; and to monitor the execution, ensuring that the resources continue to be optimally allocated, based on priority of job execution and changes unforeseen at scheduling time.

Up to this point, I have described the six basic elements that make a teleprocessing system. Though the configurations may differ widely, every system must consider and be built from these six elements. Obviously, much added detail and analysis must be considered in order to implement an advanced teleprocessing system; however, the description presented here should give the reader an overview of the general steps in the development of a teleprocessing system.

LOOSELY COUPLED VERSUS INTEGRATED NETWORK

It is helpful at this stage to view two contrasting system approaches in the teleprocessing field. The first usage pattern is termed *loosely coupled* and includes many small- to medium-size companies who have simple communication needs and will probably not require much more in the immediate future. Most of their operations stem from a single plant or complex of plants that require simple terminal communications from the remote sites to a host. Transactions consist mainly of data entry or data inquiries related to a central inventory or sales files. Orders are taken at the remote site, usually batched and communicated to the central site at the end of the day. The major remote applications are order entry, remote batch transmission, and a small amount of on-site processing. Interface protocols between the host machine and remote terminal substations are specific, finite, and well structured. Many small-to-medium companies fall into this mode of communication processing, and it is not necessary to develop a complex integrated network architecture to satisfy requirements.

On the other hand, many larger companies have a myriad of remote operations, many of a hierarchical nature—that is, suboffices or branches reporting to other suboffices or regions, which in turn report to districts and ultimately to the home office. In addition, there are a multiplicity of plants, factories, and other facilities located throughout the country. This type of organization presents a far different type of data-processing challenge than the small company environment just described.

In order to satisfy communication and data-processing requirements in systems with complex interaction, a communication framework or distributed architecture must be established. Also because the degree of data interaction (volume) is heavy, communication costs will be a significant factor in the total EDP budget. The availability of private satellite communications and value-added networks as described earlier warrant the establishment of communication protocols that enable a company to take advantage of these services. In an integrated network messages and data stream across communication lines via microwaves or satellites between terminal substations and host computers. Sometimes the network is hierarchical, where branches report to regions, and so on, as just stated, or it may be a ring structure, where branch offices communicate to one another as well as to higher-order offices.

This degree of communication complexity is far more integrated and interactive than the loosely coupled model and requires a well-thought-out long-range plan with established standards and disciplines to enable the total system to function as a network. Future growth and direction must be considered as well as industry and international standards and conventions. The standards and protocols you plan to use must interface with the broader-based standards.

Mini and micro developments have made it economically feasible to have local processing capability; thus the trend is to distribute processing to remote subunits while still maintaining the ability to talk to the host computer system and to other subunits via an established network protocol. Two examples will now be presented to give an overview of how these networks function. The first is a special-purpose network, called MULTICS, which is confined to the specific task of developing software but which is useful in explaining the elements of teleprocessing systems. The second is a generic look at the distributed-data-processing concept that illustrates the diversity and interconnectability of units of a large company, followed by a description of a modern distributed-data-processing operation in a large international bank.

THE MULTICS SYSTEM

To give you an idea of the direction teleprocessing can go, I will briefly describe a sophisticated teleprocessing system called MULTICS. This system, ten years in the making, has some unique features beyond the six elements just described.

MULTICS (Multiplexed Information and Control Service) is an advanced time-sharing system developed by Honeywell Information Systems in conjunction with the Massachusetts Institute of Technology and Bell Laboratories. The system is designed to operate without interruption seven days a week, twenty-four hours a day, the same way telephone or power systems do. MULTICS meets a wide range of user applications: scientific programs, checkout and testing of new programs, sharing of common data and program files, and such basic batch jobs as accounting and payroll.

The full list of systems objectives is:

- Convenient remote terminal access
- Continuous operation analogous to telephone service
- Wide range of capacity for growth or contraction
- Reliable internal file system
- Controlled access to allow selective data sharing
- Hierarchical storage of information
- Efficient service to both large and small users
- Ability to support variety of human interfaces
- Flexibility to incorporate future technological improvements and user expectations

The MULTICS ring protection system employs unique file protection techniques and safeguards to prevent unauthorized access to data files and programs. Combined hardware and software barricades protect sensitive data. The different levels of security are in the form of concentric rings. Particular passwords and conditions must be met each time a user requests access to a more secure ring. Thus there may be certain program files accessible only to the systems designers. Other files that exist outside this inner ring have less restrictive conditions of access. Each user determines how secure the material he controls shall be, and what other users can share it.

The system also features the concept of virtual memory. While the system has limited main memory, the hardware and software provide backing storage that can be rolled in and out of memory automatically if the contents are required by the user. The roll-in–roll-out procedure is transparent to the user; that is, the user does not have to request the procedure. If six users are using the system and another user dials up, user 7's programs can be retrieved from backing storage, placed in main memory, executed, and rolled out again in time to let the other users continue. The procedure happens in milliseconds; thus to each user the machine seems to be entirely his. This is the concept of virtual memory.

Figure 8-4 is a schematic of the MULTICS system installed at the Honeywell facility in Billerica, Massachusetts. It is similar to the MULTICS system employed by MIT, but it is dedicated to the design and testing of software. Several hundred programmers using teleprinters and CRTs compile and test advanced computer software. The system is connected to Tymnet, a value-added service network, and is available throughout Europe. Indeed programming groups in England, France, and Germany currently utilize the MULTICS facilities.

The system is built in a very modular fashion. The core of the system is four modules of 1.25 million bytes of memory (a *byte* is four data bits) linked to dual high-speed central processors. The clock allocates time to users on a priority basis and calculates usage for cost allocation and billing purposes. The virtual memory backing storage are high-speed disks connected to the memory units through a disk controller. The general input/output controller ties in the peripherals and communication terminals to the memory units. The peripheral complement includes two operator consoles, three line printers, two card readers, and a card punch. Also, there are six tape drives and thirty-two disk drives, the latter providing about a half billion

characters of on-line file storage. Some 350 terminals and teleprinters are hooked to the system. The maximum number that
can be attached at any one time is virtually unlimited. The
terminals are located throughout the Boston area, in addition to

FIGURE 8-4
The MULTICS System

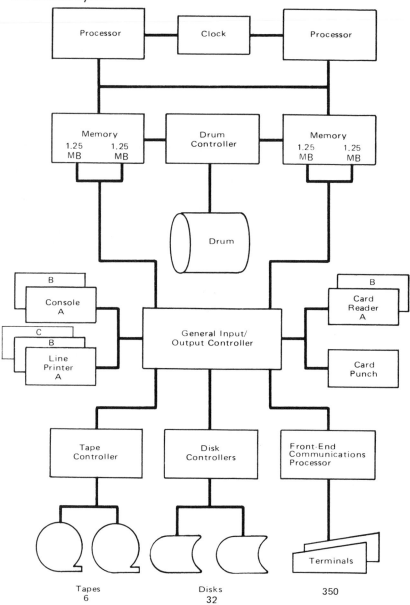

those in Europe. As an interesting aside, a number of portable terminals are taken home by programmers who work in the evening and on weekends. These terminals are easily attached to a standard telephone by a snap-on acoustic coupler.

The modular design is one element in providing round-the-clock uninterrupted service. If one memory module is inoperative, the system will run using the remaining memory module until the other module is repaired. This concept is also true for the processing units and peripheral devices. The hardware modularity and backup plus the constant monitoring activity of the software provide a capability that approaches the goal of uninterrupted operation.

DISTRIBUTED DATA PROCESSING

The distributed-processing concept is built around an approach that distributes the data base and processing capability to remote sites based on the type, number, and variety of work stations, their data-processing requirements, the degree of control desired, the type of business organization, and overall economic considerations.

The term *distributed* is a bit of a misnomer because although functions and resources are distributed, there is still a central discipline or control over the remote processing units. The key to DDP is that the host computer and distributed-processing nodes are cooperative—that is, they are designed to be able to communicate with each other for those applications that require it. The following are two examples of a DDP network, the first a generic or general illustration and the second a specific one.

The DDP Concept

Figure 8-5 is a schematic of a generalized DDP. There is an EDP center, or host computer, which is the integrating element of the entire system. A front-end communications processor (FEP) handles all of the remote communications entering and leaving the host. The FEP is connected to a variety of remote processors via one or a combination of the communication media that have been described. The company's home office utilizes graphic terminals for its executives who have access to a local data base as well as to the central data base at the host site. Administrative offices perform word processing and other office automation functions while being tied to the host system for distribution of

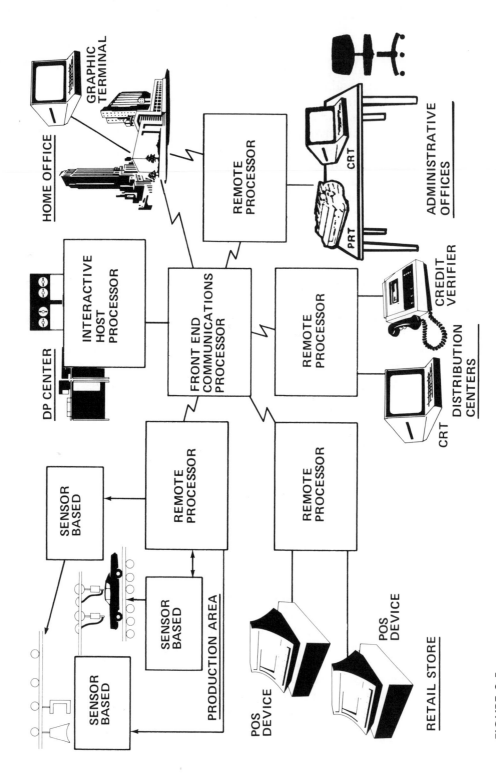

FIGURE 8-5
Generic DDP Schematic

messages (electronic mail) and a variety of inquiries to the central data base. Distribution or sales centers are also linked to the host but perform a good deal of their own local processing of order taking, invoicing, and collections.

The remaining two distributed functions, the retail store and the production area, are not found in DDP as frequently as the other subsystems. The retail store or point-of-sale (POS) area is usually a freestanding subsystem, not linked on-line to the host but to a local processor in the store or in a local warehouse. However, there is no reason why it cannot be linked if there is benefit in operating in such a manner. The same holds true for the production area subsystem. Historically this has been a freestanding entity with data delivered to the host computer in some cases, but on a batch basis after a shift has been completed. In this example, sensor-based processors are monitoring an automobile assembly process. The type of data fed to the host are defects found per car, material used, and cost information. Process control or sensor-based computers have historically been acquired and operated by engineering management rather than data-processing management, and the pressure to link the two activities has been lacking. However, the trend is for closer cooperation between the two systems and the integration of their respective functions as an overall part of a company's DDP system plan.

This, then, is a generalized illustration of a DDP network. It is a bit utopian in scope for very few companies have tied in both POS and production areas into their DDP plan. However, the trend is definitely toward this type of integration. We now turn to a more specific example of DDP, that of a large European bank implementing a rather typical hierarchical system.

International Bank

International Bank, a fictitious name for a real bank, is one of the largest banks in Europe. The bank is organized in such a way that each branch renders total banking services to a specific geographical territory. A group of branches in turn are directed by an area general manager. Each area has an average of 200 employees under its management; as business and areas grow, the company has a policy that a new division is formed when the number of employees exceeds 200 people. The current number of areas is 250, with 350 expected in the next five years as the bank continues its rapid expansion plans. International Bank believes in a decentralized mode of operation, leaving major decision authority in the hands of the area general manager, each area functioning as a cost and profit center.

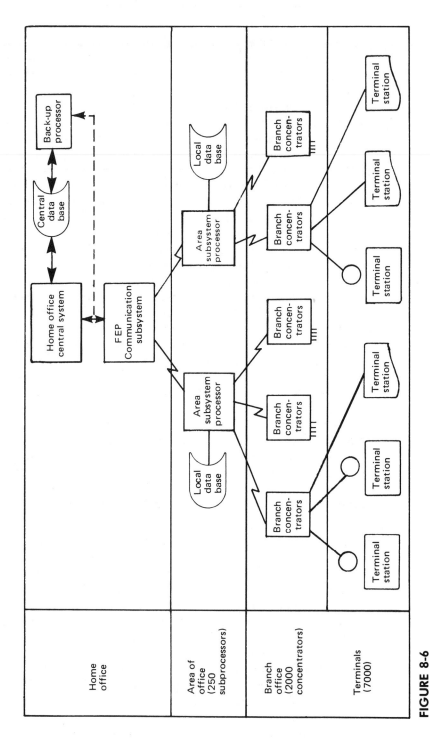

FIGURE 8-6
Distributed Processing Network of International Bank

International Bank evolved to a totally centralized system in the late 1960s and early 1970s; they started with their current distributed data-processing approach in 1975. The rationale for switching was (1) the ability to better serve the company's needs while being consistent with the prevailing decentralized mode of operation, (2) improved performance geared to higher throughput and turnaround time, and (3) improved system availability translated into higher uptime and ability to serve the growing number of users. Currently 250 areas serve 2,000 branches with a total of 7,000 terminals. It is expected that in five or ten years there will be 350 areas with 2,500 branches and 10,000 terminals.

The distributed data-processing system envisioned by International Bank is illustrated in Figure 8-6. There are four levels of distribution in the network. The first level is the home office, which has the master central data base, maintaining the names, identification key subtotals, and summary information of every account within the network. A backup processor is present in case of failure of the first processor. The second level is the area office, which communicates to the central system via a mini-processor tied into a communications front-end processor of the host system. Each area processor has a data base of the accounts within its geographical territory. The third level is the branch, which utilizes concentrators, similar to those described in the advanced teleprocessing system, to collect, edit, and prepare for transmission the data required for second-level processing. The fourth level is the terminal work stations. These work stations are a combination of cathode ray tubes, keyboards, bank teller units, printers, and the like, dependent on the specific activity performed by the branch. Thus you can see the networking effect of one home office large processor and data base communicating to area offices, which in turn communicate to concentrators at the branch, which control the variety of terminals in various locations within the branch.

The estimated total cost of this system is the approximately $125 million purchase price of the hardware complement plus about $20 million per year to operate. The latter costs include personnel, facilities rental, communication lines, power, hardware maintenance, supplies, operators, and so on. Although the distributed system is not yet in full operation, the bank feels the cost will be about equal to their previous system; as mentioned, the benefits result from improved customer service by virtue of greater system availability, capacity, and response time.

**Why Distributed
Data Processing?**

Data processing, like many other business activities, seems to run in phases. Thus the advent of computers saw individual computers at individual company sites. There was little, if any, interaction between computers and computer sites. Then the strong trend toward centralization occurred, based on economies of scale and the fact that business operations were becoming more integrated, with decisions depending on optimizing or balancing many functional activities within a company. The distributed-processing concept takes a middle course, possibly combining the benefits of centralization with those of decentralization. In the bank example, the economies of scale are obtained while maintaining a central data base of information pertinent to overall company operations, and passing down to area offices (decentralized under the company's organizational philosophy) that data used in local operation.

The basic benefits claimed by distributed data processing are as follows:

Less risk of system breakdown. In central systems, a power outage, act of God (flood, hurricane), act of sabotage, or strike can shut down the entire network. In a distributed-processing system, the local operations can continue without major service interruption; it is the summary or period reports that are affected.

Availability. Again, because of the sharing and distribution of functions, distributed data processing claims a higher percentage of system uptime over a given period.

Economy of operation. Although I find this difficult to prove either from a functional viewpoint or from actual experience, distributed-data-processing enthusiasts claim there is economy of operation. They base their opinion on the more balanced approach and the use of low-cost mini and micro processors throughout the network. A concern is the rising programming and systems cost as remote sites develop their own staffs often redundant to the host staff.

Flexibility to fit organizational philosophy. To my way of thinking, this factor may be the most important rationale for distributed processing. In the International Bank example, the information files and operational control are vested at the area-office level, where the cost and profit center responsibility resides. This can be quite important in gaining management support and involvement in the system, vital factors that can often skuttle an otherwise well-conceived approach. Also data security and privacy are enhanced by having each area responsible for securing the data and files under its control.

Less complexity of system design and implementation. This is a strong attribute of the distributed concept. Completely centralized systems have literally choked on the complexity of systems design and of operating systems aimed at accomplishing the myriad of functions required when one central processor is responsible for accessing on-line data files for the entire network. The divide-and-conquer theory is the root of the distributed approach, where jobs are off-loaded to processors specialized for handling the various subfunctions. However, reduced complexity may be a bit illusionary because complexity of another sort is introduced, the complexity of ensuring that the entire network is linked from level to level and the proper interaction pathways maintained. Whether one's approach is centralized or distributed, a strong system discipline and control is a prerequisite for success. In either case, a full understanding of the interaction patterns and information relationships are required in order to determine where decision and action optimization or suboptimization occurs.

Level of expertise required. Though some distributed-processing proponents would say the divide-and-conquer theory holds in establishing the level of expertise required of systems designers and implementers, it would seem that about the same experience level would be required whether the system is centralized or distributed. While the central system approach requires a core of highly trained and skilled practitioners, the decentralized approach requires that the system be constructed so that the disbursed personnel operating and using the system find it straightforward and simple to utilize. This adds a new challenge to systems design. Languages and inquiry methodology must be flexible enough to accommodate the different class of users; thus the application programs, the operators, the area users, the branch work station users, and the management users must all find interaction with the system effective, efficient, and easy to learn.

In conclusion, the distributed-processing approach is gaining momentum, spurred by the mini- and micro-processor developments that can provide intelligent, cost-effective front-end processors, intelligent work stations, and satellites. The approach, like many others, must be carefully evaluated by companies to see if it fits their mode of operation and their organizational environment. For most it will mean converting an existing communication system rather than starting from scratch. This will present an added challenge, since it is more difficult to restructure a going system than to initiate a new one. However, this has been a challenge faced by systems designers since the beginning of data processing.

FEASIBILITY CRITERIA

There is no questioning the potential benefits of advanced teleprocessing systems. At this point, however, I would like to consider some elements often overlooked in the planning process. I feel that too much attention is paid to the technology of teleprocessing, emphasizing the hardware and software aspects of line speeds, modems, multiplexors, concentrators, front-end processors, and terminals but grossly neglecting the nontechnical elements.

Figure 8-7 shows the three considerations of computer system feasibility: technical, economic, and operational. The technical aspects have received the most attention from systems designers. Operational aspects have received the least. More emphasis must be given to the economic and operational elements of feasibility if advanced teleprocessing systems are to be installed successfully by more companies. An article by David J. Farber in *Datamation* magazine, "Networks: An Introduction," describes seven typical computer networks with advanced teleprocessing. Six of the seven systems are projects sponsored by research or educational organizations. Considerations of economic feasibility are not as important to nonprofit organizations as they are to commercial businesses.

Dartmouth College has been a pioneer in using computers in its curriculum. John G. Kemeny, now president of the college, developed a specialized language that simplified direct communication with the computer from terminals around the campus. Kemeny has stated that "learning to use a high-speed computer should be an essential part of a liberal education."

No doubt having access to a computer in college extends the range of problems a student can tackle. For example, access to a computerized simulation model adds a new dimension to a mathematics or physical science course. I also believe students should realize that a cost-benefit analysis is needed to justify the

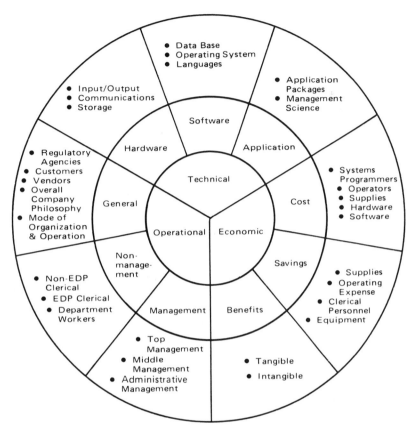

FIGURE 8-7
Computer System Feasibility Criteria

value of remote terminals and computer processing in a profit-oriented organization. Several years ago I was invited to Dartmouth's Tuck School of Business as a guest lecturer. My host asked me to direct my remarks to the cost-benefit and business considerations underlying the installation of such time-sharing systems as those at Dartmouth. He, too, was concerned with the gap between technological and economic understanding.

Operational Considerations

I am even more concerned about the gap between the technological and operational considerations. A particular application may be both technically and economically feasible and still fail to produce the predicted benefits because a company is unable to make it work. A perplexed management cannot understand why a well-conceived and -designed system is not successful in the operating departments. Some reasons for such failure are motivational and psychological. These often can be resolved by proper training and indoctrination. Other reasons, however, are serious enough to warrant placing a lower priority on a particular application area until the problem is resolved.

An example of a situation such as this might occur when a sales administration function performed by local sales branches becomes part of a centralized teleprocessing system that processes orders and bills customers. The new system is designed and installed with little or no local participation at the sales branches. The branches try to circumvent the system because they fear that account control is being removed from them. The new system develops a billing backlog, customers become irate, management becomes disillusioned, and the whole system eventually fails.

Before an application is instituted, it is necessary to assess management, nonmanagement, and general operational considerations (as indicated in Figure 8-7). The impact of the application on top, middle, and administrative management must be analyzed carefully. For example, a system such as the one in Figure 8-5 links process-control minicomputers to a general-purpose computer in order to control the production process. This approach will have a direct impact on the production manager and supervisors. A production manager who is very conservative or has been antagonistic toward computerized production systems is definitely a negative consideration with regard to operational feasibility. This problem either must be resolved or a lower priority should be given to this phase of the teleprocessing system.

In Figure 8-7 the "general" category under operational feasibility includes the system's interfaces with customers, vendors, and regulatory agencies (for example, the Internal Revenue Service). Other criteria listed under operational feasibility are overall company philosophy, mode of operation, and organization. The rest of this discussion concerns these ares.

A company's organizational philosophy may be extreme centralization, extreme decentralization, or something in between. When a company is centralized, well-defined policies and procedures are developed at the headquarters level. Local offices and plants follow these regulations to the letter; any deviations must be approved by headquarters. This type of operation usually is effective in a highly structured marketplace and where products have long production runs and fairly stable life cycles.

The decentralized philosophy places maximum leverage

and decision-making responsibility in the hands of local offices or plants. This aims to heighten an individual's motivation to succeed and develop an entrepreneurial style of operation. This approach is effective where markets and products differ according to the local environment and where quick decisions and flexibility are required.

In most cases a company's organization philosophy falls between these extremes. Also, an organization may change over time, moving from a decentralized to a centralized mode, and then possibly back toward decentralization. The changes result from normal organizational maturation, from different management styles, as well as from changes in a company's marketplace and products.

The design of teleprocessing systems must take into account the organizational mode of a company. Although theoretically a centralized computer system can be effective in a decentralized company, in practice a system has less chance of success if it runs counter to the existing organizational philosophy. Furthermore, a teleprocessing system must be amenable to change as the company moves from one stage of organizational development to another. Flexibility and modularity are important criteria in designing teleprocessing systems.

Timing is another consideration when a new system is planned. For example, if a company is planning to move to a more centralized organizational structure but hasn't yet done so, it might be wise to begin with a decentralized system that has the flexibility to move toward a centralized mode later on.

There are key systems trade-offs that must be considered during the design of any system. These should not be made strictly on technological and economical considerations. Should a completely centralized data base be developed, for example, or should subsets of the central file be maintained locally? From technological and economic viewpoints, the centralized data base might appear to be the way to go. On the other hand, operational considerations may dictate that some redundancy in file storage is necessary for the system to work. Also, local management may consider too rapid a move to centralization as usurpation of prerogatives and authority.

The claim is sometimes made that advanced teleprocessing systems solve a company's organizational and people communications problems. Experience shows that if such problems are not resolved prior to installing a new teleprocessing system, the new system might make them worse. If strict discipline is a prerequisite for successful implementation of a centralized teleprocessing system, it must be achieved before system installation, not afterward. The system will not create the needed discipline. Moreover, installing a new computer system and implementing a new operational philosophy simultaneously increases the risk that neither will succeed. The best approach is to get one's house in order before superimposing a major change. The teleprocessing system may be the catalyst, but it alone cannot resolve underlying company organization and operational problems.

Other Management Considerations

Implicit in teleprocessing is a real-time response capability—the capacity to respond immediately, whether or not immediate response is indeed necessary. Is it really necessary that the customer receive an immediate answer—or could it be sent hours, or perhaps even days, later? In a few special circumstances real-time response is vital. But in many business applications, such immediate response will rarely be required.

On-time systems, therefore, represent a much broader and more flexible approach, and probably a less costly one, to most business applications. Such systems are intended to respond to information demands, whether the demand is for immediate answer-back, or for answer-back an hour, a day, or a week later.

A basic criterion is that the review frequency must be matched to the response capability of the system. Before plunging into an expensive real-time system, examine what will be done with information once it is obtained. Don't demand split-second response just to keep up with the Joneses. Your objective should be responses available *as they are needed*.

As an example, there is quite a difference between a military control system's need for frequent review and immediate response and a grocery buyer's need to know the amount of instant coffee in the warehouse. If the course of a missile traveling at 25,000 miles per hour is not changed in a split second, it will never hit the target. However, when a warehouse has space for large quantities of instant coffee and a buyer purchases coffee once or twice a month, the split-second status of the item is not very significant. A daily inventory status report normally satisfies the on-time criterion.

The trend is not toward universal adoption of real-time operation. Rather, executives will find better ways of analyzing the objectives of their business and determining what information is needed (and not needed) to form the basis of action. The system to satisfy these objectives will be on-time, that is, the system will respond as required to meet the needs of the business. If there is cost justification for split-second responses, only then will real-time be used.

Management's perspective will play an important part in implementing realistic systems. Perspective is one of the most necessary traits in a business environment rife with reports of all types of exotic and earthshaking developments. One eye must be kept on the future, but the other must be fixed firmly on today. We must avoid the fadism that exists in many circles: the fadism of microsecond responses to inquiries, the fadism of electronic light pens, the fadism of information technologists who promise to deliver the status of the world at the feet of executives.

Perspective is vital at a time when it is common to forget tenses in talking about developments in today's market. It is easy to get the idea that what is being discussed is already in existence, when in reality it is five years off, and that what is said to be five years off in reality is a decade or more into the future.

If the benefits of a teleprocessing system justify the cost outlay, then implementation should begin. But don't forget to allow adequate time and have a careful phasing plan before you start. The project must be led by a competent manager who has had experience in teleprocessing systems. The project needs visible and high-level participation of top management.

SUMMARY

Teleprocessing systems represent the fastest growing trend in the EDP industry. Teleprocessing is a natural result of companies needing to run several plants and offices—needing to tie geographically dispersed organizations into an integrated information network. This chapter traced the beginning of communications technology and described the elements of a modern teleprocessing system. Three examples of advanced teleprocessing systems were presented—the first, a special-purpose network aimed at a specific function (software development), and the other two, examples of the distributed-data-processing concept that is so prevalent today. Finally, as they have been throughout the book, management considerations were emphasized. These considerations must be heeded if a company is to take advantage of the benefits of teleprocessing.

Future Use and Growth of Computers

9

The information-processing industry is growing faster than any other major industry. This chapter will explore what's behind that growth and, more important, the specific areas that are growing fastest in the industry and the major trends.

Figure 9-1 indicates the installed dollar value of general-purpose computer systems of U.S.-based manufacturers, as reported by International Data Corporation. The figures are not adjusted for inflation or other economic changes and do not include depreciation. The value is that at time of purchase.

The worldwide cumulative in-use figure is projected to be $208.1 billion in 1983, which is three times what it was in 1975. The international portion of the total grows from 43.6 percent in 1975 to 44.5 percent in 1983, indicating a slightly faster growth rate than in the United States. The average system price of $207,000 in 1975 compares with $125,000 in 1983, a reflection of the ability to purchase more power at less cost and also of the purchase of minis and micros by smaller companies.

These figures include mini systems and micro systems, the latter to the extent they are embedded and utilized in general-purpose computers or sold directly to the end user. Micros used, for example, in automobiles or in process-control equipment are not included. An idea of the growing significance of mini systems can be ascertained from the fact that in 1975 the value of mini shipments was less than 10 percent of the total general-purpose market, whereas in 1983 the value is projected to be

FIGURE 9-1

Installed Computer Value by U.S. Manufacturers

	U.S. Based		International		Worldwide	
	Units	Cumulative In-Use Dollars (in billions)	Units	Cumulative In-Use Dollars (in billions)	Units	Cumulative In-Use Dollars (in billions)
1975	208,000	$ 37.8	115,000	$29.3	323,000	$ 67.1
1979	492,000	$ 67.7	272,000	$53.2	764,000	$120.9
1983 (projected)	1,047,000	$115.3	616,000	$92.8	1,663,000	$208.1

about a third. The value of microcomputers included in the survey is expected to approach 5 percent of the total shipments in 1983, double that of current shipments. Though micros are still a small portion of the total dollar value, they account for a much larger proportion of unit shipments.

Another major hardware growth area is display terminals. IDC predicts the number of terminals in the general-purpose data entry-terminal equipment market will more than double its 1978 base to over 2.25 million units in 1983. This does not include special-purpose terminals for application in unique uses such as factory data collection or word processing, two areas that are expecting tremendous growth. Most assuredly, there will be more than 5 million terminals in use by 1983.

Two areas of data processing that are growing at a faster rate than the hardware are processing services and software. Processing services include computer and data-processing services ranging from carry-in and remote batch to interactive transaction processing and data base inquiry. Service companies can now provide complete on-site services, on-line services linked to a service bureau computer, or a combination of both. IDC predicts a compound revenue growth rate for processing services of 17 percent through 1983, when the total revenue will reach $10.7 billion. Service companies providing such communication facilities as VANS (value-added networks), which were mentioned in Chapter 8, are also expected to grow rapidly.

IDC predicts a compounded 28-percent growth rate through 1983 for suppliers of independent packaged software, reaching $2.3 billion in 1983, the biggest growth being that of communication software, data base software, and applications software, the latter to represent almost half of the total software revenue in 1983.

207

INTERNATIONAL MANUFACTURERS

The United States is the dominant force in worldwide computer markets, though there has been an upsurge of foreign manufacturers in particular international areas. For example, ICL is significant in the United Kingdom as is Siemans in Germany, Phillips in the Low Countries, Olivetti in Italy, and CII-Honeywell Bull in France. None of these companies has made any significant inroad into the U.S. market. The major concern of international presence in U.S. markets is Japan. They are a dominant force in the Far East with Hitachi, Toshiba, and Fujitsu each having over $1 billion in EDP revenue, but their system penetration in the United States has not yet been a factor. There are two camps of thought, one feeling the Japanese, with their technical know-how and superior price-performance equipment, will evolve their software and marketing capability to become a dominant force here as they are in the Far East markets. The other camp says the Japanese will remain a subcontractor due to their inability to develop the necessary marketing and support organizations in the United States.

Several of the less technologically developed countries, seeing the potential in information systems, are attempting to develop engineering and manufacturing capabilities of their own. This includes Yugoslavia, Brazil, and China. Russia has improved its computer capabilities but is still far behind the United States in producing a broad line of efficient commercial and scientific computer systems (particularly commercial). Their plan to import an increasing number of U.S. computers was set back by U.S. policy following the invasion of Afghanistan.

THE FUTURE OF EDP

It is now time to discuss the major technological and developmental trends that underline this impressive growth, to switch from the quantitative to the qualitative.

EDP has been viewed historically as a series of generations with specific developments characterizing a specific generation. The first two generations were easy to define, the departure point being the replacement of vacuum tubes by transistors as the principal electronic element. However, the dividing line between subsequent generation has blurred as a kaleidoscope of emerging technologies and products reached the marketplace. The approach used here is first to describe what I term *environ-*

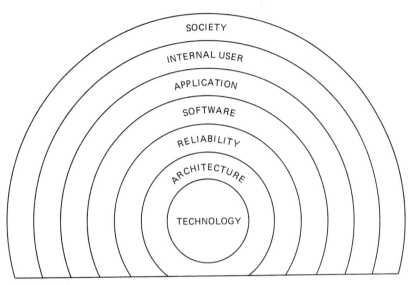

FIGURE 9-2
Environmental Rings

mental development rings, the elements that are necessary to a functioning data-processing system. I will then use these rings as a base point to trace the major developments over the last thirty years. In so doing, I will group the thirty-year commercial life of EDP into five eras, beginning with what I call the Iron Age of computers. I will spend a bit more time describing the elements of the fifth era, which is just emerging.

Environmental Development Rings

Figure 9-2 indicates by a series of concentric rings, the elements necessary for a successful information system. It begins with the raw technology at the center and fans out to include society, the outermost ring. A brief definition of each element follows.

An example of technology is the development of LSI (large-scale integration), a process that enables the fabrication and integration of logic elements on a silicon die called a chip, maybe a quarter of an inch square. The level of integration varies, but the state of the art in LSI is currently the ability to place the equivalent of 60,000 transistors on a chip.

Architecture refers to the way we put together the technology, such as using LSI to produce microprocessors that are used over a vast spectrum from powering small home calculators to controlling such specific functions as input, output, and communications within a large-scale computing complex.

The design concept of early mainframes was to place all the

logic of the system into a single central processor, but this has changed to a concept of reducing complexity by separating logical elements into micro-driven subprocessors. Architecture represents the way the system looks to users; an analogy is a prefabricated house where the floors, ceilings, and walls might be made of the same elements, but the way they are put together, the architecture, makes all the difference.

The reliability ring is an often underemphasized one, but it is quite important. Reliability, availability, and maintainability are essential ingredients to effective and productive operation of a computer system. An information system, particularly if it's an on-line one, cannot tolerate downtime and must approximate 100-percent availability.

Reliability is usually achieved by a combination of the technology and architecture rings (hardware) and the software ring. The distributed data-processing and transaction-oriented system trends are dependent on high reliability.

Software (the languages and operating systems) is needed to harness today's computer power and has been emphasized throughout the book. Historically, this element has lagged behind technology and architecture, though it has been said for years that the three should be developed as an entity.

The application is what the computer actually does, be it inventory control, maintaining patients' bills in a hospital, or scheduling school classes. The reader should be aware of the wide range of computer applications, as described in the various chapters.

The internal user environmental ring includes the management and nonmanagement end users of the information system within a company. This book has focused primarily on the management users.

Society represents the outside environment, covering (1) the economic forces such as inflation, competition, the energy situation, (2) the government forces such as laws, taxes and information demands, and (3) personal forces such as privacy, environment, and individual rights and expectations.

All seven elements are essential to an effective system; their evolution will be discussed in relation to the EDP life cycle spanning five eras.

Traditionally, EDP has been a technology-driven industry. The planning emphasis has been an inside-out approach when it should be the other way around, from the outside in. The main emphasis should not be whether or not the product will work but what kind of work it will do; the criterion should not be the ability to do something but the advisability of doing it; the concentration should be not on how something is done but on what is done.

I don't prescribe that it has to be exclusively outside-in; obviously there have been some significant, useful achievements made by technologists without outside direction; however, there have been equally significant failures and huge waste of funds working on the wrong problems. The inside-out approach often succeeds the first time, but repeated success from the same source does not occur.

FIVE ERAS OF DATA PROCESSING

Figure 9-3 lists five generations, or eras, beginning with the Iron Age, when the major emphasis was on hardware, or "iron," continuing through the second, third, and fourth generations, and leading to the fifth generation, which began in 1980, and whose general direction we are able to discern based on the evolutionary environmental development rings of the past. The eras are named a bit facetiously as there has not been enough elapsed time to attach names such as those used—for example, the Renaissance and the Golden Age.

Iron Age

This period covers the 1951–1958 time span, when the vacuum tube was the main electronic element. The hardware architecture was geared to handling one sequential operation after another. There were limited reliability aids centering on basic diagnostics such as I/O exercises which tested input-output devices during a preventative maintenance cycle. Brute force maintenance was the rule whereby field service engineering kept machines running by concentrated repair and attention. Computers employed rudimentary software with simple monitors which loaded one program at a time into memory.

The application focus was strictly on the administrative functions. In the user environment the early computers were viewed as an extension of the accounting function, and there was little if any management involvement outside the data-processing operation itself; the controller was interested, but that was all. A good deal of apprehension and doubt accompanied the installation or thought of installation. Enough said about this era; it was the beginning and few could forecast the dramatic growth of this fledgling industry.

FIGURE 9-3
Historical Computer Eras

Era	Time Period	Technology	Architecture	Reliability	Software	Application	User Impact
Iron Age	1951–1958	Vacuum tube	Mono-programming	Brute force	Simple monitor	Administrative	Accountants
Age of Expectation	1959–1963	Transistor	I/O overlap	On-site support	Multifunction monitor	Mainstream	Controllers
Age of Proliferation	1964–1970	Integrated Circuit	Multi-programming	Self-logging	Operating system	Communications	Technocrats
The Renaissance	1971–1979	MSI/LSI	Firmware, virtual system	Self-diagnosis	Interactive	Data base networking	Middle management
Golden Age	1980–	VLSI	Minis and Micros	Fail-soft operation	Transaction processing	Distributed processing	Strategic management

Age of Expectation

This era, 1959 to 1963, ushered in the transistor, which replaced the vacuum tube; it was a marvelous development. Computers decreased in size, power required, maintenance required, and, most important, cost. Although the computer had previously been considered a device for large companies, the price tag was now such that smaller firms could afford them. I do not mean to imply that they needed them in all cases. Not only did the transistor offer faster circuits and therefore more processing power, the architecture allowed the overlapping of the relatively slow input and output devices by a technique of "buffering" thus providing significantly increased throughput.

Reliability aids were improved with test and diagnostic routines enhanced to test more areas of potential hardware weaknesses. Larger sites had on-site maintenance, carrying forward the concept of brute force from the first generation. While the internal software monitors were not enough advanced at this stage to call them operating systems, they could accomplish several functions at a time; thus the monitor could be processing a payroll while printing invoices or reading transaction cards for later input into another application. The assembly language of the first generation had given way to COBOL (*C*ommon *B*usiness *O*riented *L*anguage) as well as FORTRAN (*For*mula *Tran*slation) for mathematical programming.

The predominant application type was still administrative, but there were increasing examples of such mainstream applications as production scheduling or inventory control. Application packages, preprogrammed routines, developed by the computer

212

manufacturer, were first introduced on a broad scale in this period.

The user environment found management enamored by these new devices and anxious to install and experiment; they were important as status symbols. Cost effectiveness was a secondary concern during this time frame. Organizationally the computer resided in the controller's department; he was the one who established application priorities.

**Age of
Proliferation**

During the proliferation period companies really got on the bandwagon and began installing computers wherever there seemed even a remote requirement. The technology during the time span of 1964–1970 was the integrated circuit, which continued the more power per dollar trend that the transistor had introduced. This was the era of the family concept in architecture. Machines were designed that had little brothers and big sisters such that a company could start small and upgrade to the next higher model. In addition, a company could have smaller satellite computers in division plants and offices that were compatible with the larger central computer at the corporate headquarters.

During the Age of Proliferation nationwide field engineering groups provided service in remote as well as major cities. Techniques were developed that monitored performance and recorded failures. These self-logging devices were significant aids to systems performance and preventive maintenance.

Operating systems came into their own during this period; this facilitated multiprogramming. Communication processing grew and most medium and large companies had at least several terminals that transmitted data back and forth from remote sites. Mainstream applications accounted for about as much computing time as administrative applications and some companies were beginning to integrate the mainstream and administrative functions to form the beginnings of MIS, though the design of this new approach was in the hands of the EDP personnel, or "technocrats." Management was just beginning to awake to the potential of the computer, but not to the extent where they took leadership and became heavily involved in MIS development. The advent of the operating system made computer operations much more complex than they had been under the simpler monitors and supervisors. Simplicity and ease of operation were unrealized objectives with manufacturers, and the job of understanding, evaluating, selecting, and implementing these systems was the bailiwick of the "technocrat." This period was accompanied by a proliferation of devices, particularly in the terminal and communications areas. Technical skill was a requirement if only to read and understand the literature and to analyze the claims of vendors for their newly developed products, most of which were still on the drawing board.

The overriding mood during this period was one of optimism and enthusiasm, and computers, it seemed, could solve most any paperwork problem. Indeed, every company had to have a computer; it was the Age of Proliferation.

Renaissance   Communications, networking, and the integrated data base are the cornerstones of the Renaissance era, 1971–1979, the period in which the real potential of information systems begins to be unleashed. Medium- and large-scale integration, which provide more electronic elements per square inch than the integrated circuit of the previous generation, are the principal technologies along with metallic oxide semiconductor (MOS) memory, which replaced conventional core memory. The architecture is built around firmware, which affords the ability to subdivide functions into small modular processors each specialized for a particular job. Also the concept of the virtual system, as already described, is a feature of fourth-era architecture.

The requirements for high-uptime systems dictated the use of on-line diagnostics as maintenance aids—no longer could a system be down because a field engineer had to diagnose an error or a potential error. Test and diagnostic routines become a part of the operating system, where they are called into operation routinely and without shutting down the entire system. This period also saw the extension of self-logging and self-diagnostic routines whereby potential failures can be spotted and fixed before they occur.

The software is still built around the sophisticated and complex interactive operating system, which has now been structured to handle the growing load of communication, interactive, and associated applications. The concept of management information systems comes on strong during this period and begins to have an impact on middle management. Applications are built around an integrated data base. Inquiry languages allow access to pertinent data files by both EDP and non-EDP types, the language being constructed in such a way that the users can deal directly with the system without the need to go through intermediaries. Enlightened business awareness of data processing and a sense of cost-benefit consciousness characterize this time frame.

Golden Age

This era, beginning in 1980, is in reality an evolutionary step from the fourth era. While there are and will be technological breakthroughs in basic computer circuitry, the major gains will come more from architecture, software, and application. The economies of scale and the continuing of large-scale integration should permit central processing power to show a significant performance-cost increase, consistent with past generations. Magnetic bubble mass storage will be a significant breakthrough as the data-base approach continues to mature. Architecture will take advantage of the micro and mini processor to surround the central processor itself, comprised of multi-minis with small, powerful subprocessors, specialized to do specific functions quickly, efficiently, and cost effectively.

Graceful degradation of the type described as part of the MULTICS system in Chapter 8 will be a major reliability mode. Software will feature extensions of inquiry and data-base-oriented languages, making it even easier for non-EDP personnel to communicate with the integrated data base. Applications will feature transaction processing and communications while more companies will be exchanging data and developing industry-wide methods of computer interfaces. Finally information systems will have as significant an impact on top, or strategic, management levels as they have on administrative and middle management levels today. In some companies managers will communicate with the computer much as they now use the telephone.

We now take a closer look at the environmental development rings of the fifth era. As can be seen, many of the developments had their genesis in the fourth era and some even in the third. This is not surprising, for as computer vendors and users alike have developed a greater sense of business perspective toward this rapidly changing technology, it has become obvious that evolutionary growth without traumatic transition and conversion between generations of equipment is an important criterion. Figure 9-4 indicates the key areas of development during the fifth era.

```
Technology                      Software

. VLSI                          . Efficient multirunning
                                . Design modularity/simplicity
. Bubble domain                   (ease of use)
  mass storage                  . Enhanced data base
                                  management
. Point of sale optics          . Management inquiry languages
  (OCR and laser readers)       . Conversion/expansion
                                  emphasis
. Voice input/output

. Flat screen display
  technology & color
  graphics                      Application

. Data transmission
  enhancements                  . Management information
                                  systems
                                . Mainstream functions
                                . Distributed data processing
                                . Transaction processing
Architecture                    . Decision support systems
                                . Office automation
. Virtual machine               . Home computers
  extensions

. Mini/microprocessor

. Distributed data processing

. Firmware extensions

. Data orientation/security     User impact


                                . Results orientation
                                . Aid in decision making
Reliability                     . Integration/unification
                                . Reduced application
. Fault logging                   gestation
                                . Information as a resource
. Self diagnosis                . Cost/performance

. Online testing

. Graceful degradation

. Replace in lieu of repair


                                Society

                                . Increased regulation
                                . Security/privacy issue
                                . Rise of the knowledge worker
                                . Socially useful as a criterion
```

FIGURE 9-4
Fifth Era Environmental Development

TECHNOLOGY

As previously stated, greater densities of electronic elements will be utilized on silicon chips; mass production techniques will make these chips extremely inexpensive and therefore their use will spread as processors, input/output controllers, memory, and firmware. Bubble domain mass storage, which can store billions and even trillions of information bits for massive data base systems, will shortly be on the scene. This bubble memory, smaller, more reliable, and eventually less costly than disk memory facilitates the storage of data in binary form on tiny

216

magnetic domains in semiconductorlike chips. Optical disks, with extremely high density as a result of laser beam technology, will also become a mass storage medium.

The grocery front-end checkout counter utilizes a laser reader to interpret the bars of the universal product code that was developed by the food industry. Optical readers are being used in retailing and banking operations. These optical/laser readers will cause a proliferation in point-of-sale devices. Associated with this trend is the development of the electronic funds transfer system made possible by the use of a money card or credit card that can be optically read.

In conjunction with the foregoing, the punched card has slowly been replaced as the principal computer input medium by direct on-line data entry. Keyboards or transaction terminals will transmit data directly to the computer, which will react immediately to verify the input and affect the particular transaction in real time. Voice synthesis will be used both for input and output in such a way that verbal commands can be recognized by the system, and synthesized voice messages will emanate from the system.

On the output side, flat or plasma screens will begin to replace cathode ray tubes as the principal output device. Plasma screens improve registration and allow graphic and pictorial matter to be displayed; for example, executives will be able to see product or profit movement projected graphically over a five-year long-range plan period based on alternative assumptions. Design graphics will also be available with the use of color increasing in both design and business graphics.

The cost of communicating digital data will fall as volume picks up and such private companies as Satellite Business Systems and Microwave Communications, Inc., enter the picture. Satellite and packet switching will make data communications more efficient and will support the increasing growth of networking systems. Packet switching technology is developing as a result of the need for rapid response time, high reliability, low error rate, dynamic allocation of capacity, and the ability to change in relation to traffic volume. Packet switching breaks down messages into packets, which are then sent over communication lines. Fiber optics, utilizing optical or glass fibers produced from silicon and upon which light beams (light-emitting diodes or lasers) can travel simultaneously in both directions, will begin to replace copper both in telephone lines and coaxial cable.

ARCHITECTURE

The virtual-machine concept of the fourth era is still in its infancy and will mature in the fifth era. The objective of a networking system is to have each user interact with the computer system as if he or she were the only one using it—and this remains so despite the number of users. In order to do this in an economical manner, the virtual machine will have to load and unload programs rapidly from fast "backing storage" and be able to access hierarchical storage devices in a microsecond time frame.

As mentioned, the mini and micro processor will be utilized for specific functions. The mode of architecture will follow a divide-and-conquer objective; that is, in order to make operational the growing complexity and variety of functions that must be performed by fifth-generation computers, the concept of sub-processors, each performing a specified portion of the task, will emerge. By dividing up the job and delegating it to mini or micro processors, the complexity is overcome and viable networking systems become possible. This is really the basic premise of distributed data processing (described in Chapter 8), where functions are delegated to remote units based on usage patterns and on overall economy.

The firmware-oriented machine is a cost-effective, flexible way to build machines. It affords the opportunity of suboptimization of languages (for example, ALGOL, COBOL, FORTRAN, PLI), operating systems (for example, pushdown stacks, table handling, and priority queuing—all essential for effective multirunning systems), emulation of other machines, and the possibility of application packages or at least some portion of them. However, a prerequisite is that the process to be incorporated within the firmware (usually etched chips) be well enough known so that it is not subject to frequent change. Firmware lies somewhere between software and hardware; it is not as flexible and easy to change as software, but it is not hardwired or as permanent as hardware. Figure 9-5 indicates how increasingly complex functions can be performed by firmware from the microfunction level to the application package level. However, the accomplishment of an application such as a payroll would not appear to meet the criterion of infrequent change, thus application firmware may prove illusive even in the fifth computer era.

Figure 9-6 illustrates the fifth-generation architecture that separates data from instruction through the use of an intermediate "data descriptor." This type of architecture facilitates the

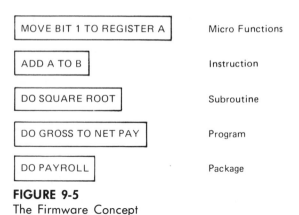

MOVE BIT 1 TO REGISTER A	Micro Functions
ADD A TO B	Instruction
DO SQUARE ROOT	Subroutine
DO GROSS TO NET PAY	Program
DO PAYROLL	Package

FIGURE 9-5
The Firmware Concept

application of the virtual-machine concept to data and increases data security by applying a ring number or security code to each piece of data.

RELIABILITY

It has become increasingly expensive from a maintenance standpoint to keep communications-oriented systems operable, particularly since many require twenty-four-hour-per-day uptime. Because maintenance is a labor-intensive activity, the cost has risen with the rise in wage rates and has not followed the downward curve of electronic circuits, where mass production techniques have reduced labor requirements dramatically. The key to fifth-generation reliability is ensuring high uptime through the use of fault logging, self-diagnosis, and the use of on-line test and diagnostics while controlling costs. T&Ds will become integral parts of the operating system, periodically being called upon to test the entire system automatically, check logs and counters, and print out or display instructions if manual intervention is required or fix the problem automatically if it is under machine control. The test routines will cover central processors, peripherals, and terminals, as well as the communication lines themselves. Thus the entire computer network will undergo periodic and regular on-line testing.

In order to control costs, the repair of packages and circuits will give way to replacement. Packages, boards, and circuits could be so inexpensive that it could be more economical to replace a circuit rather than expend the labor to repair it; furthermore these packages would be replaced on a scheduled basis

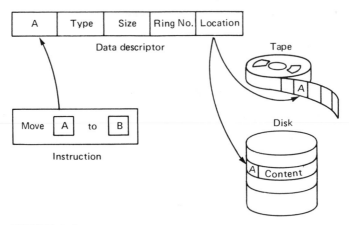

FIGURE 9-6
Data Orientation

as with light bulbs, often in the coactive mode, where the user would do the replacing based on simple cookbook-style instructions rather than calling in a maintenance engineer.

The concept of graceful degradation, or fail-soft capability, will become an important attribute of future transaction-oriented systems. This concept means that if a machine failure occurs, there is backup circuitry that can keep the system operational. In certain cases, cost factors will make it more practical to switch off the failing circuit and simulate it via other circuits while the failure is repaired. The point is that even though there is a system malfunction, the redundant, or simulated, circuit takes over until the failed unit is fixed or replaced. The system may be slowed for a period of time, but it continues to operate and the system degradation is usually not noticed by the users. This is the meaning of a soft failure.

SOFTWARE

Multirunning, a combination of multiprogramming and multiprocessing, will continue to become more efficient. Operating systems often have more impact on throughput rates and turn around time than the internal speed of the circuitry. Operating systems will be designed more flexibly and simply, utilizing the mini and micro processor and firmware architecture concepts. By dividing up the functions while embedding many in firmware, efficiency will be greatly improved.

The data base systems of the fourth era will be further enhanced to produce the highly interactive data files required of distributed data processing. They will utilize virtual-machine concepts and hierarchical file structures to economically store huge data files required by the growing number of data base users. The concept of shared files, which are integrated for use locally or in concert with a host system, will be a feature of this generation of data bases.

When one talks future data base systems, the key new concept is relational. The relational data base takes its name from the mathematical theory of relations. Simply stated, it is a way of arranging files that separates the user view of data (the language he or she uses to access data) from the physical representation of data such that one can be changed without altering the other. The goals of relational data base are to construct the files so that the user sublanguage that is employed is easy to learn, has the ability to readily expand or alter files, and allows the flexibility to access data in formats that were not anticipated at file development time, either in batch or spontaneous mode.

An important phrase heard more and more in the data-processing industry is *ease of use*. With the widening circle of computer use as a result of distributed data processing, both EDP and non-EDP users demand a straightforward simplicity of operation. As someone has said, computer systems must become friendly, tranquil, and forgiving. Terminals must be operated by nondedicated users using simple menu selection and screen tutorial instruction. The user must be able to recover from seemingly out-of-control conditions with the press of a specified function key. Systems must be human-engineered; they should work for people and not the other way around.

Inquiry languages have been of the structured variety, which may be efficient for dedicated administrative users who have learned the structured language but which are not useful for casual management users who desire system access. The advent of natural language inquiry which, in the case of a U.S. installation, is the English language, will facilitate a much broader system use. Natural language allows nonexpert end users to access the company's data base in a language that is completely natural, free of form, without regard to syntax, grammar, or spelling.

Finally, more attention will be given to protecting the user's investment in software, which far outweighs his investment in hardware. Vendors will become more conscious of compatibility and the ability to grow and upgrade without traumatic conversions involving serious interruptions in computer operations. Standardization of data formats and common languages will play a big part in this evolution.

One last comment on software is the need to develop better testing and quality methods. It is my opinion that software quality has seriously lagged behind the improvements in hardware. The fifth generation should see the development of improved quality and testing tools not only to accelerate the development cycle but to improve the final product.

APPLICATION

The object of the book is to focus on management and it is a thesis that the fourth era only tapped the surface of management information systems (MIS). The fifth era will see the extended use of MIS. The distributed-data-processing concept will expand and will develop around a transaction-driven system, where events that trigger paperwork activity and supervisory actions will be processed as they occur. This will be coupled with new point-of-sale or point-of-transaction devices. In many cases the closed-loop type of operation employed in process-control operations will be applied to business information systems.

One emerging and quite important new application area will be the use of decision support systems, described in Chapter 6 and just now coming into use on a broad scale. Managers will be able to activate simulation models that have access to relevant portions of the data base to aid them in decision making. It will be an interactive, trial-and-error type of activity, where the manager can experiment and see projected results of alternate action plans. This single application area may produce more benefits to a company than the sum of the other computer applications combined.

A major application growth area in the 1980s will be office automation. Studies show that capital investment per white collar or office worker has not changed much over the past decade from the current $5,000, whereas capital investment per blue collar or factory worker is in excess of $20,000. A major increase in computer use in offices is forecast for this period. Most medium-to-large companies are establishing office of the future departments, and those concepts will trickle down to the offices of smaller companies as well. Figure 9-7 indicates a confluence of word processing, business data processing, plus other office

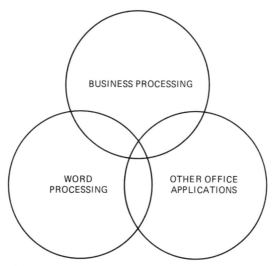

FIGURE 9-7
Office Automation

applications. The word processor or smart typewriter is the cornerstone of office automation. Information keyed into electronic media can be easily edited, stored, indexed, and accessed for later use. Adjuncts are electronic mail where, based on distribution indices, data can be automatically dispersed throughout a building or around the world. Also links to intelligent copiers can produce large-volume manuals or periodicals. Once installed, the computer used initially for word-processing application can be upgraded to include management calendar-time scheduling, project control, information retrieval, and other business-related functions. A. D. Little states, "We think that the shipment of office information systems, taken as an aggregate, will be as large in 1982 as all computer shipments were in 1977, which is to say that a business that is now at about six or seven billion dollars a year, most of it in photocopy equipment, will become a business of $15 billion a year in 1970 dollars by 1985."

Another area of computer growth will be in the home, though it will be a while for this to really take off. The harbingers of the home computer are the TV games and the growing amount of microprocessor intelligence in such appliances as the microwave oven and the thermostat. A service that started in England under the name of VIEWDATA allows subscribers to receive selected information and to make travel arrangements, restaurant reservations, and the like all via the home television screen. Home computers will expand from their current hobby use by engineers and professionals to their use in controlling environment and home security, and in providing interactive entertainment and educational modules via the video screen.

USER IMPACT

This area summarizes the type of requirements that have been continually stressed throughout the book; I feel it is the type of thinking that will direct the fifth era of data processing. Management wants information systems that produce results rather than promises, and they want the system to aid them in the real money-making areas of a business—strategic decision making. Business operation relies on integration and unification of activities to optimize decisions across the functional areas, the type of result produced by efficient MIS and data base systems.

Users want to see applications developed quicker with the gestation period, defined as the interval between application conception and successful implementation, cut down to reasonable limits. As mentioned, they want protection of their programming investment as they advance to the MIS and DDP stages. Users want the benefit of these advanced systems, but the systems must not be so complex and multifaceted that no one can understand, much less use, them.

A subtle, but important development is occurring in EDP management with the full recognition of information as a resource. The distinction between the computer and information is analogous to the distinction between the railroad business and the transportation business or the telephone business and the communications business. Focusing, in both cases, on the latter recognizes the scope and significance of the business. It puts things into proper perspective. The future EDP manager will become an information resource manager, having broad responsibility for maximizing the effectiveness of that most valuable business commodity—information.

Finally, cost-performance is still a major criterion for any business investment and particularly for EDP, which has withstood the normal ROI measurements for so many years. It can no longer be rationalized that computer technology and information systems are changing too fast to warrant strict cost justification; therefore cost-performance becomes a major criterion in the fifth era. Management wants the DDP transaction processing and the decision support systems, but these developments must pay their own way in a reasonable time frame.

SOCIAL CONSIDERATIONS

As national attention is drawn to the sociological and psychological implications of technological events these days, it seems appropriate to conclude with a discussion of this area. Sometimes these considerations are taken for granted, but both the computer professional and the non-EDP person who works with computers are remiss if they neglect this area, particularly when many of society's ills are blamed on automation. Sociological factors are pertinent to the broad spectrum of computerization. As in any area of automation, I believe that these factors should be heeded.

While societal issues were not that significant in the early decades, their role may prove in this decade to be the most vital of all the environmental rings. The first major impact is that of governmental regulation. EDP has become so all-pervasive that it is a direct target for government surveillance. First, a single company, IBM, has held a 60-percent-plus share of the computer market almost since its inception, and a government suit against the company has gone on for the past ten years with still no major resolution. It is an example of government involvement if not intrusion. The government has instituted commissions to investigate computer applications with broad citizen impact, such as electronic funds transfer and the use of the Universal Product Code in grocery stores. Probably the most significant area is in communications. Communications has been a regulated industry, dominated by AT&T, but recent decisions of the Federal Communication Commission have allowed independent companies to provide microwave and satellite communication services. The most recent decision allows AT&T to enter the data-processing market through an arms-length subsidiary and on a nontariff basis (in other words, the prices will be competitively determined). It proposes that U.S. business and residence telephone subscribers will purchase or lease all voice (telephone) and data terminal equipment located on their premises. The proposal has major impact on the availability and costs of communication and terminal equipment. Not only the business office but the individual who uses a telephone is affected as well.

Individuals have feared the intrusion of the computer, in the guise of huge corporate and government data bases, creating a Big Brother type of society. The Privacy Act of 1974 provides specific safeguards for the individual by requiring federal agencies to permit an individual to examine his record, question and

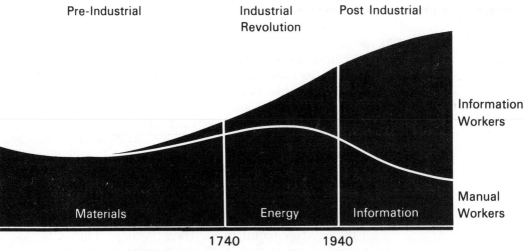

FIGURE 9-8
Technology and the Industrial Revolution

contest specific data, and to ensure that the data are current and accurate for their intended use. Federal agencies are subject to damages if an individual's rights are violated.

In very general terms the Industrial Revolution has had pre and post phases. The preindustrial phase was characterized by humanity's mastery over material (stone, iron, bronze, and so on). The Industrial Revolution itself is tied to the invention of the steam engine around 1740 and is characterized by humanity's mastery over energy (steam power, then coal, electricity, the jet engine, and so on). Peter Drucker, an authority on management and technology has coined the word *knowledge worker* and states, "The substitution of knowledge for manual effort as a productive resource in work is the greatest change in the history of work." He points out that in 1900 eighteen out of twenty workers were manual workers, whereas by 1965 five out of twenty of a vastly increased work force did manual labor, and this trend continues. Figure 9-8 points this out with the post-industrial phase, centered on humanity's growing mastery over information, tied to the development of the computer around 1940.

In the information era it behooves us to avoid the Luddite syndrome. The Luddites were an organized band of English rioters who campaigned against and destroyed labor-saving equipment in the early 1800s as a protest against lost jobs and the poor quality of work produced by the machinery. Their leader was called Captain Ludd, and the aftermath of this activity was a series of shootings and hangings and then strict legislative control before the movement finally came to an end. Today the term *Luddites* is used to refer to an individual or group who are against automation or the use of machinery to replace people or even to augment individual effort.

Modern-day Luddites and Captain Ludds are prevalent in the computer age. The original Luddites attacked the initial products of the first phase of the Industrial Revolution, namely textile machines; modern-day Luddites find computers and the information systems they power targets for their twentieth-century fear and anxiety. Today's Luddites do not use physical means (though there are still intermittent instances of computer destruction) but rather more subtle methods, geared to the information era. One government worker programmed a condition in a computer program that would occur exactly sixty days after he retired. The data would trigger the execution of a program subroutine that would destroy the department's program file and central data base. In this case, a backup file system prevented this hoax from becoming a complete disaster.

Other businesspeople, including some high-level executives, secretly resent the intrusion of computers into their business sphere, changing the way they perform their functions and causing them to learn complicated new procedures whose effectiveness they question in the first place. The mode of battle here is often to avoid involvement altogether or to subtly withhold key information parameters that are vital to successful system operation.

It is obvious that we should be as interested in what computers can do for us as what they can do to us. The answer is not resistence, recalcitrance, and sabotage. Everyone is aware of what technology brings to a society—in transportation, communication, medicine, industry, education—yet there is urban blight, traffic jams, pollution, radiation, crime, juvenile delinquency, schizophrenia, depression, and loneliness. As Peter Drucker says, "The only positive alternative to destruction by technology is to make technology work as our servant. In the final analysis this surely means mastery by man over himself, for if anyone is to blame, it is not the tool, but the human maker and user. 'It is a poor carpenter who blames his tools' says an old proverb."

The feasibility of computer applications was discussed in Chapter 8 under the headings of economic, technological, and operational feasibility. These three categories consider whether an application is profitable, whether it can be accomplished, and whether it can be effectively installed. An additional feasibility consideration might be whether it is socially useful or acceptable.

A statement on a personal résumé I received several years ago indicated that the individual's objective was to pursue a challenging, rewarding, and socially acceptable job in the computer industry. As businesspeople, we expect an individual to be interested in challenging and rewarding work; we are a little surprised to see socially acceptable in a résumé. It raises a valid question, one that we should all give more thought to.

There is a social difference between using computers in the aerospace industry and in the medical industry. We have learned the system and calculations for sending men into space, but we have not developed the calculations for diagnosing and curing illness. There are obvious reasons why it is easier to use computers in aerospace than in medicine; however, there is an imbalance in the amount of money devoted to each. There is more profit in developing computers for aerospace and for industry. It is reasonable to assume that profit was necessary when the companies were getting established. But the industry is maturing, and manufacturers and users should be expected to dedicate a greater portion of their resources to the more socially oriented industries even if the profit is less assured.

I would like to add a word as to where I think the application emphasis should be in such industries as medicine. I believe that there are things that people can do better (and probably always will) and things that machines can do better. The EDP industry has wasted a good deal of money trying to tackle applications that were not technologically or operationally feasible. A computer can aid the medical profession in recordkeeping and in the business end of operations; hopefully, it can help reduce the spiraling medical costs. It can aid in scheduling scarce facilities and in assisting nurses and doctors in the administrative aspects of their jobs. The computer can maintain historical information about patients and act as an extension of the doctor's recall system to uncover similar cases. It can maintain an index and retrieval system for medical articles, books, and journals. The computer can aid in the initial testing and screening of patients who are either ill or are undergoing routine checkups. I do not think the computer can accomplish surgery or develop the final diagnosis for a patient with neurological disease. I do not think a computer can replace a doctor or the major part of his job, which requires judgment, wisdom, experience, compassion, and manual dexterity.

Electrocardiograms by computer is a case where a computer is capable of measuring, calculating, and analyzing medical data quicker, more accurately, and perhaps more economically than a doctor. It is an area that deserves attention and investment. It is an area where the computer can be superior to people. This is the way the system, as developed by the TELEMED Corporation, works.

A mobile electrocardiograph unit is installed at the location (hospital, clinic, nursing home, doctor's office, and so on) where the ECG is to be taken. While the signals from the ECG machine are being used to drive a conventional chart recorder, they are also used to frequency-modulate carrier signals that are in turn transmitted to the computer center over normal voice-grade telephone lines. Telephone lines transmit ECGs to the computer with no clinical distortion, and noise in the lines can be readily filtered out.

At the computer center, the analog telephone signal is converted back into its original analog form, then converted into digital form and entered into the computer system for analysis. The computer will then perform an analysis that will: (1) measure all pertinent ECG amplitudes and duration; (2) characterize the wave forms from each of the twelve leads of the scalar electrocardiogram; (3) calculate such factors as rate and electrical axis; and (4) produce an interpretation of the status of the electrical function of the heart based upon these parameters. The resultant interpretation is then teletyped back to the location at which the ECG has been taken, in digital matrix format with a summary set of correspondent interpretive statements.

Extending this type of computer application to other types of diagnostic tests is a sound and feasible social usage of technology. It promises major advances in preventive medicine.

I remember reading an article that, in my opinion, illustrates the potential misuse of computer resources and is a classical case of working on the wrong problem. The article talks about surgery in the year 2001. I would like to think the article was science fiction, but I believe that the intent was serious. It describes a patient who receives a kidney transplant from the robot doctor using laser beams after his problem had been diagnosed and the size of the artificial kidney calculated by determining his weight and body volume, the latter by a system of photosensing devices. The computer calculated the patient's survival chances without the operation, versus his chances while undergoing the operation, versus his survival chances as a result of having had the operation, and then mathematically selected the best statistical course of action. The patient leaves the hospital with a new kidney five minutes after he enters.

I think investment of computer resources for computerized operations or for full computerized diagnosis is rather absurd. Although both the electrocardiogram application and operation by computer are socially useful, we must use intelligence and our knowledge of machines to direct their use to those applications that are technologically, operationally, and economically feasible. I intended that "socially useful" be a fourth feasibility consideration and not be used *in lieu of* the other three—in other words, that computer applications be directed to areas in which all four criteria are considered.

WAY-OUT THINKING

Referring back to Chapter 1, we might project the lives of each of our computer protagonists (or antagonists) into the world of 2001.

The turn-of-the-century Sam Curtis has reviewed his data-processing needs with several vendors and has selected the Alpha system. Sam's manufacturing business had reached a stage where paperwork was beginning to pile up and he knew a computer system was required. The Alpha system features a customized turnkey system that requires no programming or systems personnel on the part of the user. Sam and his controller indicated their particular application requirements and via a menulike selection process the relevant application chips were plugged into the processing unit and the system customized for Curtis's unique requirements. The chips are chosen from a program library and can be exchanged or updated as conditions dictate. This feature is important to Sam as he anticipates growth from inside and also from acquisition. The application chips provide economical processing power that is optimized for Curtis's particular method of operation—thus the software is bent to serve the user and not the other way around. The application chips offset the increasing people and programming cost that has paralleled the inflationary economy since 1980. The Alpha system is customer-installable and comes equipped with self-diagnosis and maintenance routines such that the average machine failure is once per year. Sam is looking forward to the installation of his first computer system.

When the investment counsellor, Carole Harrison, enters her office one morning in the year 2001, her duty for the day is to review the customer portfolios assigned to her and the stocks under her surveillance. The portfolios of her clients are under continual computer control. The stocks were selected based on the individual investment profile, income status dependencies, future objectives, and the like. Each day the closing prices of the various stock exchanges are screened against the updated customer profiles. When change points are hit, automatic buy and sell orders are issued to maintain the desired profile of the portfolio. Harrison has access to a computerized econometric input-output model of U.S. business. The model immediately reflects the various investment factors, such as new housing starts and inventory positions. The model projects the impact of these elements on current and future stock market prices and investment decisions. In addition, Harrison can obtain a projection of future economic patterns based on her own judgment of what she thinks is likely to occur. The model can simulate the complicated interaction of many variables and can print out the results in a matter of seconds on Harrison's office terminal.

The twenty-first-century Dr. Lloyd Carson is able to spend far more time in medical research and in enjoying his family because of the patient monitoring system installed at his hospital. (In addition, his squash game has improved with added practice.) Every patient is continuously monitored for thirty different biological functions, from temperature and blood pressure to brain wave patterns and metabolic balance. Between visits a two-way video screen enables Dr. Carson to communicate with his patients. After reviewing the monitors, he then indicates the various medication and tests for each patient via a special terminal. To request a test or medication he need only point with a light pen to the name of the requested test or prescription. Dr. Carson's orders are transmitted immediately to the on-line terminal in the lab or clinic where they are queued by priority and then carried out. Patient records are automatically updated when the drugs are dispensed. Diagnostic tests also are conducted via an on-line telemonitoring system that projects the most likely diagnoses along with the statistical odds of each possible diagnosis based on case histories. The computer can suggest courses of treatment and project the duration of the illness.

It is 8:00 A.M., April 6, 2001, and Harris P. Updike enters the executive offices of the Blocker Electronic Company. He quickly summons management information specialist Calvin Sharpe, Jr., to his office. Updike asks Sharpe to review the last night's operations. Sharpe picks up the electronic stylus and writes an instruction on the screen of the terminal in the corner. Through an on-line hookup to a remote computer the screen indicates in three columns the scheduled production, the actual production, and the reasons for the variances. The screen also displays standard costs and actual costs, by item and by department. Updike then asks Sharpe for a report of yesterday's sales activities. A touch of the electronic stylus lights up sales by item, variance from plan, and reasons for the variances. Updike now wants to look at the financial situation. Another movement of the stylus indicates the company's cash position as of that morning. By 8:20 A.M. Updike has dictated orders to his production and sales management people, as well as to the treasurer and controller. He tells Sharpe to return at 10:00 A.M., and they will review the early morning activities and take any necessary action. He also indicates that Sharpe should input the latest results as well as the current GNP economic indicators into the integrated company model to see if any long-range action is necessary.

Helen Swindell looks at the calendar and sees that today is May 26, 2001. Helen is an early riser and often sits down at the family computer control center with her first cup of coffee to get chores out of the way before the rest of her family stirs. The kitchen is already comfortable because the house temperature has been programmed to respond automatically to the outside environment. First she asks the computer to list the notes and reminders for today on the display screen. (The family uses the computer as a message board.) Helen finds a note she left herself that she needs to buy a few clothing items for her daughter. Helen decides to order them via the terminal, since she has a business luncheon in conjunction with her job at the bank. Monday is grocery day, so Helen asks for a price update and then checks off the items she wants. Pressing a transmit button delivers the order to a terminal at a local supermarket. Because of the home computer control center, it is no longer necessary for one member of a family to devote full time to running the household. The Swindells are living in what was called the "cashless society" back in the 1980s. For every purchase made, whether at home or in a store, Mrs. Swindell inserts an ID card and her index finger into a special identifier unit. Her social security number and fingerprint provide the necessary identification. The computer checks her credit status and automatically debits or credits her bank account.

A FINAL WORD

The computer trends discussed in this chapter may or may not lead to the vignettes just described. In the long run, I feel the future role of computers will be dictated by the interplay of four feasibility criteria. The first three criteria (technological, economic, and operational) were mentioned before. A fourth (social) was added in this chapter.

All four criteria must be met for a computer system to be a positive factor in our society. The industry has made great technological strides, and there appears to be little reason to doubt that from a technical viewpoint, most of our data-processing requirements can be met. We must analyze the economics of each situation to see if the resulting benefits offset the added costs and produce a satisfactory return on investment. Operational aspects involve the ability to install the system successfully in the existing environment. A system that is technically and economically sound may fail because the human factors have not been reflected in systems design or implementation.

More and more, the social worth of something is increasing in significance. The social consequences of data processing and computers can rule out otherwise feasible applications. For example, there is a fear that using a single identification code (such as a social security number) will enable or encourage the government to hold all data about citizens within a massive central data base. This could result in invasions of privacy and in situations where a minor criminal offense could remain a lifetime part of an individual's file to limit freedom and opportunity severely. Proper administration of the Privacy Act described in this chapter could alleviate this fear.

It is my belief that use of the four feasibility criteria discussed earlier will determine whether the 2001 worlds of Sam Curtis, Carole Harrison, Lloyd Carson, Calvin Sharpe, and Helen Swindell resemble the world of our children and grandchildren. When one criterion is ignored, growth is malformed and unhealthy. It takes consideration of all four to produce sound progress.

Having referred to Alvin Toffler's book *Future Shock* in

Chapter 1, it is appropriate to conclude with a reference to his latest book, *The Third Wave*. It is interesting that Toffler sees a significant shift in the forces of technology, for while in his prior book he saw a depersonalized, highly automated massified society, Toffler now talks about the power of the new technology to demassify. Interactive, personalized computer systems will provide increased options and alternatives in business, education, and our leisure pursuits. Individual preferences will be accommodated by the variety of entertainment, education, and business modules that we can select from a stored data base; further we can tailor these modules to our own taste and rate of learning by interactive dialogue with the system. Thus the third-wave humans, the twenty-first-century knowledge workers, can have more choice, extended flexibility, and greater freedom. On this positive note our story ends.

Bibliography

ANTHONY, ROBERT N., and JOHN DEARDEN. *Management Control Systems.* Homewood, Ill.: Richard D. Irwin, Inc., 1979.

ANTHONY, ROBERT N. *Planning and Control Systems: A Framework for Analysis.* Cambridge, Mass.: Harvard University, Graduate School of Business Administration, Division of Research, 1965.

BONELLI, ROBERT ALLEN. *Executive Handbook to Mini-Computers.* New York: McGraw-Hill Book Company, 1979.

BROOKS, F. P., JR. *The Mythical Man-Month: Essays on Software Engineering.* Reading, Mass.: Addison-Wesley Publishing Co., Inc., 1975.

CLARK, JON D., and ARNOLD REISMAN. *Computer System Selection.* New York: Praeger Publishers, Inc., 1980.

DERTOUZOS, MICHAEL L., and JOEL MOSES, eds. *The Computer Age: A Twenty Year View.* Cambridge, Mass.: The MIT Press, 1979.

DOLOTTA, T. A., and others. *Data Processing in 1980-1985.* New York: John Wiley and Sons, Inc., 1976.

DRUCKER, PETER F. *Technology, Management, and Society.* New York: Harper & Row, Publishers, Inc., 1970.

———. *Managing in Turbulent Times.* New York: Harper & Row, Publishers, Inc., 1980.

FRIED, I. *Practical Data Processing Management.* Englewood Cliffs, N.J.: Prentice-Hall, Inc., 1979.

FUORI, W. *Introduction to the Computer: The Tool of Business* (2nd ed.). Englewood Cliffs, N.J.: Prentice-Hall, Inc., 1977.

GOLDSTINE, HERMAN H. *The Computer from Pascal to Von Neumann.* Princeton, N.J.: Princeton University Press, 1972.

HOUSLEY, T. *Data Communications and Teleprocessing Systems.* Englewood Cliffs, N.J.: Prentice-Hall, Inc., 1979.

KANTER, J. *Management-Oriented Management Information Systems* (2nd ed.). Englewood Cliffs, N.J.: Prentice-Hall, Inc., 1977.

LAVER, MURRAY. *Computers and Social Change.* Cambridge: Cambridge University Press, 1980.

LECHT, CHARLES P. *The Waves of Change.* New York: McGraw-Hill Book Company, 1979.

MACIARIELLO, JOSEPH. *Program Management Control Systems.* New York: John Wiley and Sons, Inc., 1978.

MARTIN, JAMES. *Computer Data Base Organization* (2nd ed.). Englewood Cliffs, N.J.: Prentice-Hall, Inc., 1977.

————. *Introduction to Teleprocessing.* Englewood Cliffs, N.J.: Prentice-Hall, Inc., 1972.

————. *The Wired Society.* Englewood Cliffs, N.J.: Prentice-Hall, Inc., 1978.

McLEAN, EPHRAIM R., and JOHN V. SODEN. *Strategic Planning for MIS.* New York: John Wiley and Sons, Inc., 1977.

MILLER, ARTHUR R. *The Assault on Privacy.* Ann Arbor, Mich.: The University of Michigan Press, 1971.

MORTON, SCOTT, and PETER KEEN. *Decision Support Systems.* Reading, Mass.: Addison-Wesley Publishing Co., Inc., 1978.

MURDICK, ROBERT G., and JOEL E. ROSS. *Introduction to Management Information Systems.* Englewood Cliffs, N.J.: Prentice-Hall, Inc., 1977.

MURDICK, ROBERT G. *Management Information Systems: Concepts and Designs.* Englewood Cliffs, N.J.: Prentice-Hall, Inc., 1980.

PETER, LAURENCE J., and RAYMOND HULL. *The Peter Principle.* New York: William Morrow & Co., Inc., 1969.

ROGERS, WILLIAM. *Think: A Biography of the Watsons and IBM.* New York: Stein & Day Publishers, 1969.

SANDERS, DONALD H., and STANLEY J. BIRKIN. *Computers and Management in a Changing Society* (2nd ed.). New York: McGraw-Hill Book Company, 1980.

STEWARD, DONALD V. *Systems Analysis and Management.* New York: McGraw-Hill Book Company, 1980.

TOFFLER, ALVIN. *Future Shock.* New York: Random House, Inc., 1970.

———. *The Third Wave.* New York: William Morrow & Co., Inc., 1980.

WEIZENBAUM, JOSEPH. *Computer Power and Human Reason.* San Francisco: W. H. Freeman & Company Publishers, 1976.

Index

ABACUS, 11-12
Accounting subsystem of management information system, 155, 158-59
Administrative applications, 23, 24, 128
Administrative management role, 82, 83-84
Addresses, 113-14
Advertising application, 132-33
Aetna Insurance, 179
Agricultural planning applications, 61-62
Aiken, Howard, 14
Air studies, 138
American Standard Code for Information Interchange (ASCII), 187
American Telephone & Telegraph Co., 102, 179, 186, 187, 225
Analysis phase, 78-80
Apple Computers, 95, 99
Applications (*see* Computer applications)
Application software, 125-26
Architecture:
  defined, 209-210
  1951-1958 period, 211
  1959-1963 period, 212
  1964-1970 period, 212, 213

1971-1979 period, 214
1980 period, 218-19
Arithmetic operations, 8-9
Assembly languages, 121, 212
Asynchronous transmission, 196
Automatic telegraphy, 178

BABBAGE, CHARLES, 12, 13
Bandwidth, 185-86
Banking applications, 30, 37-40, 168
  teleprocessing, 195-97
Banking terminals, 184
Batch processing, 25
Baudot five-level code, 187
Bell, Alexander Graham, 178
Bell Laboratories, 140, 190
Bell System, 187
Bender, William E., 122-25
Benefit/cost justification (*see* Cost/benefit justification)
Binary numbering system, 113
Boards, replacement of, 219-20
Boole, George, 14-15
Break-even analysis, 75
Brilliant terminal, 95, 183
Broadband Exchange Service, 187
Bubble memory, 216-17
Burroughs Corporation, 16, 17, 93

Business applications, 30, 34-37
Business data processing, 222-23

CARLSON, WALTER M., 41-42
Cathode ray tube (CRT) terminal, 95, 118, 120, 181-83
Central data base, 122, 164-66
Central processing unit, 8, 120
Chief financial officer, 84
CII-Honeywell Bull, 208
Circuits, replacement of, 219-20
Club of Rome, 60-61
COBOL (Common Business Oriented Language), 114-18, 121
Communication line, 185
Communications, 9-10, 14, 225
  case histories, 47-50
  types of, 176-80
  (*see also* Teleprocessing systems)
Communication satellites, 179
Compilation, 114
Compiler program, 114, 121
Computer-aided decision making (*see* Management science)
Computer-aided manufacturing, 100, 101
Computer applications, 22-64, 120, 121
  administrative, 23, 24, 128
  banking, 30, 37-40, 168, 195-97
  business services, 30, 34-37
  decision making (*see* Management information systems; Management science)
  defined, 210
  distribution, 31, 52-53
  education, 30, 44-46
  federal government, 30, 40-44, 169
  finance, 30, 37-40
  growth of: 1951-1958 period, 211; 1959-1963 period, 212-13; 1964-1970 period, 213; 1971-1979 period, 214-15; 1980 period, 222-24
  health care, 31, 55-57, 228-30
  information categories, 26-27
  insurance, 30, 46-48, 168-69
  inventory (*see* Inventory control)
  management attitudes and approach, 27-28
  manufacturing, 29-34
  miscellaneous, 59-63
  operational, 23-24, 128, 129

personnel services, 30, 34-37
printing and publishing, 31, 58-59
retail, 30, 57-58
selecting and implementing, 65-89: cost estimation, 69-73; feasibility criteria, 66-69; management guidelines, 84-87; management involvement, 81-84; phases of, 78-80; savings and benefits, 74-78
society considerations, 225-30
state and local government, 30, 50-52
strategic, 22-23, 24, 128, 129
transportation, 31, 53-55
types of, 22-24
use by industry, 28-31
utilities, 30, 48-50, 168
Computer decades, 16-20
Computer from Pascal to Von Neumann, The (Goldstine), 15
Computer professionals, 84-85
Computer retail stores, 99
Computers:
  applications (*see* Computer applications)
  communications (*see* Communications; Teleprocessing systems)
  decision making and (*see* Management information systems; Management science)
  future use of, 215-30
  growth of, 206-30: environmental development rings (*see* Environmental development rings); international manufacturers, 208
  hardware (*see* Hardware)
  history of, 11-20 (*see also* Environmental development rings)
  impact of, 1-5
  programming (*see* Programming)
  software (*see* Software)
  as systems, 7-9
  systems theory, 5-7
Computer service center case history, 35-36
Computer-Tabulating-Company (C-T-R), 13-14
Comsat, 179
Conditioning, 186
Control Data Corporation, 16, 93
Controller, 84
Cooperative computer system, 44-46

Cost/benefit justification, 65-89
  cost estimation, 69-73
  feasibility criteria, 66-69
  management guidelines, 84-87
  management involvement, 81-84
  phases of, 78-80
  savings and benefits, 74-78
Cost estimation, 69-73
Credit card applications, 6-7, 36-37
Criminology application, 60-62
Cybernetics, 15

DATA BASE MANAGEMENT SYSTEMS,
    122-25, 164-66, 169-70, 214, 221
Data descriptor, 218-19, 220
Data monitoring and control, 100, 101
Data-processing costs, 70
Decision making (see Management in-
    formation systems; Management
    science)
Decision support systems (DSS), 129,
    222
Defense, Department of, 41-42
Design graphics, 217
Device intelligence, 185
Dial-up (switched) network, 186-87
Difference engine, 12
Digital Equipment Corporation, 16,
    18, 92, 99
Disk storage devices, 110-11
Distributed data processing, 94, 95,
    100, 101, 193-200, 221
  concept of, 193-95
  examples of, 195-200
Distribution applications, 31, 52-53
Distribution channels:
  mainframes, 72
  minicomputers and microcompu-
    ters, 98-102
Dollar benefit estimation, 75-76
Drucker, Peter, 226, 227

ECKERT, J. P., 14
Eckert-Mauchly Computer Corpora-
    tion, 16
Economic feasibility, 200, 201
Economic order quantity calculation,
    142-43
Educational applications, 30, 44-46
Electrocardiograms by computer, 229
Electronic data processing (EDP), 7
Electronic mail, 223

ENIAC (Electronic Numerical Integra-
    tor and Automatic Calculator), 14
Environmental development rings:
  defined, 209-11
  1951-1958 period, 212
  1959-1963 period, 212-13
  1964-1970 period, 213-14
  1971-1979 period, 214-15
  1980 period, 215-30: applications,
    222-24; architecture, 218-19; re-
    liability, 219-20; society consid-
    erations, 225-30; software, 220-22;
    technology, 216-17; user impact,
    224
Exponential smoothing, 140
External information, 26, 27

FAIL-SOFT CAPABILITY, 220
Faraday, Michael, 177
Farber, David J., 200
Farm management applications, 61-62
Feasibility criteria, 66-69
  economic, 200, 201
  operational, 200-204
  society considerations, 225-30, 233
  technical, 200, 201
  in teleprocessing, 200-205
Feasibility study, 79-80
Federal Communications Commission
    (FCC), 186, 225
Federal government applications, 30,
    40-44, 169
Feedback control, 6-10
Fessenden, Reginald, 179
Fiber optics, 180, 217
File storage, 110-11
Financial applications, 30, 37-40
Firmware, 98, 218
Flat screens, 217
Flint, Charles R., 13
Flowcharts:
  programmer's logic, 111-14
  system, 109
Food distribution application, 52-53
Forecasting methods, 139-41
Forrester, Jay W., 60
Freestanding processing, 99, 101
Front-end processor (FEP), 187, 193,
    194
Fujitsu, 208
Full duplex mode, 186
Future Shock (Toffler), 11

GAMBLING APPLICATION, 61
General Electric Company, 16, 19, 93
General Telephone and Electronics
    Corporation, 102, 186, 187
Geometric organizational syndrome,
    165
Gleiser, Molly, 13
Global problems application, 60-61
Goldstine, Herman, 15
Graceful degradation, 220
Graphic terminal, 183

HALF DUPLEX MODE, 186
Handheld terminal, 185
Hardware, 120
    architecture (*see* Architecture)
    costs, 70, 71
    microcomputer, 97
    minicomputer, 93-94
    teleprocessing, 180-88
Harrison, Carole, 3-4
Harvard-IBM automatic sequence-con-
    trolled calculator (Mark I), 14
Health care applications, 31, 55-57,
    228-30
Hewlett Packard, 92
Hitachi, 208
Hollerith, Herman, 13
Home computers, 223-24
Honeywell, Inc., 16, 17, 93
Honeywell Information Systems, Inc.,
    190
Host computer, 187-88
Household applications, 62-63·
Hull, Raymond, 2

IBM CORPORATION, 16-17, 73, 93, 99, 121,
    179, 225
ICL, 208
Implementation modes, 24-26
Implementation phase, 79
Industrial Revolution, 226
Information categories, 26-27
Information security, 165-66
Input, 6-10
Input format documents, 109-10
Insurance applications, 30, 46-48,
    168-69
Intangible benefit, 74
Integrated data base, 214
Integrated information system, 151-52
    case history, 33-35

Integrated network, 189-90
Intelligent terminal, 95, 183
Interfaces, standard, 72-73
Internal information, 26
Internal users, defined, 210
International Data Corporation, 27,
    28, 70, 71, 72, 92, 175, 207
International manufacturers, 208
Intuition, 144-45
Inventory control:
    case history, 53
    programming, 107-18
    statistical, 139-43
    as subsystem in management infor-
        mation system, 156, 158
    teleprocessing, 175-76

JUSTIFICATION, 79, 80 (*see also* Cost/
    benefit justification)

KEMENY, JOHN G., 200
Knowledge worker, 226

LEASING, 72-73
Leibnitz, G. W., 12
Life-cycle costing, 69-70
Linear programming (LP), 132-33
Line printer, 120
Little, A. D., 223
Local government applications, 30,
    51-52
Loosely coupled network, 188-89
Lovelace, Ada, 12-13
LSI (large scale integration), 95-97
Luddite syndrome, 226-27

MAGNETIC DISK, 110-11
Mainframes:
    distribution channels, 72
    evolution of, 16-20, 91-92
Management attitudes and approach
    to computer applications, 27-28
Management checklist, 87, 88
Management guidelines, 84-87
Management information systems
    (MIS), 149-74, 213
    case histories, 33-35, 40-42
    characteristics of, 150-54
    defined, 149-50
    environment for development of,
        167-69
    growth of, 214-15, 222

implementation of: elements in, 162-66; management considerations in, 169-74
management science implementation, 145-47
model of, 154-62
payoffs of, 166-67
Management involvement, 81-84
Management science, 129-48
defined, 129-30
impact on decision making, 143-47
linear programming, 132-33
queuing theory, 133-35
simulation, 42-44, 73, 135-37, 222
statistical analysis, 137-43: environmental, 137-39; inventory control, 139-43
Management steering committee, 85-86
Manufacturing applications, 29-34
Marconi, Guglielmo, 179
Marketing subsystem of management information system, 159-60
Mark I, 14
Massachusetts Institute of Technology, 190
Mass marketing, 99
Materials control subsystem of management information system, 156-57
Mathematical processing, 8-9, 66-68, 122
Mauchly, John W., 14
Medical applications, 228-30
Memory, computer, 8, 9, 112-14, 118, 119, 214, 216-17
Metallic oxide semiconductor (MOS) memory, 214
Microcomputers, 19, 90-91
decision criteria, 103-5
defined, 97
development of, 94-95
distribution channels, 98-102
future, 218
growth of, 206-7
markets, 99-102
software, 97-98
Microwave Communications, Inc., 217
Microwaves, 179
Middle management role, 82, 83, 173
Mihalasky, John, 144-45
Minicomputers, 90-91

decision criteria, 103-5
defined, 97
development of, 18, 19, 92-96
distribution channels, 98-102
future, 218
growth of, 206-7
markets, 93, 99-102
software, 94, 97-98
Modem, 185
Monthly labor summary, 67
Morse, Samuel F. B., 177
Morse code, 177-78
Motorola Communications and Electronics, Inc., 95
Moving average, 139-40
MULTICS (Multiplexed Information and Control Service), 190-93
Multiplexor, 185
Multiplying machines, 12
Multiprogramming, 213
Multirunning, 220

NATIONAL AERONAUTICS AND SPACE ADMINISTRATION, 169
National Cash Register, 16, 17, 93
National Institute of Health, 169
National Semiconductor Corporation, 95
New London simulation facility, 42-44

OFFICE AUTOMATION APPLICATIONS, 222-23
Olivetti Company, 208
On-line processing, 25
case histories, 37-39, 47-48, 54-55, 58-59
Operating management role, 82, 83
Operating systems, 122-25, 213
Operational applications, 23-24, 128, 129
Operational feasibility, 200-204
Operations research (OR) (see Management science)
Optical disks, 217
Optical readers, 217
Optical terminals, 183-84
Order-processing, 67
as subsystem in management information system, 154-55
teleprocessing, 175-76
Output, 6-10
Output format documents, 109-10

PACKAGES, REPLACEMENT OF, 219-20
Packet switching technology, 217
Pascal, Blaise, 12
Payroll applications, 67
Peccei, Aurelio, 60, 61
Personnel costs, 70, 71
Personnel services applications, 30, 34-37
Peter, Lawrence J., 2
Peter Principle, The (Peter and Hull), 2
Phasing plan for management information systems, 172-74
Phillips Company, 208
Physical systems, relationship to information systems, 170-71
Plasma screens, 217
Point-of-sale devices, 184-85
Poison control center application, 56
Printing applications, 31, 58-59
Privacy Act of 1975, 225-26
Private (leased) network, 186-87
Processing, 6-9, 25-26
Product vendors, 100, 102
Programmer's logic flowchart, 111-14
Programming, 106-26
  case problem, 107-8
  computer operation, 118-20
  software (*see* Software)
  steps in, 108-18: computer compilation, 114; computer programming, 114-18; file storage, 110-11; input-output format documents, 109-10; programmer's logic flowchart, 111-14; program operation, 118; system description, 109; system flowchart, 109
Program operation, 118
Prudential Investment Company, 3-4
Public education applications, 50-51
Public health applications, 50-51, 137-39
Public Health Service, 137-39
Publishing applications, 31, 58-59
Purchase of computers, 72
  decision criteria, 103-5
Purchasing subsystem of management information system, 157-58

QUANTUM SCIENCES, 28-29
Queuing theory, 133-35

RADIO, 179

Radio Corporation of America (RCA), 16, 19, 93
Radiological diagnosis system, 56-57
Radiological studies, 138-39
Real-time processing case history, 36-37
Relational data base, 221
Reliability:
  defined, 210
  1951-1958 period, 211
  1959-1963 period, 212
  1964-1970 period, 213-14
  1971-1979 period, 214
  1980 period, 219-20
Remington Rand (the Sperry Corporation), 16
Rentals, 72-73
Repetitive transactions, 66-68
Retail applications, 30, 57-58
Return on investment analysis, 76-78
Rodgers, William, 13

SALES VOLUME, COMPUTER EXPENDITURES AND, 73
Satellite Business Systems (SBS), 179, 186, 217
Scientific processing, 67-68
Self-logging, 212, 213, 214
Sequential processing, 25
Service bureaus, 102
Services, costs of, 70, 72
Service vendors, 100, 102
Shared files, 221
Siemans Company, 208
Simplex mode, 186
Simulation, 42-44, 75, 135-37, 222
Small-business computers (*see* Microcomputers; Minicomputers)
Smoothing constant, 140
Society considerations, 210, 225-30
Software, 10-11, 120-26, 210
  application, 125-26
  assembly, 121, 212
  compiler, 114, 121
  defined, 120
  growth of, 207: 1951-1958 period, 211; 1959-1963 period, 212; 1964-1970 period, 213; 1971-1979 period, 214-15; 1980 period, 220-22
  microcomputer, 97-98
  minicomputer, 94, 97-98

operating system, 122-25
Source documents, 66-68
Sperry Rand Corporation, 17
State government applications, 30, 50-51
Statistical analysis, 137-43
  environmental, 137-39
  inventory control, 139-43
Stibitz, George, 14
Storage, 7
Stores control subsystem of management information system, 154-56
Strategic applications, 22-23, 24, 128, 129
Strategic planning, 67, 68
Strategic planning subsystem of management information system, 159, 160-61
Student scheduling, 67-68
Supplies, costs of, 70, 72
Synchronous transmission, 186
Synthesis phase, 78-80
System:
  computer as, 7-9
  defined, 5-6
System builders, 99
System description, 109
System flowchart, 109
Systems design, 79, 80
Systems study, 79, 80
Systems theory, 5-7

TABULATING MACHINE COMPANY, 13
Tandy Corporation, 95, 99
Tangible benefits, 74
Tax reports, 67
Technical feasibility, 200, 201
Technical management information systems, 169
Technology:
  defined, 209
  1951-1958 period, 211
  1959-1963 period, 212
  1964-1970 period, 212, 213
  1971-1979 period, 214
  1980 period, 216-17
Telegraphy, 177-78
TELEMED Corporation, 229
Telenet, 187
Telephone toll-rating system, 49-50
Telephony, 178-79
Teleprocessing systems, 175-205

distributed data processing, 94, 95, 100, 101, 193-200, 221: concept of, 193-95; examples of, 195-200
elements of, 180-81
feasibility criteria, 200-205
future, 217
history of, 213, 214
loosely coupled vs. integrated network, 188-90
MULTICS (Multiplexed Information and Control Service), 190-93
terminals, 181-88
types of long-range communication, 176-80
Television, 179
Terminals, teleprocessing, 181-88
Terminal subsystem, 183
Texas Instruments, 95
Think (Rodgers), 13
Third-party participants, 72-73, 94, 98-100
Third Wave, The (Toffler), 234
Toffler, Alvin, 11, 233-34
Top management role, 81-83, 84, 86-87
Toshiba, 208
Transaction input, 100, 101-2
Transaction-oriented approach, 184
Transaction processing, 25-26
Transactions, volume of, 66-68
Transaction terminals, 217
Transistor, 212
Transportation applications, 31, 53-55
Transportation subsystem of management information system, 156-57
Turnaround time, 67
TWX (Teletypewriter Exchange Service), 187
Tymnet, 102, 187, 191

UNIVAC I, 16
User impact:
  1951-1958 period, 211
  1959-1963 period, 213
  1964-1970 period, 213-14
  1971-1979 period, 214
  1980 period, 224
Utilities applications, 30, 48-50, 168

VANS (VALUE-ADDED NETWORKS), 187, 207
VIEWDATA, 223